ABOUT THE AUTHOR

TRACY MCMILLAN is a film and television writer, a veteran of such shows as the NBC series *Chase*, AMC's Emmy– and Golden Globe–winning series *Mad Men*, Showtime's Emmy Award–winning series *The United States of Tara*, the ABC drama *Life on Mars*, and the NBC drama *Journeyman*. She lives in Los Angeles with her thirteen-year-old son.

For my dad, who never let me go. And my fourth husband—

wherever you are.

Everything works out in the end. If it hasn't worked out yet, then it's not the end.

—UNKNOWN

Contents

Acknowledgments

First and foremost, I thank my dad, who has fearlessly supported me in the writing of this book. I love you.

This book would not exist without Andy Mcnicol, Alan Rautbort, Nancy Miller, and Hope Innelli—each of whom has gifted me with their encouragement, professionalism, guidance, and expertise. Special thanks to Jill Soloway, who blessed me with the best three words of advice a writer could ever hear ("be more you") and has mentored me in the funniest and most generous way. Thanks also to Kevin Falls, Diablo Cody, Josh Appelbaum, Andre Nemec, Scott Rosenberg, Nancy Josephson, Tom Wellington, Margaret Mendelson, Jennifer Grisanti, Ava Greenfield, Jaclyn Lafer, Dana Calvo, Amy Turner, Mishna Wolff, and the writing staffs of *Journeyman*, *Life on Mars*, and *The United States of Tara*, for proving that Hollywood is filled with good people.

Deep gratitude goes to the friends and loved ones who have given my life shape and meaning: my foster family for teaching me love and trust; my great friends Katie, Mary, David, Tracy Renee, Jane R., JoAnna, Karin, Joe, Stacey, Bevin, Chala, and Susie; all the beautiful souls at Saturday Night Atwater for their unfailing love and support; my son's stepmother for her cooperation and caring; and most especially my son's dad and grandparents, who truly have been family to me.

To Jon, Anil, Carla, Wynne, and Norma at the Casbah for the coffee and camaraderie, not to mention the necessary distractions. You guys are truly in this book.

And most of all, to my son, whom I love beyond words just for being himself.

Introduction

I LIKE TO THINK I'M NORMAL. I'm from the Midwest, I'm a mom, and I drive a Toyota.

But I'm not. Aside from my big hair and my ADD, there are two major facts that separate me from the average chick. 1) My dad was a pimp and a drug dealer and is doing twenty-three years in a federal prison as we speak. And, 2) I've been married three times.

This book is about the connection between those events.

If it were a math equation, it might look like this:

$$Pimp \leq Womanizer + [Sex^3] + Incarceration$$
$$\mathbf{x}$$
$$Daughter + Daddy - Security + Foster\ Homes^{12}$$
$$=$$
$$MAN\ ISSUES$$

So how, more precisely, does one define Man Issues? Well, the story of my three marriages is a pretty compelling place to start. In my defense, it's not quite as bad as it sounds. There were thirteen years between my first marriage and my second one. And five years between my second marriage and my third. Sometimes I think I married the boyfriends whom other, better-parented girls would have had the good sense just to cohabit with.

In any case, it's obvious I didn't learn *everything* I needed to know in kindergarten. I think I must have been absent the day they covered "Topics in Serial Monogamy: From Mayhem to Matrimony," because my man-ventory also includes:

- Four live-in lovers
- Five guys I was "in love with" but who wouldn't have sex with me
- More depressives than you can hook up with at a poets' convention
- 1.5 agoraphobics (one of whom was considered half-functional because he at least had a job)
- A host of other assorted addicts, whose dependencies included but were not limited to work, food, sex, heroin, and, um, motorcycles

Then, of course, there were those long stretches with no man at all, though not in a good way.

But the thing that truly convinces me that I have Man Issues and not just man problems (a difference similar to that between weather and climate—one is a cold spell, the other is Greenland) is this little paradox: at heart I'm totally conservative!

I know what you're thinking right now. *How can she* possibly *think she's conservative when she's a three-time divorcée?* It's a question I've had to ask myself. And here is the answer: because at my core, all I've ever wanted is to be in a committed relationship with one man. Who else do you know, without a burka, who has "settled down" at age seventeen? While my peers were out sowing their wild oats, racking up conquests, and sampling one, two, even three flavors of man each month, I was packing lunch for my husband. And loving it!

What's more, I have never *ever* had any interest in casual sex. (Not even in France! Or on ecstasy!) It's not a moral thing—on the contrary, more than once over the years I have *wished* I had the capacity for no-strings, uncommitted fun. Then I could have explored the whole subset of super-hot guys who've never met a string without a "G" attached to it. Alas. It's just not my temperament. Maybe it's nature—I'm one of those people who go to the same restaurant twice a week and order the exact same thing every time. Or maybe it's nurture, and I'm just an emotional wreck from too much childhood. Either way, I'm in total agreement with my gay friend Mark-David, who says, "No ring, no ding, honey."

It's all about the relationship for me.

Which is why I've spent months, nay, *years* on the phone with cauliflower-eared girlfriends—fleshing out scenarios, detailing facial expressions, recounting exact bits of dialogue—trying to figure out if he likes me, what he's thinking, when he's going to call, or if not, why not. And that's *before* the relationship starts. Once it's going, it's all about getting him to 1) stop doing what he's doing, and 2) start doing what I want him to do, or if that's not an issue, wondering 3) if he's going to leave or 4) whether I should stay.

And my dad Freddie's in all of it. Way up in it.

Not like that's a new thought. Any chick old enough to have acquired a Diet Coke habit has heard that your relationships with men will be based—one way or another—on the one you had with your father. But I arrogantly dismissed this as the kind of folk "wisdom" you get at the nail salon between the polish and the top coat. So trite, so clichéd, so lowest-common-denominator. Helloooo, what about free will? Women have choices. We're not just programmed to seek out Daddy 2.0. At least that's what I thought. But three wedding dresses later (a tea-length, a two-piece, and a big traditional white, in that order), I'm here to say that I'm not that special. It did, indeed, all come down to Daddy.

So this is my story. It's about how a girl from Minneapolis whose dad was obsessed with women became a woman obsessed with men. How having a pimp for a dad taught me to love men, leave them, fear them, fuck them, and yes, marry them. Over and over. Until I met "the one." The one who went wrong in exactly the right way, making it possible for me to finally see who I had been emotionally wrangling with all along: my dad. It's a story about a father and a daughter who managed to love each other despite one of them spending thirty years behind bars. And about how raising a son taught me everything I *really* needed to know about loving men.

Maybe you'll relate.

i love you

and

i'm

leaving

you anyway

One

If You Love Me,
Please Press "5"

MY THIRD EX-HUSBAND CALLED me today.

He wants to see me. "Why?" I say, genuinely curious. It's been just over two years since I last ~~had sex with~~ saw Paul. That's when we gamely tried to paste our marriage back together in time to celebrate our one-year wedding anniversary. In bed.

We failed at the reconciliation. The bed part, as always, worked out great.

Since then, we've spoken on the phone from time to time, and lately he's been calling more often. But he's never asked to see me. Until right this second.

"I've been thinking . . ." He pauses, unsure if he's really going to say what he's about to say. "I was wondering—" He stops short. "It would be kind of like a before-and-after thing. You could see me before. And after. For comparison purposes."

I should mention that Paul's getting electroconvulsive therapy next week.

"If it works"—he means the electroconvulsive therapy—"would you maybe . . ." He stops once more. There's something really vulnerable in his voice. Something I haven't heard in a long time. Like, since we were married and manic depression took over his life, driving him all kinds of lying, cheating crazy.

"I was wondering if maybe you would . . . like me again?" He says "like" in the fifth-grader sense of the word, as in *boy-girl* like. "I know I blew it."

It's not as though I've been waiting to hear a mea culpa all this time, but this, I must admit, feels like a very nice start to one. Still, this man—this adorable, brilliant, sexy man—has got mental problems. Don't, as they say, get it twisted.

"Oh, Paul," I sigh doubtfully. "I don't know."

"Please, I really want to see you." He's almost begging, and what woman doesn't find that kind of irresistible?

I take a long, deep breath. What do you say when your ex-husband asks you ~~on a date~~ to coffee?

SOMETHING'S DEFINITELY GOING ON. Because that's the second plot-twisting phone call I've gotten recently from a key man in my life. The first was a week ago.

I am walking out the door to work, when the phone starts to ring. I know better than to answer it (when I get distracted leaving the house I usually end up forgetting something important, like my kid), but I pick it up anyway, because for me a ringing phone has always had a Wonka-bar quality to it, like, *You never know, it might be something really, really cool, like a great job offer or a new man or a million dollars or . . .* So I press the "on" button.

"Hello?"

Pause. Beat. Beat. Institutional recorded voice: *"This call is from a federal prison."*

Oh, shit. It's not a million dollars.

It's my dad, who's serving twenty-three years for conspiracy to distribute cocaine. He calls me every two weeks, like clockwork, and we talk mostly about what I'm doing in my life. We already know what he's doing in his. Sitting there.

"This call is from—"

"FREDDIE." He says his name so perfectly, like he's just arrived at, say, Hyde or Villa or Beatrice Inn (or whichever "It" club you prefer) with two totally hot chicks and he knows he's on the list.

"—an inmate at a federal prison. To decline this call, hang up. To block all future calls from this inmate, press '7.' To accept this call, press—"

Don't think I haven't got a recurring morbid fantasy about accidentally pressing "7" and never again getting another phone call from my dad. But that would leave letter writing as the only available means of communication, and if that happened, he might as well be doing time on the International Space Station. Because I am the worst letter writer in the history of jailed fathers. In the fourteen years my dad has been incarcerated this time around I have managed to send exactly three letters. (In my defense, each contained a picture of my son.) And I call myself a writer! I am somehow sure Nelson Mandela's kids coughed up more than three letters in fourteen years. Of course, *their* dad was a hero. Mine was a pimp.

I press *FIIIIIIIIIIIIIIVE*. Good and long to make sure Automated Prison Recording Barbie hears me. Then I wait. There's always a weird moment where I'm not sure which of us—Freddie or me—is going to speak first, which leads to some awkward "you-go-no-you-go" overlap. I've learned to just be silent and let him speak first.

"Hey, baby!"

Freddie always says hello like this. With a certain forced brightness that makes me feel obligated to sound happy in return. Sometimes I don't feel like sounding happy. And I don't bother to try to hide it. This is a relatively new development. For years I urged myself to sound cheerful. Then one day I overheard a friend on the phone with her mother and realized that normal adult children are annoyed when their parents call. And all I really, really want to be is normal.

But nothing about this is normal. Our phone calls are timed, fifteen minutes apiece, to the second. I think the inmates buy some kind of phone card, but exactly how it works is one of those federal-prison mysteries you just don't bother to inquire about when you only have a quarter of an hour two times a month in which to conduct an entire father-daughter relationship. There's a necessity to get straight to whatever talking points you're in the mood to get to.

"I watched the show again last night," Freddie offers.

This makes me feel all warm toward my dad. I was a journalist for a long time, but now I'm a television writer and he has been faithfully watching the show I write for, every week. I recognize this as a dad-in-prison act of love. There is a separate scale for what constitutes an act of love for a dad in prison, because dads in prison can't do normal things like carve the Thanksgiving turkey or fix your leaky faucet or give you money for a down payment on a house. In this case, simply watching my show qualifies, because I know he must have had to pull some serious strings to commandeer one of the communal televisions every Monday night, especially since the show does not fall into a felon-friendly genre. I imagine he had to give away a lot of cigarettes. And he doesn't even smoke.

"Well, what did you think?" I'm only asking for the sake of conversation.

But Freddie breaks it down, and he doesn't spare my feelings. "The ending was good, but you lost half of us before you got there."

Ouch. Really? I'm visualizing the inmates getting up in droves, preferring to go back to their cells (!) rather than find out what happens to Dan and Katie at the end of the episode. Obviously, this is not a good sign. Genre notwithstanding, you want them to be loving your shit at the federal penitentiary. Because if the captive audience isn't interested, how are you going to hang on to the regular Americans? The ones with the Internet and Halo 3?

"This call is from a federal prison."

There's Barbie with the two-minute warning. Already?! This always happens. Just as I get over my mild dad-in-prison petulance and am really starting to enjoy his company, the call is almost over. "Now listen," he says, "we're running out of time. I got something to talk to you about. Guess what today is?"

My mind goes blank. *What day could today possibly be? A holiday? No. His birthday? No.* Our birthdays are exactly two weeks apart, and they had just passed. (We are Virgos together, which must explain something.) No one has died, that I know of, and besides, he would have led with that.

"I give up. What is today?"

"October twentieth," he says.

I plug October 20 into my mental search engine, but even after .091 seconds, nothing comes up. "I give. Tell me. "

"It's my release date!" Freddie's excited, exultant even. He slaps his hands together and chortles—a big, giant, James Brown–like shout of *HAH!* "I'm coming home, baby! October twentieth, 2012. Five years from today!"

Mind you, my dad has been "getting out" since he got in, back when I was three. Usually any minute now. I have learned over the years to just say "Yeah, yeah" and go on with my life. But this time is different, I can tell. For starters, he gave me a date. A specific one.

This has a surprising effect on me. Kind of like the time I got my nose pierced. My mind thought, *Okay, cool, that was easy,* but the moment I tried to stand up my body was like *JEEBUS PRICE, SOMEONE JUST PUNCHED A HOLE IN ME WITH A NEEDLE THE SIZE OF THE ONES IN A SEWING MACHINE!* My insides are spinning and racing and rolling in all kinds of directions like a bucket full of marbles thrown on a cement floor. It's one thing to have your dad in federal prison. It sucks, yes, but at least you know where he is, and you know he can only drive you crazy long-distance, and if you really really must, you know you can always press "7" to refuse all future calls.

But he just said that in five years—no, in four years, 364 days,

23 hours, and 59 minutes (and counting)—prison officials will give him a set of clothes, and $200, and a box packed with those three measly pictures I managed to send him, and they will lead him down a hall, and usher him through some doors, and then, finally, they will open the last door and he will walk through it. He will have served eighteen years. He will be seventy-six years old. And he will be a free man.

And all I can think is this: *I wonder where he's going to live?*

SO THAT'S WHAT I'M THINKING about while I'm sitting in this café, waiting for Paul to arrive. How I'm not ready for my dad to get out. How even though Paul is from an affluent family, is white, and went to Harvard, he's a lot like my dad. Too much like my dad. Exactly like my dad? Yes, exactly like my dad. They both loved me and left me anyway. Then, once they were gone, they refused to let me go.

The two of them are the continuum of men in my life: from the very beginning until the very end, until . . .

Now.

As the minutes tick by, I consider that I don't exactly know what I'm doing here waiting for Paul. On one level it's simple: He asked to see me. I said yes. On another, more mysterious plane, there's something bigger going on. It's an intuitive flash—like when you've lost something, and you suddenly realize where you might have left it, even if it makes no sense to look there. It's the precise opposite of what I usually do when I lose something, which is to look over and over in the same place, the place I think it *has to be*, even though I already know it's not there, because I've searched that spot seven times already. When it comes to men, that describes me perfectly. Someone looking over and over in the same place for something that isn't there. But, sitting in this coffee place, waiting for my third ex-husband to arrive, thinking about my dad coming home, it hits me all at once—

I think I know where to look now.

Two

I Love You,
This Is Just How I Am

BY PRETTY MUCH ANY CONVENTIONAL standard, my dad was bad. (And badass.) Terrible even.

For starters, he was a pimp.

A fur-coat-wearing, El Dorado–driving, sharkskin-suit-clad, pinky-ring-sporting, mustache-smoothing P.I.M.P., straight out of a blaxploitation picture. Eventually, he promoted himself to drug dealer, and there he also fit the stereotype, becoming a large-scale, conspiracy-heading, recidivist heroin and coke dealer just like on *Starsky and Hutch,* or maybe cooler, like in *Goodfellas,* if they were black. It sounds awful, right? Deplorable. Appalling. Immoral.

You dislike him already. I understand.

But here's the thing about my dad. If you didn't know anything about him, and I brought him over to your house for dinner, you would like him. You just would! First of all, he would be exceedingly polite. "Pleasure to make your acquaintance," he would say upon meeting you. And he would say it in this mellifluous, almost singsong voice that would strike you as remarkably kindhearted and agreeable. That would cause you to take a closer look at his face, and you would notice the pleasing symmetry of his features, the sparkle in his eyes, and his overall warmth. He would offer to help you in the kitchen, and you would accept. You'd discover that he's a great cook, and so easy to talk to! You would feel that he liked you, and you would be correct. You'd feel like this was a particularly good hair day.

After dinner, he'd help clear the table and just start doing the dishes. Without even being asked! The two of you would tootle around the kitchen, cleaning up, and he'd ask you about the man in your life. If there wasn't one, he'd say something about how "a beautiful and charming young lady such as yourself" won't be single for long, and you'd believe him. Mostly because it's true! You are beautiful and charming. We all are. Freddie knows that.

At the end of the evening, as we were walking out the door, he'd say, "Thank you," with genuine gratitude, and off he would go, leaving you to think to yourself, *What a nice man . . .* You'd be so dazzled, you'd call me the next day to tell me how much you liked him. Just like I knew you would.

This is the fascinating dichotomy of my dad. It is what made him such a great dad. And, of course, what made him such a great pimp.

I NEVER WANTED GUYS WITH "GAME"—the kind of smooth talkers who obviously know their way around a woman, or five. Quite the contrary. I spent the vast majority of my life with men at the other end of the continuum. Dating nice guys. Really nice guys.

Ultra Nice Guys.

Until age twenty-five, I was like someone who grew up with two fat parents and knows she will likely spend the rest of her life on a diet. Deep down, I knew that if I took even *the first bite* of Bad Boy, I would never want vegan pizza again. So I didn't.

I just said no.

This wasn't as difficult as it might sound, because I had two things working in my favor: I was afraid of sex (and of men in general); I was also extremely insecure. Which was kind of perfect really, since super-sexy guys naturally want sex (a frightening fact if you're scared of sex), and they almost always want it *now* (an even scarier reality if you're insecure). What's more, sexy guys don't make any commitments (a truly intolerable condition if you're still dealing with a lot of posttraumatic stress surrounding your years in foster care). The combination made them totally repulsive to me.

So, I dated Ultra Nice Guys instead. UNGs are a whole tribe of men who are generally just as they seem: they're polite, they open your car door, and they don't pressure you for sex. They commit after a certain period of dating (usually thirty or sixty days, about as long as one is allowed to let an invoice languish before it is considered past due), they take you home to meet their (totally nice) families, they have steady jobs and good credit. They like their mother but they don't feel *responsible* for her and (probably as a result) they don't use women as a drug, because they're not out there trying to reclaim the power over women they didn't have as a boy.

They drive defensively.

There is only one problem with these men: they are boring. Scratch that. It's not that they are boring, it's just that they aren't exciting. I used to think that if excitement was a coin, the flip side would be boredom. Now, almost thirty years of dating later, I've decided the flip side of excitement is intimacy. Without all those "exciting" ups and downs, two people can actually build a stable relationship and eventually experience closeness. Something my subconscious was determined never to let happen to me.

There is this Jungian thing I learned, where if you look at a woman's choice of mate (or even date) you will see the male version of herself. And if you look at a man's partner, you will see his inner female.

Take a quick look around—it's a pretty G-D interesting theory, right?

I have two Inner Males—the pastor and the pimp. And for a long time, it was confusing as hell, dawg. Seventy-five percent of me is an upper-middle-class white boy—a commitment-oriented intellectual who got an IRA with his first job and thinks strip clubs are lame and slutty girls are just that: slutty.

The other 25 percent of me is really, really horny.

My UNG side would put together a relationship, a home, and a future. Then my inner pimp would trade it all away for one night in Bangkok. Or even Portland, Oregon.

Which explains how Paul, bless his heart, was my perfect match. We each had a side of ourselves that wanted desperately to make a home. And we each had a side that would not, or could not, allow that to happen. But more on that in a moment.

I NEVER REALLY KNEW MY DAD until I visited the place where he was born—a no-stoplight town in rural Alabama called Midway, two highways from anywhere, with maybe a few hundred people, almost all of them black.

I had always imagined the Deep South as this perspiring, mythic place of plantations, Spanish moss, and houses up on cinder blocks. A place where two slices of white bread are always served with dinner. Not long before my fortieth birthday, while on a solo visit to Atlanta, I decided to find out for myself.

I hop in a rental car and make the two-hour drive.

I find the town without too much trouble. I take the left turn off the county road and then, typical of me, suddenly realize I had absolutely no plan for Finding My People.

Up ahead there are four guys sitting on lawn chairs, stuff spread out on the ground for a yard sale. *A fine place to start,* I figure. I come to a stop right in front of the driveway and get out of my car. The four men, who I now see are drinking Budweisers, are wearing expressions like something out of the movie *Close Encounters of the Third Kind.* They're Richard Dreyfuss. I'm the alien.

Not quite sure what to say, I just launch into my introduction.

"Hi, my name is Tracy McMillan, and my dad is from this town originally, and I was over visiting in Atlanta and I just decided to just drive down here and check it out." I take a breath, aware that I am probably coming off like a sorority girl, and a white one at that.

One of the men, in his late forties maybe, looks at me a long spell. Then he turns to the guy next to him and they exchange a glance that says something like *Are you seeing what I'm seeing?* They are still thinking about how to respond when a large eighties Oldsmobile four-door sedan—the kind of thing a Los Angeles hipster would drool over—pulls up. Two more guys, waistlines courtesy of too many trans fats and not enough leafy greens, get out. "We saw *her*," the Oldsmobile driver drawls, gesturing toward me, "and decided to stop." Apparently, it doesn't take much to be newsworthy in Midway. Big hair, skinny arms, and premium denim will do it.

I turn to the two new guys and repeat my pitch. "Hi, my name is Tracy McMillan and I'm visiting from Los Angeles, and my dad is from this town. I wanted to come and check it out." They, too, look at each other. Then they look at the other four guys. I see that the main older dude has changed his expression slightly, to something like *Amusing, isn't she?*

"What did you say your name was?" Oldsmobile queries. Slowly.

"Tracy McMillan." At this point, I can tell these guys think I am just about the funniest thing that's happened all year. I start to play along. Big smile. Tilted head. Exaggerated arm gestures. I can get a pretty good airhead thing going on when I want to.

The lawn chair guy points at Oldsmobile guy. "He's a *Mack*-Millan." I love how he says "Mc" like it has an "a" in it.

"I sure am," says Oldsmobile. "Who'd you say your daddy was?"

"Freddie McMillan. I think he left here when he was about eight and moved to Birmingham. His mother was named Thelma?"

"Is he white or black?" asks one of the until-now-silent lawn chair brothers.

This question surprises me. I have light skin and features some have sworn were Greek (or whatever) but my hair is pure Soul Sister.

"Black!" I answer indignantly. I can only guess that at this moment my German farmer side is shining pretty bright.

Oldsmobile sizes me up. "I'll take you to meet my mama."

One would think I would be circumspect about following a man I have known less than ninety seconds to some unknown location, but—unless I am intensely sexually attracted to a guy—my People Assessment System (standard equipment for every foster child) is absolutely foolproof. (Actually, it's foolproof all the time. If I am intensely sexually attracted to a guy, I can be 100 percent certain having sex with him would be a bad idea.) Since I am not at all sexually attracted to Oldsmobile, I have no hesitation about following him to meet his mother. I get in my car and trail him a mile down the road.

Oldsmobile's mom turns out to have a vague recollection of my grandmother. "But you should really talk to my sister," she advises me. "She know ever'body around here."

I'm totally interested in talking to anyone who knows everybody, so I get back in my car and caravan to the next house. I'm amazed that Oldsmobile has so much patience for this, but then again, I am pretty much the gossip of the day.

A few minutes later I'm standing in the kitchen of the sister, who apparently functions as a sort of town memory bank. She knows a bunch of my relatives, people whom I've never met but have heard of. Then she shows me a picture of her dad, a McMillan, who has sloping shoulders *identical* to my dad's, and I have them, too. Who needs a DNA swab? Sometimes things are just obvious.

I spend an hour with this woman and her son, Oldsmobile (I don't remember his name, or hers). She serves me a warm-ish Coke, and I sit in her dim but orderly living room and look at her family pictures. It is a strange and lovely afternoon. After a while, I leave, feeling a little bit guilty that I am going back to the Big City, leaving them (decades) behind.

Not until I am almost halfway back to Atlanta, after eating ribs off a plastic plate with slices of white bread at a roadside barbecue joint and blasting soul oldies on the radio, soaking in the "realness" of the true South, did I have a deeper revelation.

My dad was born in that place.

How he somehow had a child—me—who, in only one generation, found her way into the world of journalism, film, television, private schools, and pool houses was a testament to something essential about my dad.

And that something about him is something about me, too.

FREDDIE WAS BORN IN 1935, the sixth or seventh of nine children. His dad was a traveling preacher named Booker who went around to neighboring towns and counties, spreading the word of God. I suspect, too, that, being a McMillan, he had a little extra something special for the lady believers.

At some point Booker abandoned the family. Details are sketchy, but I think that's when my dad moved away. The other story goes that my grandmother Thelma was accused of stealing jewelry from a white lady she washed clothes for, got raped and/or beaten in retaliation, and that's when they left. However it happened, Thelma and the kids lived in Birmingham until the early 1950s, when one by one, they all migrated north to the tough industrial town of Gary, Indiana, outside of Chicago. Aside from steel mills and high crime, Gary became famous as the hometown of the Jackson 5. Then, as now, Gary was a black city.

Sometime in the 1950s, my grandmother's sister, Aunt (pronounced "Ain't") Sallie, moved with her husband to Minneapolis, for a job in a flour mill or something like that. Aunt Sallie soon reported back to all the Indiana family members how fantastic Minnesota was. Sure, it was cold, but it wasn't *that* much worse than Chicago, and the quality of life and relative lack of racism made it a *whole* lot better. She urged the family, one and all, to relocate to the Upper Midwest.

My dad and his posse came first.

There were four of them, still calling each other by their child-hood nicknames: Cadillac, Big Dog, Shugger, and Far-Out Freddie. They'd been friends since they were kids shooting marbles and dice back in Birmingham. In those days, the Upper Midwest was to a hus-tler what China is to Philip Morris: one ginormous untapped market, just waiting to be exploited properly. They all worked loosely together, running cons, kiting checks, and dealing small-time marijuana.

And pimping.

Because there was one thing above all else that made Minneapolis unlike any other city in America for a black man in the mid-1950s: white women.

Not just any old white women. These were white women from Scandinavian and northern European backgrounds, relatively liberal and open-minded—for Americans, that is—and raised in a culture where "Socialist" is just another word for a first-generation Swede. A culture where people don't really give a great big hoot what you do, since you're inside a good five months of the year anyway.

For a guy who spent the first twenty-odd years of his life drinking from separate water fountains than the white folks, moving to Min-nesota must have been the sexual equivalent of the riots you always see in developing nations right after they overthrow the despotic leader. Par-*tay*!

Freddie once told me a story that illustrated the enormity of the cultural jolt. Not long after he arrived, he was riding a city bus, sit-ting in a window seat, near the back. The bus, already almost full, stopped to pick up more passengers. Last to board the bus was a white woman, attractive, probably in her late twenties. She took the seat right next to Freddie. Just sat down right next to him, like it was a completely normal thing to do.

It was the closest physical proximity he'd ever had to a white woman. Ever! And he was going on thirty. He burst into a cold sweat, his heart racing, his hands shaking, with an overwhelming urge to get up and run. That's how deep the taboo went against even *sitting* next to a white woman, and how well he had internalized it. After all, where he grew up, his life had depended on it. You could get lynched for way less—like just *looking* at a white woman.

To think that, shortly after that incident, my dad had not only met a young white woman and introduced her to prostitution but impregnated her too is to realize how deeply transgressive an act my conception was. My dad was doing something he could have *died* for just a few hundred miles to the south.

It tells me just how ballsy Freddie and Linda really were. How nonconformist. How rebellious. How totally punk rock. A black man getting with a white woman in 1964 was better than having a Mohawk in 1978 or a pantyless crotch in 2007. It was a way to say, *Your rules don't apply to me, and by the way—fuck you.*

What a way to start a life.

I'M AMAZED I NEVER TURNED A TRICK. I never even stripped! Not that I would blame me if I had. Many, if not most, girls of my provenance find themselves trading sex somewhere along the way for cold hard cash (as opposed to engaging in the less overt quid pro quo of a serious relationship with a man of some—or any— means). And to be honest, I always secretly thought I would, too.

But I didn't, and I'm not sure why.

Fear of sex was definitely a part of it. But there was another intangible thing, a force almost, that prevented me from being able to tap into my sexuality in order to make money or further my career. I was not terribly happy about this thing, either. Mostly because it meant Prince would not be building his next girl group around me. (A pause here for all of those who care to mourn the loss of Tracy Renee 6, the great girl group that would have come after Vanity 6 but before Apollonia 6 . . .)

I remember the exact moment I discovered this predicament. It was seventh grade, the year of my sexual awakening. I was spending a lot of time alone, and, probably because that year we were living in one of those neighborhoods with the poor-people zoning laws, where XXX theaters are right at the end of the block and the corner store carries as much T&A as PB&J, I'd come across sexually explicit materials on two different occasions. First, I found a book of hard-core pornography on the bus, wedged between the seats. I took it home and, with remarkable speed, managed to think up uses for it.

A short time later, as I walked to school on a snowy day, I happened upon a stack of girlie magazines dropped off outside the aforementioned corner store. Titles like *Cheri, Oui,* and *Hustler.* I stole a couple and stashed them under the bed, where they, too, became interesting reading material when I was bored.

As I said, I had a lot of free time that year.

The thing about it was, there was something very familiar about pornography. Not necessarily the pictures—some were highly explicit and shocked me at first—but the *energy* in the pictures; it was familiar, almost normal. I should say I'd been sexually, er, awake ever since I could remember. Without going into crazy details, let's just say even at age four, when given a "time out" I knew how to make the minutes pass quickly in ways that were probably not what my foster parents were thinking when they named the time-out spot "the naughty chair."

Back to my moment of choice, though. I was in the basement with my friend Jody and this kid named Keith, who was somebody's cousin or nephew and who just happened to be visiting. As happens with seventh graders, the discussion turned to sex, and a dare was put forth: I should French-kiss Keith. In theory, I really liked the idea. I was going to get to kiss this boy (and he was cute) without having to risk "liking" him, with its attendant possibility of rejection. Furthermore, since he was visiting, I would never have to see him again.

Well, my mind may have been in agreement, but my body most definitely was not. As soon as the kiss became imminent, my heart began to pound and an unbelievable fear took hold. I couldn't move.

"Go!" Jody urges me. "Kiss him!"

I'm looking at Keith, and he's just standing there. Waiting. Ready.

"*Kiss* him!"

And . . . I . . . just . . . couldn't . . . do . . . it . . .

I couldn't do it.

I couldn't even *force* myself to do it.

Jody, ever the bolder of the two of us, muttered something about my being a loser and stepped right in front of me with a confident, "Okay, then, I'll do it." She put her arms around Keith's neck, and he put his arms around her waist, and right in front of me, they started going at it.

A tsunami of shame washed over me. *What is wrong with me? Why couldn't I just kiss the guy?* He was standing *right there.* He wanted me to. It would have been so easy.

But something really deep inside had just frozen me to the spot—like a wet tongue on metal when it's ten below outside—unable to carry out the command that Jody Jeffs, and my mind, had just given.

Even though *I wanted to do it!*

It would take me, oh, a couple of decades to figure it out exactly, but eventually I would come to realize that I had two separate but interrelated sexualities: one with myself, and one with men. Two different selves I would spend the next twenty years synthesizing: the one who knew too much too soon and was hypersexual and kind of perverse, and the other, more powerful one that would keep me in check, up to and including trading sex for money.

MY DAD *SWEARS* THEY VOLUNTEERED. Every last one of them.

"Not *once* did I ever walk up to a woman and say, 'I'm a *this* and I want you to be a *that.*' That's not how it happened."

He swears it. And I guess I believe him.

Here's his side of the story:

One night in 1956 he was sitting at a bar, and a woman came up to him. "Can you come upstairs with me?" she asked. "I have a piece of furniture I need help moving."

My dad, ever the gentleman, was eager to be of service. "I was twenty years old," he remembers. "A square. Just off the bus. I honestly thought I was going up there to help the girl out."

So upstairs he goes, to a small room in a building over the bar. Once inside the room, he says, she broke it down for him.

"I want you to be my man," she told him, point-blank.

"What do you mean?" Freddie asks. Recounting the story, he articulates every word, like "What. Do. You. Mean." He really sounds like he had no idea what she was talking about.

"I'm a working girl," she explained. "I make money, and I'll give it to you, if you'll be my man."

Freddie gives a big throaty laugh at the memory. "Man, I didn't know a hooker from a loaf of bread," he says, clapping. "I'd heard about them, but I'd never actually *seen* one. But this girl, she just . . ." He stops. Then he finishes: "I said, 'Sounds good to me.' And boom! I was in bidness.

"We went around to all the clubs in Minneapolis, the Key Club and Moby Dick's. And she made money and she gave it to me. And she fucked me silly."

Freddie goes on to tell some version of this story—*She came up to me and said she had decided to become a hooker, but she needed a man, and would I do it?*—for every woman he ever "worked" with. The way he tells it lends credence to the adage "There are no victims, only volunteers." But even though these women were in agreement with trading sex for money, it doesn't change my mind about the real costs to them of doing so.

Not that anyone has ever asked, but as the child of a prostitute, I don't really believe there is such a thing as a happy hooker. Even the ones making thousands a night. Yeah, maybe sex work is cool in the short term, in the same way it's awesome to smoke cigarettes in your early twenties. It looks cool and feels glamorous. But poll any smoker over the age of forty-five. They all want to quit.

TURNS OUT MY MOM WASN'T REBELLIOUS so much as she was crazy. This might have been predicted. My dad once told me that when Linda found out she was pregnant she wanted an abortion, and the only reason she didn't get one is because he essentially locked her in an apartment and kept her there until I arrived.

I was born in Hennepin County General Hospital on September 12, 1964. In fact, one of the first things I asked my mom when I met her was the time of my birth. I'm one of those chicks who's into astrology (which is a little like saying "I'm one of those guys who's into blow jobs") and I'd been waiting a lifetime to find out the hour and minute of my birth so I could calculate my rising sign, which in astrology is the equivalent of *You Are Here* on a map.

"It was in the afternoon," Linda remembers, sounding quite certain.

"Really?" I'm breathless. I've been wondering about this since I cracked my first astrology book, in my teens. "You're sure?"

"Yep. Positive. I remember because your dad was at the hospital and I was nervous that my mom was going to show up any moment because school was out for the day." Linda's mom, Helen, was a second-grade schoolteacher. She could print like nobody's business. "My mom hated your dad, you know. Hated him."

Of course she did! My dad was black *and* a pimp. To Helen he must have been a rolling, strolling, overdressed billboard announcing the fact that she was not a typical college-educated elementary schoolteacher, but rather an abandoned wife who raised her only child to be a welfare mom and prostitute. There is, as we say in the news business, a story there. We may never know the details, but figure the story is the approximate size and shape of Linda's insanity. Or Freddie's diamond rings.

"Do you know what time? I mean, exactly?" I've tried to find out on a number of occasions by obtaining a copy of my birth record, but Hennepin County General Hospital was torn down in the 1970s and all the actual birth certificates were packed away when the data was computerized, so now when you request your records, they just send you a piece of paper that essentially says, *Yeah, you were born, on September 12, 1964.*

Thanks. I knew that already.

There's no time of birth on there, or little footprint, or doctor's signature. Nothing that would say, *You're specific, there's only one of you, you are special and wanted.* This is the kind of indignity you suffer when you're too poor to be born in a hospital with an actual name. *General Hospital.* It means no one claims you, not the Seventh-Day Adventists, or the Methodists, or the Catholics. You don't really have a tribe. Unless indigents and welfare cases are your tribe.

No wonder I've always felt like I was hatched, not born.

"Four ten in the afternoon," Linda says adamantly. "Yep. School was already out."

Now *this* is something I can work with. Later, I ask my dad, and he corroborates the Helen part of the story, including the part about seeing her in the waiting room after school. He thinks the time was a little bit earlier, though. Perhaps around three thirty P.M.

I run off to do my birth chart and immediately discover my birth time is right on the cusp between rising signs. If I was born at 4:10 P.M., I'm a Capricorn rising. If I was born at 4:30 P.M., I'm an Aquarius rising.

Great. You'd think that would settle the question, but it doesn't. A teensy bit more research reveals that my parents are either liars, or dimwits, or both. (Surprise.) And here's how I know.

Because I was born on a Saturday. There's no school on Saturday.

* * *

MY DAD WAS AHEAD OF HIS TIME. Thanks to his, er, nontraditional job and my mother's complete inability to take care of me due to her bipolar-y/alcoholic problems (think Britney, early 2008), my dad was my primary caretaker.

Freddie played Mr. Mom twenty years before Bob Saget ever met an Olsen twin. He cooked for me, fed me, bathed me, dressed me, and took me everywhere with him. Pictures from that time consistently show me—always with a fierce look on my face, always dressed to *work* in the RuPaul sense of the word—being toted around in my dad's arms. Except for when he was dropping me off with a babysitter ("babysitter" being another word for some chick he was fucking), I was his constant companion. His sidekick, talisman, and ultimate accessory. We were inseparable.

Presumably I even attended a drug deal or two.

Later, when I had my own (stroller-hating) son, I started to realize what it might have meant to be carried around by him all the time. When you are a baby being held by someone, you absorb all their energy, you see the world from their viewpoint, you smell their hair. They, in turn, have full access to your face. They can kiss you whenever they want, and you can see all their expressions in extreme close-up, like being in the first row at a movie theater. I don't know about you, but I get motion sick in the first row.

It's no wonder, then, that I've always felt so connected to my dad. For the first three years of my life I was literally closer to him than I was to anyone else, emotionally, physically, and metaphysically. I'm so close to him, every choice he makes in his life reverberates through mine in a very big way. So when he gets his first major prison sentence, there is only one word for what I am.

Fucked.

Three

I Love You,
but I'm Stuck in Here

I ALWAYS GET A NEW DRESS for visiting day. June Ericson takes me to Dayton's Velvet Coach and we pick out something special to wear to see Daddy. This time I get a dress the color of cotton candy with a full skirt and a big sash. I'm pretty confident I'm going to be the best-dressed girl at the prison.

Leavenworth is a long way away. Four hundred forty-eight miles, and those are circa-1970 miles, before the interstate was built. We take a very impressive Braniff 747 and get there in two hours. I'm one of the only kids at my school who has been on a plane, so I feel really special. Even though the only reason I got to go on one is because my dad is stuck in prison for the next four years.

June is my new mommy. She is forty-one years old, pleasantly plump, and wears her hair just like Carol Brady in the early episodes of *The Brady Bunch*. She is the nicest person I have ever met. The fact that she promised my dad that she would drag me all the way to Kansas to see him twice a year gives you an idea of just how nice. This is probably because she is a minister's wife. I forgot to mention, I am a Lutheran now, baptized and everything. I'm not sure what I used to be.

Last summer, we came here in a car, detouring a couple hundred miles out of the way on our family vacation to see June's sister in California. I spent most of the journey in a Dramamine-induced stupor on the floor of our wood-paneled Ford station wagon. I regained consciousness just long enough for June and me to pop into the prison for a quick visit. My dad totally mentioned how calm I seem now.

The rest of the family—my new dad, Pastor Gene Ericson, and my three new sisters, Faith, seventeen; Sue Ann, sixteen; and Connie, eleven—waited for us in the prison parking lot. My other new big sister Elin doesn't live with us because she married a guy with serious facial hair and moved to St. Paul. Neither does Carl, my new older brother, who is studying to be a minister, just like Daddy Ericson. I'm not the only kid the Ericsons picked up in an act of Christian kindness. My new sister Connie was adopted from Korea when she was four. We share a bedroom, which is unfortunate for her since she's super-perfect and quiet and neat, and I am Pippi Longstocking without the monkey or the chest of gold doubloons.

In Leavenworth we always stay at the Cody Hotel, which was once owned by Buffalo Bill's mom. I think that might be her behind the front desk, with a tall chestnut-colored beehive and a twang to match. The lobby crawls with large men reading newspapers and exhaling thick blue smoke from filterless cigarettes. Who knows what they're doing here? They don't look like their daddies are inmates.

We call a cab to take us to the prison, about a fifteen-minute drive away. Just outside of town, the road gives you two choices: go straight to something called Fort Leavenworth, which has to do with the army, or take a left and go to the prison. I don't know exactly how—maybe it is the cab driver's expression—but I can tell that if you go forward, it means something entirely different than if you turn left. One way and you're sort of a hero; the other way and you definitely are not.

A couple of minutes after the turn we come to a stop in front of an electronic arm. A guard's voice booms out of an intercom:

State the purpose of your visit.

June quickly rolls down her window and speaks into the intercom while gazing upward at the two-story tower where the voice is apparently coming from. It looks like there is a gang of air traffic controllers up there.

"We're here to see an inmate, sir."

Do you have any firearms, blah blah blah, narcotics, or other contraband?

Maybe it's just me, but that seems like a stupid question. "Why would we tell them if we did?" I ask loudly. The driver smirks.

"Be quiet, honey," June shushes me. She's not at all harsh about it, but she says it in such a way that I'm definitely not going to be raising my hand for a follow-up question. "No, sir," she says to the guard. "We don't."

Go ahead.

The arm lifts and the taxi pulls up to the drop-off area. We get out, and June pays the driver. "Thank you," she says politely. He takes off without saying anything in response, glad to have these prison-visitor types out of his cab.

I gaze up at the prison. I am wowed by this building! It's massive and white, with a big dome—not quite as grand as the Minnesota state capitol, which I visited on a field trip for school, but close. With its white marble and neoclassical lines, Leavenworth is both flashy *and* severe. As if Nurse Ratched was being played by the lead singer in an eighties hair band. And the windows! There must be a thousand of them. As we climb the steps, I pick out a window and wave and smile in case my dad is watching me from his cell.

I'm secretly proud my daddy lives in such an impressive place.

Right inside the front door is the guard station where you check in, which looks like a cross between a drive-up bank and a single-room-occupancy hotel—a few guards behind bulletproof glass and a little silver vent to talk through. June fills out some paperwork saying who we are and which inmate we're here to see.

Then we're off to the waiting room to cool our jets for a while.

The waiting room is a medium-size institutional square with built-in molded chairs in shades of olive, mucilage, and rotten sherbet lining the wall. At one end of the room is a bank of vending machines. The Pepsi machine takes thirty-five cents and of course I want one, but June says no. So instead, I go around in a frenzy, checking all the coin returns, hoping someone else's forgotten nickel or dime will turn this into my lucky day. June rummages through her bag, pulling out the coloring books, Rook playing cards ("real" cards would be, like, the Devil), and Barbie dolls that I'm allowed to take into the visiting room.

There's a clock staring down from the wall, and I watch the second hand sweep around and around. This part of the visit always seems to take forever, but today it's taking forever and a day. It's not just me, either, because I can see that June is starting to lose her patience as well.

"*What's* taking so long?" June glances at her tiny wristwatch, the one that I play with in church on Sundays, which leaves deep indentations in her cushy wrist. "Man alive! You'd think they went to China to get him."

We are not allowed to say "gosh," "golly," "gee," "gee whiz," and *certainly* not "god," "jeez," "Jesus," or anything else that even comes *close* to taking the Lord's name in vain. That doesn't leave much except "man" and "man alive," which isn't much to work with at a time like this.

(June told me that when I first came to live with her, I used to sit on my suitcase and swear a blue streak. Just reel off a litany of crazy swear words, the kind pimps, drug dealers, hookers, and other less god-fearing individuals tend to favor when provoked. I don't know what she did, but I learned real quick. *We don't say those words here.*)

After what seems like forever, we hear our name called over the intercom.

"*Ericson,*" the voice says. "*To the guard station.*"

June gets up. She's got a stricken look on her face. She grabs my hand and puts it in a Lutheran death grip, where her pinky wraps around the outside of my hand so tightly, it chokes my palm. Usually, this particular handhold only happens at the Brookdale Mall. I loathe it, since it ensures that I cannot so much as turn around to look at the lady with the especially interesting makeup and hair.

"What in the world could be going on?" she mutters worriedly as we make our way back to the guard station. She leans forward to speak into the silver vent, and then it speaks back to us. Worrisome things.

"Mrs. Ericson, the inmate you're trying to see is not allowed visitors today."

"I beg your *pardon*?" June is aghast. "There must be some kind of mistake—"

"His privileges have been revoked. Until next week. You can come back then." The guard says it with a straight face. They don't give *anything* away around here. Not even smiles. "I'm sorry." The guard shakes his head.

"He's not sorry," I pipe up. June yanks on my arm. It's obvious the guy's not sorry.

June looks around in that way people do when they suddenly find themselves in a moment they could never have expected and are therefore totally unprepared for. A moment without a map. Her shoulders heave, and it looks like she might be about to cry. There's a lost-slash-wild look in her eye. Something I've never seen there before. She's usually a rock.

She pulls me away from the guard window, her breath laboring hard against the constricting polyester dress, the nylons, and the boxy-toed heels. Even her clip-on earrings look strained. She closes her eyes for a second. She's probably talking to god right now. And he must have said something back, because suddenly, her energy changes. She makes her way back toward the guard booth.

"I need to see the warden," she says through the silver vent.

You can see the guard, with his Smokey the Bear hat and heavy golden badge, perform a quick calculus: *Likelihood of getting this woman out of here without a scene, times likelihood of the warden seeing her, times risk I'm taking by putting my ass out there even to ask.*

He looks from June to me. I call upon my deep reserves of Dickensian ragamuffin pathos and gaze back at him with my most heartbreaking expression.

"Wait here," he says.

THE WARDEN'S OFFICE IS QUITE LARGE. I have been deposited in a chair toward the back and June is sitting across from the big man's desk, looking fierce. Make that as fierce as a pastor's wife can look.

"Warden, *what* is happening here?" The words come out like a plea; there's a beseeching tone, like you might have when speaking to god after, say, a hurricane.

"Mrs. Ericson, the inmate, Mr. McMillan"—he shuffles some papers on his desk looking for the right one, the one with the answer to why I can't see my dad, and finally finds it—"is in solitary confinement."

Ooh, that doesn't sound good. June sits back, unsure how to respond to this bit of information.

"He's being punished," the warden adds for effect. He looks like any other sixties white guy—Brylcreem, gray two-toned glasses, short-sleeved dress shirt, and pants that are fashionably too short. He's not an unreasonable man, but even a first grader can tell that there is something about his absolute power as the warden that he enjoys. No—gets off on.

"We came here all the way from Minneapolis, warden." And just to show our level of financial investment, she adds, "By plane."

June has a way of sighing while she talks that is both very affecting and sort of exhausting at the same time. You can just *feel* how much good she's doing every day out there on the front lines—and for people like my dad, who really haven't done a thing to deserve it. They're just the lucky beneficiaries of her serious Christian love. That shit is no joke.

"Ma'am, I'm sor—"

"I brought this little girl five hundred miles to see her daddy"— pan over to me, looking cute in my pigtails and felt hair ribbons— "and I just *can't* get back on that plane without this visit."

"Ma'am," the warden says feebly, "I appreciate your circumstances. We have rules."

"She only sees her daddy twice a year. Are you going to do that to this child?" June is starting to raise her voice, something you don't really want to make a minister's wife do.

"Ma'am—"

June stands up. She leans over the desk. She's really up in the warden's face now! I've never seen her like this. I think she's . . . she's . . . *angry*.

"I don't care what he's done. We've come all this way to see this child's father. You are the warden. You are in charge here. I am asking you, *please*, can you find it in your heart to let this visit happen? Please." She's not begging, she's *appealing* to the warden. To his sense of decency, of family, of god, justice, and all things good.

The warden doesn't answer. Instead, we are ushered out of his office and back into the waiting room. It's now been almost two hours since we arrived. June is slumped in one of the olive-colored chairs, her hankie in her right hand. She's not crying, but she's misty, more out of frustration than anything else.

"Are we gonna get to see Daddy?" I ask. I'm awfully concerned about whether I'm going to get the Kentucky Fried Chicken they order in for the inmates and their families on visiting day.

"I don't know, Tracy. We're waiting to see what the warden says." There's no mean-spiritedness in her. She's a woman of faith, so this must be what faith looks like. No bad-mouthing, no calculating odds, no wavering at all. Just a simple standing up for yourself and holding on to an inner yes just one more time than you hear a no.

A guard shows up in the doorway to the waiting room. The one with the Smokey the Bear hat. We look up at him expectantly.

"The warden says to tell you the inmate will be right down." The guard smiles.

June lets out a loud sigh. "Oh, thank you, Lord." When she says it, it's not taking the Lord's name in vain. *"Thank you, Lord."* No, she's praising the Jesus she knows who can walk on water and multiply loaves and fishes and convince the warden at a maximum-security prison to let a man out of solitary to visit his little girl. She scoops me into her arms and nuzzles me close. "You're going to get to see your daddy after all."

And she sways back and forth as she hugs me tightly.

Good thing, too, because this is a really cute dress I have on, and my dad's really going to like it.

I JUST FELL IN LOVE AT FIRST SIGHT. Accidentally. With a guy on my computer screen.

I am at my TV news job, killing time while waiting for the next car chase or plane crash to happen, when my girlfriend Lisa and I start talking about guys. Specifically, how I should find myself one. I am, after all, thirty-nine years old. The odds of having a marriage that lasts for a lifetime are getting better every day.

I've been single for a few months, since I broke up with Bryan, a musician who came over one evening "just to jam" and basically never left. He and I started a band together, and while our music was actually pretty amazing, we found out why people say to never date your bandmate. You'll want to kill them, that's why.

The relationship ended when I discovered we'd been having a little misunderstanding for the past three years: I thought we were more or less engaged, and he thought we were just filling time until the real thing comes along.

Whoopsy-fuck!

"You should date online," Lisa says, sensing that enough time has passed since the Bryan debacle.

"No, I shouldn't," I say. "Look at me. You think there's any guy *I'm* going to be interested in online?" Sometimes I think I'm so different from everyone else just because of my unusual childhood and my alternative hair.

"Yeah, I do," she snaps back. "Here." She turns the computer toward me. "Have a look. You can use my login."

Filling the screen of her computer is the home page of a popular dating website—the one that's like meeting someone at the office. I guess it's better than the site that's more like meeting someone in a bar, but not as good as the one that's more like meeting someone at Starbucks. There's nothing else to do at the moment, however, so I think to myself, *Fine, I'll check it out.*

I start clicking around, paging through men. Dozens and dozens of them. Click. Click. Click. Not *one* of them is interesting to me. There are UNGs galore—chubby, balding, a little past their prime. There are even some "cute" guys, but they're not really my type. Too long on working out and too short on working in. There's nothing. Nada. Zip. Until . . .

Wait. Who's *that*?

(Don't click it. You'll never be the same.)

The picture stops me in my tracks. There's something so wide-eyed, so woodland-creature about him. He's like a magical elf king, with satyr rising. Equal parts indie-rocker Beck and Brit-rocker Liam Gallagher. Which is to say, he's a guy a normal American girl probably would have paged right by with little more than a note to self saying *25 percent gay, 35 percent freak.* She most certainly would *not* have said *45 percent big dick.*

Me, though, I'm not normal.

No. I am having a moment of Total Recognition. I am connected to this photograph! I *know* this person! Even though I've never met him! If the gods of love could whisper in my ear, this is what they would be saying:

You have just laid eyes on a man who is going to trigger every single childhood wound you have, who is going to bring those wounds to the surface, and who will, in the process, bring you to your knees, all for the purpose of your healing.

Like I said, love at first sight.

Quickly, I scan his profile—as if what I read will even matter. It is exceptionally well written. In it, he talks about living downtown in a loft, and all I can think is *I wonder how I'm going to like living downtown.*

Even as I'm thinking these thoughts, I'm aware that they are quote-unquote insane. *I've never even* met *this guy!* But obviously I'm not crazy. Crazy people don't know when they're thinking crazy thoughts. I *know* this is crazy. Totally different.

I call out to Lisa, who is busy writing something profound, like "(PAUL) *Good evening, I'm Paul Magers.* (LAURA) *And I'm Laura Diaz. Our top story tonight . . .*"

"Now *here's* the kind of guy I like," I say.

"Show me," she says. "What kind of guy do you like?"

I swivel the computer screen in her direction. "This kind." She looks at the picture of Paul. She wrinkles her nose.

"He looks like Beck," she says.

"I know. Isn't he awesome?"

"Whatever gets you off," she says. "Just invite me to the wedding."

I click the page closed and go back to my stupid newswriting. But for the next half hour, I can't seem to stop myself from thinking about how much I'm going to like living downtown . . .

I ONLY REMEMBER A COUPLE OF THEM. Of the dozen or so foster homes June says I bounced through before landing in their lovely four-bedroom contemporary (the nicest house on the block), memories of all but a few have faded.

Actually, "remember" is not quite the right word.

What I have are impressions. Some of them are visual—pictures of scenes, of rooms, of people's faces where the centers are blurry like if you had glaucoma. Others are aural, like the house near the train tracks where the man came into my room at night, or olfactory, like the place that smells of Charlie perfume and unchanged diapers. Whichever sense the images are connected to, they are not so much clear as they are indelible and unchanging over time. That's how I know they're real.

I have memories going back to age three, which isn't really amazing when you consider how much was going on. My personal theory is that when people don't remember their childhoods, it's because not much was happening that a kid would consider newsworthy. When things are crack-a-lackin'—Mom's a-leavin', and Dad's a-gettin' jailed—you remember plenty.

The first place I remember is my grandma McMillan's in Gary, Indiana. But it's not her house I remember so much as the restaurant where she worked. Thelma was a short-order cook at a coffee shop around the corner. While she fried eggs and bacon and sausages and hash browns and served them to the neighborhood people, my cousins Russell and Ray and I used to jump on a pile of old mattresses in a back room. A scene that sounds (and was) superghetto but that I remember as being superfun.

I stayed at Thelma's only a couple of months. The story of exactly how I came to leave there would make a great first episode in a TV series I should pitch about a detective who traces the lives of kids from broken families back to the source of their original dysfunction. In the show, a couple of smart detectives (one of them me) would run around putting together all the pieces of how someone's life (okay, mine) got so fucked-up.

My real-life investigation starts with a phone call to Phyllis, the longtime girlfriend of one of my dad's posse members, who still lives in South Minneapolis. I get her number from Cadillac, who is still my dad's best friend on the outside. Cadillac lives in Los Angeles, and though I don't see him often, we speak regularly on the phone. He became an actor in his fifties and now has a cool career playing character parts in movies and television. He's the only posse member who never did time. He's like a godfather to me.

"You call her," he says of Phyllis. "She knew your mom. And she likes to talk."

He's so right. As part of the inner circle, Phyllis was good friends with Linda, which means she had a front-row—or should I say ringside—seat to my early-life drama. When she picks up the phone, it's like we've known each other forever.

"Girl, I knowed you since before you was born." Phyllis's got a tenor sax for a voice—bright and reedy and impossible to ignore. "I sure did. I knew your mama and your dad's girlfriend Yvonne, too. I loved Linda. *Mmm-hmm.*"

Phyllis says "mmm-hmmm" the way teenage girls say the word "like." Like, constantly.

Mmmm-hmmm.

There's a thing in writing TV cop shows—it's the first thing you learn—where the detectives go looking for A, but they always find B. It's how you keep the story surprising. It's also what happens, apparently, in real life.

Before talking to Phyllis, I thought I knew all about My Life, the Early Years. I've had countless conversations with Cadillac—about pimping, hustling, my dad, my mom, and Minneapolis in the 1960s. But talking to Phyllis is different—she's a chick, so she has all the chick-type information. Like what folks were wearing.

"Linda was *sharp*, girl," Phyllis enthuses. "Mmm-hmm. She was *sharp*. She had herself a mink coat. You know they had the coats made out of the females and the coats made out of the males? She had the *really* expensive one." Actually, I didn't know this. Learn something new every day. "I used to call her Miss Jackie Kennedy, 'cause she look just like Jackie."

Well, maybe not quite *just* like Jackie. I've seen pictures from this era, and indeed, Linda had a bouffant (on a good day—on a bad day a bouffant is just a rat's nest), and a couple of cute Oleg Cassini knockoffs. With her big orangey-hazel-brown eyes and wide smile, Linda definitely had her something. And charisma to match my dad's. But she was a good couple hundred miles, at least, away from Miss Porter's.

After some more reminiscing about female minks and sixties hairdos, Phyllis gives me the twist. "You know Linda's mother ruined her life, girl," she says casually. *"Mmmm-hmmm."*

No, I didn't know this.

"She shore did."

"Do you mean Helen?" I prod.

"*Yeah,* I mean Helen. Linda's mother. That woman, she took it to the *limit*. The *limit*, girl."

"The limit?" (I make a mental note to resurrect the use of the phrase "the limit" by overusing it until it catches on. Kind of like "right on" circa 1997.) "What did she do?"

"*Mmmm-hmmm.* She got all dressed up and visit Freddie in the prison and tell him she gon' take you home with her. And she went down to Gary and got you from your grandmama—"

Oh, yeah. Now I remember. One of my indelible images is a plane ride I took home from Gary. I remember the plane. I just never knew who was sitting next to me.

"And when she got you back to Minneapolis, girl . . ." Phyllis pauses. I can feel her shaking her head on the other end of the line, and all at once, I know this is the moment—the big reveal—where the final fact drops and the villain is unmasked.

"She put you in a foster home." Phyllis's voice is clogged with disgust. "And didn't nobody know where you was. *Mmmm-hmmm.*" She lets it sink in, good and long. "She took it to the limit."

So this *is why my dad's family didn't take me?* I always thought it was because my dad didn't want me to be raised in Gary—that it was too poor and too dangerous for his taste, a conclusion I came to knowing that my aunt Florence and cousin Rochelle were murdered the year after I left.

But if Phyllis was right, and she sounded mighty right, it was my own grandmother who gave me away. Not only did she *not* want me, she didn't want anyone else to have me, either.

Why? Or, more accurately, *why not?*

Phyllis must be able to read my thoughts, because she's already explaining it to me. "See, you was the bond between your mom and dad. Your grandmama didn't want them to have nothin' to do with each other. Some womens would do *anything* not to have they daughter mixed up with no black man. Prostitutin' and stuff.

"Helen hated your dad. She thought if she got ridda you, they wouldn't have no reason to be together. *Mmm-hmmm.* But didn't matter where they put you, your daddy always tracked you down. I never *seen* a man so crazy about his child." I'm still trying to process all this, but Phyllis's on a roll.

"Linda had no life when her mother got done with her. She don't dress no more. Her feet was dirty under the bottom. You know what I'm sayin'?" Her voice rises at the end of the sentence for punctuation.

Yeah. Not really. But, yeah, I guess so.

"She didn't care about her life no more. Her mother tore her life *up.*"

I'm stunned. For a minute I slip into that defended state where it seems like it all happened to someone else. Growing up, I lived in that space all the time. Completely detached from everything. I would tell my life story as if I were talking about a character on *All My Children.* But over the years, I have reconnected the wires—many of them, anyhow—and now have an ability to experience my life from the inside outward.

Still, I cannot fathom how my own mother's mother could dispose of her own flesh and blood. Cute flesh and blood! I can see how much more comforting it has been to imagine my crazy mother being unable to take care of me than my super-rational grandmother making a calculated decision to just . . . give me away. It's the difference between manslaughter and premeditated murder. One's fundamentally human. The other is fundamentally not.

I also can't help but wonder exactly *how* Helen carried out her plan. Did she simply get out the phone book, jot down an address, drive there, put some money in a meter outside a sterile-looking building downtown, and walk in with a three-year-old girl, then walk out without one? Or did she bring me home from the airport and, after deliberating for a while, call social services, then wait an hour and forty minutes for some idealistic codependent (who didn't know what to major in at the University of Minnesota and picked social work out of a hat) to knock on the front door, talk briefly with her, then take me by the hand, put me in the backseat of a car, and drive off with me?

Did I know what was happening? Did she give me a kiss? Did I wave good-bye as the car pulled away from the curb?

Something tells me I didn't even cry.

I MEET HELEN ONCE AFTER THAT, at the age of thirty. It's one of the few occasions where I see my mom, on a trip back to Minneapolis. Helen comes over to be part of the visit and brings a box of old pictures with her.

I've never seen myself as a baby before.

There are a dozen or more photos of me with my dad—him always holding me, me always adorably dressed—and five or six of me with Helen. She was attractive then, with remarkably long, pretty arms. Besides her tight smile, she seems to like me okay. There are only two photos of me with Linda, both at Christmas. I'm about four, so it must have been my last Christmas with her. As far as I know I was already in foster care, but maybe they let me see her, just for the holiday. In one picture, I'm on the floor, opening presents. In the other, I'm sitting on her lap, my smile especially big and bright. As I study the photograph, I notice that this feeling of sitting on her lap is like an heirloom I accidentally put out at a yard sale for a dollar. It's long gone. And I'm a little sick about it.

Helen watches as I go through the pictures, here and there filling in names, and details, and places. She's sitting in a nearby armchair, nursing a whiskey-Seven. But even though we are only three or four feet apart, she hardly even looks at me, I mean *really* looks.

After talking to Phyllis, maybe I know why.

JUNE AND I ARE JUST TWO DOORS AWAY from seeing Daddy—our door and his. The guard is unlocking ours right now, and we are ushered into a large visiting room, perhaps seventy-five feet long and twenty feet wide. There are chairs lining the walls, and each is paired with another chair that faces it, separated by a little brown Formica-topped table with silver legs. The table is the Rio Grande. It looks like just a hop, skip, and a jump to the other side. But it's another country over there. You can't put your body on the other side, except to hold hands.

Unless you are a little girl. Then you can sit on your daddy's lap all day, and no one says a word.

The waiting room is full—since we're so late—and we have to cram ourselves near the far end of it. Once there, it's another ten minutes or so, while the inmate goes through whatever process is required before the door at the other end of the waiting room opens and he walks through it. The anticipation could kill a person.

Seeing him appear behind that door is just like when a contestant is introduced on a game show. The door slides open and Daddy's standing there, with a giant smile on his face. I watch him stride toward me, giving a handshake or two to fellow inmates who are also receiving visitors that day. I can't help but notice his impossibly shiny shoes and freshly pressed shirt and pants. Freddie always looks fabulous. It's part of his brand.

By this time, all that excitement has turned on me and I am quaking with bashfulness. June is giving me a little shove at the rump, but my legs aren't cooperating. The closer Daddy gets, the harder it is to make eye contact, until—

I'm swept up toward the ceiling in a large arc, and before I know it I am flying overhead, looking down on my dad, my feet artfully outstretched. All those hours I've been logging down at the Jenny Lind Elementary ice rink (it's just the baseball field flooded with water) have obviously paid off. Everyone's watching us like we're the 1971 Russian Olympic pairs champions. Then, just as gracefully, my feet land back on the floor.

That's when he attacks me with smothering kisses.

"Give your dad some sugar!" He's shouting. *"How's my little gyurl?"*

Honestly? I could use a Dramamine. This is all way too much. I stand there, staring at a crack on the floor, with a stupefied smile on my face.

"Let me get a look at you, gyurl." My dad steps back and gives me the once-over. He's got a checklist of things we have to go over about my appearance before we can get started. Sort of like when you get a rental car and you have to initial any dings before you drive off the lot or pay dearly for them when you get back.

"Didn't I tell you not to stand like that? C'mon now." He tilts my hyperextended knees from their weird double-jointed position back to straight. This is always the very first thing he says to me, so it's not quite as harsh as it sounds. Besides, I agree with him. It looks really dumb when I stand like that. (I've never thought to tell him this, but he'd be proud to know I *never* stand like that in my adulthood. Parents try, you know. And sometimes it works.)

There's a first prize for my dress and an honorable mention for my anklets-and-patent-leather-shoes combination. Then we take our seats, June on the visitor's side and Daddy on the prisoner's side. The visit has officially begun.

And we're in time for the Kentucky Fried Chicken. Man alive! Things are gonna be okay after all.

The visit passes in a blur of playing cards, vending machines, cigarette smoke (other people's, not ours), paint-with-water books, Barbies, and whatever else I brought in there to play with. There's the occasional frown from the guard when I get too loud or too rambunctious. I can't help it if it gets dull when June and Freddie are talking about grown-up things like attorneys, and sentences, and parole, and my dad's case. They also talk about other McMillans, Linda, me, my schoolwork, my social workers, and the Hennepin County Welfare Department.

And before you know it, it's over. Usually, not a moment too soon. Visiting is exciting, but in the most boring possible way. I get a wavy feeling in my stomach when it's time to say good-bye. It's a little harder and more forceful than the sick feeling I get on my way in. I guess because I know I'm not going to see my dad again for another six months.

At the end of visiting hours, the inmates are allowed to make physical contact with their visitors. Since most of the visitors are women in love with inmates, the closing minutes can be quite an eye popper. I think I even saw a boner or two. Or at the very least, felt a lot of boner-type energy.

I, for one, am okay with that.

Because all that intensity gives me something to pay attention to besides this terrible feeling, already traveling up my arms and through my ears and into the back of my eyes:

I miss my dad.

IT'S BEEN THREE MONTHS and I haven't looked at that dating website again, but I haven't forgotten about it, either. I've been too busy working my way through the tail end of this stupid breakup with Bryan, which is turning out to be a much bigger deal than I would have thought.

There's a saying: "If I'm hysterical, it's historical." Any time my reaction to a thing is wayyyy bigger than the thing itself, chances are I am dealing with a core issue, something deeper perhaps than losing the best guitar player I've ever collaborated with.

Lately, it's all I can do to go to my part-time TV news job, make my son's peanut-butter-and-jelly sandwiches, drive him to kindergarten, and cry my eyes out until it's time to pick him up again.

I've cried so hard and for so long I know it can't possibly be about Bryan, since he was actually a little bit of a dweeb who may have been smart and handsome and talented but was hardly a guy anyone would mistake for my true partner. Except maybe me.

Obviously, I am grieving a much bigger loss. Of Daddy. And Mommy. It shouldn't surprise me that this breakup has triggered it— this is the first of all my breakups since college where *the guy* dumped *me*. No wonder I've never allowed this to happen! To paraphrase the old saying, it's better to have loved a little bit less than to have loved a lot and been left afterward.

I am doing all kinds of things to "get over it," not realizing that there *is* no getting over it. There's only getting through it. I spend my thirty-ninth birthday naked, in the pitch-blackness of an Indian sweat lodge (improbably located in a backyard in Van Nuys), getting in touch with my spirit animals and working through my abandonment issues. I would put quotes around "spirit animals" and "abandonment issues" but I'm not even joking. I broke it down in there. Or maybe I just broke down.

There's another saying: "Don't worry about getting in touch with your feelings, because eventually, they'll get in touch with you." Yeah, they will. Through your spirit animals.

Fall of 2003 passes in a veil of tears, and by New Year's Eve leading into 2004, I'm ready to let it all go. I leave a lame party at

12:02 A.M. and go home to perform a ritual I heard about where you write down every single thing that you want to let go of from the past year on little slips of paper. Then you officially Let Go™ of those things by burning the papers in the flame of a candle. You feel like you are in a New Age bookstore when you do this, but you don't really care because you also feel like you are *doing something* to bring about desperately needed change, too.

Then, on another set of little slips of paper (this ritual involves a lot of little slips of paper, which is way better than involving chicken blood), I write down everything I want to bring into my life in the coming year, setting the intention to receive it now. *NOW!*

At the top of my list: a love relationship.

It's a big deal that I can even acknowledge this. I've spent my life looking for and finding relationships (or is it hunting down and killing them?), but nevertheless, it's hard for me to say out loud that having a man, loving a man, being in a long-term, committed relationship with a man, is really important to me. Maybe because I grew up in the seventies, where I heard that a woman needs a man like a fish needs a bicycle.

Well, fuck that. I'm tired of being politically correct. I need a man; I'll just say it.

So yesterday, I went back on that website, ready to not just try harder but to try differently. The first thing I did was search for "that guy," the one I'd seen while using Lisa's password.

He's still there. In his loft, downtown.

My heart beats a little bit faster as I get out my credit card and pay the fee, then upload my picture and write a short, sweet profile.

I like pale blue water, vintage things, and places I've never been.

Then, I "wink" at him.

I'm nervous because once I click that mouse, I know that I am stuck—I can never get that wink back—and whatever happens from here is out of my control.

But I shake that feeling off and go on with my day.

Four

I Love You, and
I Can't Live Without You

MY DADDY IS HOME! He got out on parole, after four years in Leavenworth. All of us—June, Gene, and the five Ericson children—went down to the airport with balloons and a hand-painted banner reading WELCOME HOME FREDDIE! When he stepped through the airplane door into the terminal, I rushed into his arms. It was a lot like my favorite TV show, *Truth or Consequences,* where guys coming home from the war are reunited with their trembling wives on national television. The only thing missing was Bob Barker.

Daddy has moved into a halfway house and we've been ~~dating~~ seeing each other regularly. Sometimes, he comes for Sunday services at Hope Lutheran, looking fly. After church we walk down the block to the parsonage (that's what the minister's home is called)—my dad in his platforms and Qiana shirt, surrounded by the Ericson girls, who are all dressed for a Billy Graham Crusade. At home June has a pot roast surrounded by carrots, potatoes, and onions in the oven for Sunday dinner.

Other times Daddy and I go out together, just the two of us. Mostly, we like to drive around. We say we're going shopping, or fishing, or to the zoo, but what we really do is turn the radio up and roll the car windows down, and get our cruise on.

My dad's car is huge, with doors so big I can't shut them by myself unless I'm standing up. The seats are white leather and the windows go up and down automatically when you push a little metal doodad on the armrest. It's awfully cool. And a long, long way from that new Mercury Comet the Ericsons just bought.

"Can we get some beef jerky?" I ask.

I love beef jerky. It's salty and chewy and I like to chew on things. It gives me something to do with my nervous energy.

"Absolutely," my dad says as he single-handedly swings the steering wheel, the size of an extra-large pizza, in the direction of the corner store. "Whatever you'd like, darling."

I don't ask my dad for things as much as I put in a request. There's never any question that I will get what I have asked for, as long as it's within reason. It's just a matter of time, which means there's no need to wheedle and no manipulation necessary. It's not that he's trying to buy my love. It's that he doesn't see any reason to deny me.

"And can I get some Pixy Stix, too?"

I love beef jerky, but I'm *obsessed* with Pixy Stix, the powdered SweeTart-like candy that comes in a paper tube decorated with a colorful swirl. Pixy Stix are the crack cocaine of candy. Pure, unadulterated sugar, laced with tangy ascorbic acid. So addictive, you might as well just smoke the motherfuckers. Or shoot them up.

"Sure, little gyurl. Pixy Stix, too."

We head over to Humboldt Drug, where usually I have to shoplift my candy because I need much more than the Ericsons think is reasonable. In minutes I am contentedly munching on leathery beef as we drive around North Minneapolis, listening to soul music on the radio.

Until my dad and I started chilling together, I didn't even know Minneapolis *had* a soul station. "Me and Mrs. Jones" is my favorite song. It has a sad melody that matches the way I feel inside a lot better than Andy Williams's "Raindrops Keep Fallin' on My Head" or whatever it is that June is always listening to in her car. I also like

"Back Stabbers" by the O'Jays and "Reach Out (I'll Be There)" by the Four Tops. My musical taste apparently hints at my emotional life—all about lying, cheating, and being left.

"Can we go to the record store?"

"Sure, baby," my dad says, "we can go to the record store." It's just a normal sentence, but when my dad says it, it sounds like he's about to start laughing. My dad thinks everything that comes out of my mouth is terribly amusing. He has this way of looking at me when I talk—he pays very close attention, much more than adults usually do, and he listens very carefully, smiling but not mocking. The most accurate word for it, I think, is "delight." He delights in pretty much whatever I say.

I already know what I'm going to get—the new Sonny and Cher record. My dad has bought me every single one of their albums, except for the one from Cher's fur-vest-and-straight-bangs era, which I don't want. The new album has pictures of the inside of Sonny and Cher's Beverly Hills mansion—all blue velvet upholstery and sump- tuous furnishings—which I will spend hours poring over, in an early intuitive form of creative visualization. I wouldn't dare tell anyone this, but what I really want to be when I grow up is Cher. One time I told one of my social workers this and she gave me a very funny look. So now whenever anyone asks, I just say I want to be a nurse.

We walk out of the record store loaded with music. In addition to my new Cher porn, I've got a half-dozen 45s: "Little Willy" by Sweet, "Tie a Yellow Ribbon Round the Ole Oak Tree" by Tony Orlando and Dawn, "The Night the Lights Went Out in Georgia" by Vicki Lawrence, and "Sing" by the Carpenters. I'll play them on the tur- quoise portable record player my dad bought me a few outings ago.

"Hey, baby. You want to go fishing?"

"Yeah!" I shout. My dad knows I love to fish. It's pretty much the only time I'm able to sit absolutely still.

But it's too late to go get our fishing poles and buy some worms and head to Cedar Lake to get in a boat for some real fishing, so my dad pulls over near Shingle Creek (locally pronounced "crick"), a tiny riverlike body of water that wends its way through North Minneapolis. (South Minneapolis has its own crick, called Minnehaha Creek.) It's sunny out, and little bits of gold dapple the surface of the water where the light is filtering through the elm trees. The creek is too cold to really step into, but there are little pools of shallow water near the edge where it's fun to stick your hand in and pull out a pretty rock. Sometimes if you break them open, they have the mesmerizing concentric circles of an agate.

"Look!" I blurt out, pointing at a school of minnows that has taken up residence in a tiny eddy. "Baby fish!"

I'm really excited. But it's not enough for me to just witness the beauty of the minnows. I want to catch one. I try to trap one of the wriggly little suckers in my cupped hands. I'm not even close.

"Wait a minute," Freddie says. I turn to see him trekking back up the short embankment toward the car. "I'll be right back. Don't move."

He's back in a jiffy, toting a glass jar. I have no idea where he got it. Maybe he just drives around with old jars in his big car. Probably it had something disgusting in it that he likes to eat, like pickled pigs' feet or some other nasty Southern food.

"Go ahead and catch one," he says encouragingly. He gives the jar a quick rinse by swishing cold, clear Shingle Creek water around inside of it. "You can put it in this," he says, tossing me the jar.

Ghetto aquarium in hand, I run along the creek's edge, stopping every so often to scoop up a jarful of water and checking to see if there are any wriggling little fishes in there. My dad runs along behind me.

"Did you get one?" he asks. He's almost as excited as I am.

"No," I say, submerging the jar again. I pull it up to eye level to see if there's a minnow in there. Nothing. Except leaves, and sticks, and dirt. I am bereft. "I'm *never* gonna catch a minnow!"

Freddie laughs at how emotional I am. "Just try again," he says.

I do try again, and again, but each time, I come up empty. "I *can't*," I wail.

I'm not a little girl with a lot of perseverance. I think if I don't get something the first couple of times I try for it, it means the gods have chosen some *other* little girl for the honor of catching a minnow in a jar. Like maybe Buffy from the TV show *Family Affair*. She (and her ilk) seem to have been chosen for *most* of the honors.

"Keep trying," my dad offers. "You'll get one." He seems so certain.

But every attempt is coming up empty, and it's starting to feel personal. "They won't let me catch them!" I'm frustrated now and getting near tears. My feet are soaking wet, and the watermark on my jeans is hitting somewhere around the knee. I'm cold, too. Spring in Minnesota is like winter everywhere else.

"Tracy Renee," he says, sounding almost impatient, "put that jar in the water and catch a minnow." He's really firm about it, which takes me by surprise. *Catch the damn minnow;* that's the tone of voice he just used. I find it scary and liberating to be expected to succeed and not allowed to fail, simultaneously. It gives me permission to let go of my well-worn view of myself as the helpless little foster child who can't get what she wants and fully commit to the idea of having the minnow.

Of *owning* the minnow. I rent everything. Even parents. (And later, husbands.)

I don't know how to get what I need, much less take what I want. And the Ericsons can't teach me—they're much too Swedish for that sort of thing. But my dad knows how. In fact, he's so sure he deserves what he wants that he's even willing to steal it (which I don't con-done). In a strange way, his willingness is exactly what I'm going to need to survive the life he has, through his choices, tossed me into. It's not that I need to be willing to steal, it's that I need to be willing to go for it, to want something and to think I deserve it.

"There they are!" I spot the school of minnows again and pitch myself forward, almost falling in as I bail a full jar of water out of

Shingle Creek. Like a desperate forty-niner panning for gold, I hold the jar up and there, swimming contentedly in the murky water, is a tiny little minnow.

"You got it, baby!" My dad's jubilant. "You got one!" Freddie's gotten a little messy in all the excitement: his green leather shoes have a ring of water damage, and there are specks of gray water spots on his polyester pants. "Bring it here. Show it to your dad."

He peers into the jar. "There he is! Your minnow." He claps and takes a big swig of air that makes a deep resonant sound of glee in his throat. He obviously approves. "A good-lookin' son of a gun, too." Freddie laughs big. "What are you going to name him?"

Name him? I never thought of giving him a name. But it only takes me a second to come up with something. "How about Mrs. Jones?"

Freddie looks like he's going to fall over with fatherly pride. From the expression on his face, I'm the smartest, most amazing girl on the planet. "Mrs. Jones it is, then," he says, without mentioning anything about gender reassignment. He gives me the cover to the jar and I screw it on, so I can take my trophy home. June and Gene are going to be so impressed. On the way home we listen to Stevie Wonder sing about the sunshine in his life and I think to myself that I got one.

It might be the first time in my short little life that I got one.

PAUL WRITES BACK RIGHT AWAY. *"Could you be more gorgeous?"* That's what he writes.

Could.

You.

Be.

More.

Gorgeous.

Um, yeah. I probably could be. Or at least I could *have been,* until this moment. Now I'm suddenly feeling pretty gorgeous. The rest of his note is short and sweet and to the point: *"I would like to take you to coffee."*

And so you shall. Take me to coffee.

I meet him in the Art and Architecture stacks at Borders. His idea. Which I think is inspired, romantic, and creative. I don't think it means he prefers fantasy over real life. It also has the added advantage of being a relatively discreet place since I'm pretty mortified to actually be hooking up with someone I met online.

I'm careful to get there just a few minutes late. For my outfit, I've managed the neither-here-nor-there, not-too-much-or-too-little, not-too-sexy-or-too-prim, not-too-high-of-heels-in-case-he's-short blind date outfit conundrum so well, I will not even remember what I was wearing a week later.

"You're beautiful," he says sometime in the first minute. He's gazing at me.

I blush. "Really?" I think this is such a charming and vulnerable thing to say. I don't think it's seductive or calculating.

"Yeah, really." He's still gazing. "Really," he repeats. That awkward date feeling descends upon us, but he, thankfully, breaks the silence. "Would you like to get a cup of coffee?"

"Sure!" I'm grateful for the distraction of being able to walk and talk.

We head for the café, which gives me a chance to check out his outfit. There's a green vintage dress shirt, which I'm liking, topped with a corduroy vintage casual overcoat. Nice start. His bottom half could use some work, though. He's wearing "designer" jeans, which (unfairly) I have a terrible prejudice against, even though I own a dozen pairs. I'm partial to slightly oversize Levis 501s on men. Anything else seems vain. Like they succumbed to a Diesel ad, unconsciously hoping they would get that Amazonian Brigitte Bardot–lookalike chick if they wore those jeans. And his shoes—a zip-up ankle boot with a little too much heel—are also a bit suspect. But the rest of him is pretty cute, so I decide to let it go.

At the café, there's a line, so we stand in it.

He starts telling me about his four-year-old son and the "great" relationship he has with his baby-mama, who is also "really great." I'm not thinking that if it was really that "great" a relationship they'd still be in it. Nor do I know yet that he would regularly like to murder his ex and that she would like to murder him right back. I won't find that out for a while, and by the time I do, I'm pretty sure that, since my love is so awesome, it will all get resolved.

We get our coffees and sit down at a table near the window. He's jabbering—literally—about the presidential election, John Kerry, and the primary, but I don't think this is because he's obsessive. To be honest, I'm not really listening. I have a borderline hand fetish, which means I'm paying an inordinate amount of attention to his fingers, which are long and slim (but not pointy), the kind I like, maybe because mine are thicker and more square. His nails are dirt free and clipped to the quick, which I'm also partial to. I can just tell he has good handwriting.

The "discussion," quite frankly, is one-sided and boring, and he hasn't really asked me anything about me yet, but I don't think this is because he's narcissistic. He also has a strange quirk—he punctuates his conversation with cartoon noises, like *woo-hoo!* or *hee-hee,* said in the manner of Dudley Do-Right on a day when he was doing wrong. It's kind of annoying, but I don't think it's part of what noted psychologist Donald Winnicott would say is an overdeveloped false self. Or in this case, possibly underdeveloped.

It's time to do something else, so we walk over to Amoeba Records, one of the world's biggest (and noisiest) record stores. It's much too loud for conversation, but we do wander around the store for a little while. I buy the new Cat Power record, and then he walks me back to my car. Absolutely nothing eventful happens—standing in the long line at the record store doesn't count—but on the way back to the parking lot, I do notice that I kind of like the way he walks. There is a jauntiness and certainty to his gait—like he knows where he's going and he's determined to get there.

That said, the date is a disappointment, really. I mean, for a guy I fell in love with at first sight, online.

"Well, thank you for the coffee," I say, a little relieved to be getting into my car. "I had fun." I did have fun, I think. But I'm honestly not sure I want to see him again.

"You're welcome," he replies with a slight bow. "So, does that mean that I may have another date with you?" He slips into a purposeful formality (hello, Freddie? Is that you?), which I don't think is a tad manipulative.

Something about me wants to say yes. (Maybe it's just that he asked?) "Sure," I say, hesitant to disappoint.

"Great," he says, beaming. "I'll call you."

Later, after I put my kid to bed, I spend the evening on the phone with my various girlfriends, telling them that I'm not sure I want to date this guy. "He was kind of weird," I reason.

"Oh, he was just nervous."

"But he didn't ask me about *me* at all!"

"Guys talk about themselves on first dates; that's just what they do."

"He wouldn't stop talking about the presidential primary."

"Then he was *definitely* nervous."

"He made strange cartoon noises."

"He's quirky! Were you attracted to him?"

"Yeah. I guess."

"Just see what happens."

Okay, I'll just see what happens. No rush, either. Now that my son is older, his dad has fifty-fifty custody. I have two days before it's even possible for me to see Paul again. And knowing me, that's a good thing.

JUNE HAS CALLED ME INTO her room. She's got a super-serious expression on her face, one I can't quite figure out. "What is it?" I ask as I follow her up the stairs and down the hall to the master bedroom. I'm a little worried that I'm in trouble.

"Honey, I need to talk to you."

As a foster child, and a misbehavin' foster child at that, I learned early on to distinguish between various tones of voice for their likelihood of leading to a punishment. And I've had lots of practice, since in the four years I've been living with June and Gene, I have wreaked all kinds of havoc.

Here is just a partial list of things I have done:

- dismantled an entire sewing machine during Saturday-morning cartoons
- unscrewed a water main, flooding the basement with several inches of water
- set a medium-size fire inside a cupboard
- picked up and smoked cigarettes left behind in public ashtrays
- deconstructed the arm on a brand-new console stereo
- broke the refrigerator
- tried to get hit by a car so I could ride in an ambulance
- picked every single baby apple off Pastor Ericson's beloved apple tree

This is in addition to the normal juvenile-delinquent-in-training-type stuff, like playing doctor during naptime at my fundamentalist Christian kindergarten; compulsively shoplifting candy from the corner store; stealing ice cream bars in the middle of the night, eating one, and hoarding the rest under my bed, only for them to be discovered days, weeks, or months later; stashing my shoes in another kid's lunch box—forcing me to go home on the bus stocking-footed, (in *Minnesota*); "secretly" unwrapping my Christmas gifts and putting them back under the tree; getting left behind at a truck stop in Arizona; and much, much more!

No wonder they called me Racy Tracy. And put me on Ritalin.

No wonder it worked.

June and Gene are stern traditionalists, and spankings are a normal consequence for misdeeds, but this voice is different. This isn't a spanking voice. It's not a Naughty Chair voice, either. This is something else entirely. At the same time, I'm picking up an energy that seems oddly, faintly familiar.

I trail June into the master suite, a place I only rarely visit. Lavender is June's favorite color, and her bedroom is an homage to its dulcet coolness. Late afternoon light filters through the sheer curtains, giving everything a purply, shadowed glow. If it were a photograph it would be underexposed. In a beautiful way.

June sits down on her flowered bedspread. "Come here, Tracy," she says, patting her lap. I plop into her, almost but not quite too lanky for June's five-foot three-inch frame. Everything is incredibly still.

"Honey . . ." June's lungs have been troubling her lately; when she draws a breath, they fill only halfway with air. It gives her speech a halting, labored quality. "Your daddy wants you to come live with him." She leaves the sentence just dangling there, like it's too painful to finish.

I know what this is about. And it's something I am unwilling to experience. Again. So I'm casual. I retreat into my formidable little intellect.

"Why?" I ask. This is the only safe thing to say right now. Reasons are safe. Explanations are safe. They're like watching news video of a terrible snowstorm when you live in California. You're kind of like, *Huh, that doesn't look too good.* You can see it, but you can't feel it.

"I guess your daddy just can't live without ya, sweetheart." June says this in her customary wry yet upbeat manner. Her joyous Christian love is made better and more interesting by a fat dash of sardonic humor. Like Dr Pepper, a combination of two things, one sweet and the other unexpected. She says it again: "He just can't live without ya."

June doesn't say how Gene, Faith, Sue Ann, Elin, my big brother, his new wife, Missy, and their almost-born baby are going to live without me. I already know how Connie's going to do it—happily. She's probably had just about enough of Pippi Longstocking in her bedroom.

"Where am I going to live?" I'm not really sure why it matters right now where I'm going to live. Maybe I'm just practicing for my future in journalism, where it's all about the Five Ws.

"With your dad and his girlfriend Yvonne. She has a house in South Minneapolis. Near Lake Harriet." Lake Harriet is a definite draw. It's nice over there. "You remember Yvonne?"

Of course I remember Yvonne. She wraps birthday gifts with felt ribbon, the kind I used for my ponytails before my curls got too complicated and June chopped them off. Yvonne's also tall and thin and pretty—no, striking—and wears fantastic clothes. How could I forget her?

I look closely at June. She's holding me tight, and she looks like she's crying, which I don't get at all. If I play my cards right, this could actually be really good news.

"Maybe *they'll* let me get my ears pierced!"

This has been a point of contention for some time. June thinks I have to be thirteen to pierce my ears, but I'm ready *now*. Daddy's a total pushover. He'll definitely consent. I'm stoked. It's just like me to look on the bright side. That's what you get with a Sagittarius moon. "That would be so cool!"

June's kind of surprised by my reaction, but she goes along with it. "Maybe they will, Tracy. Maybe they will."

I scramble down out of her lap. "Is that what you wanted to talk to me about?"

"That was it," June says with some tragicomic amusement at my *Well, what's the big deal?* reaction to this news. Maybe she's a bit confounded by this unpredictable child the Lord brought to her and is now taking away. But she knows children well enough to index her emotional reaction to mine, not the other way around.

"Whaddaya say we go to Dairy Queen?" She claps her hands together and stands up, smoothing her dress. She's ready to go get Gene and the kids. They probably had this planned.

"Yayyyy! Dairy Queen!" I am jumping up and down. There's not much a vanilla ice cream cone dipped in chocolate can't make you forget.

At least temporarily.

WHAT HAPPENED WAS, Paul asked me out again. We had a long talk on the phone last night and I don't know exactly what changed, or when, but I decided I like him. A lot.

Now I have this feeling of intense anticipation, like someone's gone to get the drugs and they are due back any minute. It's almost painful, in a hurts-so-good kind of way.

Paul is waiting downstairs when I arrive. He takes me to a sushi spot where the fish rolls by on a conveyor belt and you just grab what you want. Again, there's not a lot of conversation, but for some reason I'm okay with it. He tells me I'm beautiful, and we make light conversation about current events, and that's enough for me for right now.

We go to hear my friend's band. He seems totally smitten. With me. "You're the most beautiful girl in the room," he says again. I've never had a guy say cheesy stuff like that to me. Especially not over and over. If I had, maybe I would know to watch out. Instead, I'm kind of like that girl in the horror film who's innocently wandering around the house, looking for the source of the strange noise.

Paul pulls out a tiny digital camera. "Let me take your picture," he says playfully. I *hate* having my picture taken. I feel like pictures of me always turn out badly. People with expressive faces don't tend to photograph well, and I'm one of them. But I don't want to be disagreeable. What to do?

I let him take my picture but cover my face.

"It's good!" He shows me the picture, and we laugh. "Look"—he flips through the other photos on the camera—"you want to see my mom's car?"

It's kind of a non sequitur, but I say sure.

He hands me the camera. There's a photo of a 1950s Mercedes convertible. Black with caramel interior. It's beautiful.

"She gave it to me when she died," he says evenly.

"Oh, I'm sorry." I'm not sure what to say. The band is about to go on. "That's sad."

"It's okay."

"When did she die?"

"Nineteen ninety-six." That's a long time ago. I know Paul just turned thirty-nine. That means he must have been in his mid-twenties when she died. "She was great. She always said, 'You're a lover, not a fighter, Paul.'" He pauses, looking at the picture of the car. "I'm almost done having it restored. I've got an Armenian guy in Pacoima who's been working on it for more than a year. I know she wouldn't want me to just let it sit there. She would want me to drive it."

He turns and gives me a vulnerable smile, a boy's smile.

It's the most personal thing he's said in my three days of knowing him, and I'm touched by it. But before the conversation can go any further, someone with an asymmetrical haircut steps onto the stage and begins strumming wildly on a Fender Stratocaster. The moment is gone.

As we listen to the band, Paul takes my hand and my heart jumps a little. I hold my breath—it scares me sometimes, to make actual contact with another human being. Not in the way that a monster running after me would scare me. More like, *What if I like him? What if I don't? What if I don't feel anything at all? What if I do?*

It's immediately clear that he's an excellent hand-holder. Expert, really. During the band's set he takes me through his whole oeuvre: from mindless caressing to some quite sensuous finger-play. If this is a preview of coming attractions, I definitely want to see the movie.

And it looks like I'm going to get the chance. As we pull up to his curb, he invites me upstairs.

THE ERICSONS WERE GOING to put up a fight. They wanted to keep me, like my dad promised they could. But fate, or whatever, intervened. Years later, June told me what happened.

"We went to the Hennepin County Welfare Department people and asked them what we could do," she explained. "They said to gather all the information I could on the promises your daddy made to me that we could raise you until you were eighteen."

The promise had been part of the deal. When the Ericsons adopted Connie from a Korean orphanage (just four years before I came to live with them), they made a decision to stop doing foster care, to protect Connie's sense of security in her new home. So when my social worker called June one night and told her there was this child—me—whose mother couldn't care for her and whose father was in prison, June agreed to take me in. But only if the placement was permanent.

"I stayed up late one night, going through all your daddy's letters"—a long process, since June was a major letter writer—"looking for the places where he said he'd never try to take you out of our home. But before I even finished, Children's Services called and told us we just weren't going to win this. We had two big strikes against us: we weren't your relatives, and we weren't black."

With two strikes, there's still hope, right?

THEN COMES THE THIRD STRIKE.

I literally stumble into the news. We are in Los Angeles, visiting June's sister Auntie Anne. I have just come through the sliding back patio door, a contraption that, on the scale of Exotic California Things, falls somewhere between avocados and Jack in the Box. In

Minnesota the indoor and the outdoor are kept as far apart as girls and boys in Saudi Arabia. And like girls and boys in Saudi Arabia, where they do come together, there is always some type of intermediary—a screen door, a foyer, a little porch—to run interference. That you can simply step across a threshold and be indoors seems . . . outrageous. And cool.

It also makes it possible to hear something you're not really old enough to process. As I enter the room at the far end, I see June hang up the phone and do one of her characteristic deep sighs, except deeper. Gene hovers protectively. He always looks different, less powerful, on vacations, probably because it's the only time he's not wearing his black pants, black shirt, and white minister's collar. There's a feeling in the room—it's both electric and morbid.

"He says it's lupus," June says simply.

I'd been picking up a lot of chatter about this lupus lately, along with talk about prednisone, the room-a-tologist, staying out of the sun, and tests, tests, and more tests. I don't know anything yet about lupus—that it's an autoimmune disorder, that it could put you in the hospital ten times in one year, that it would cripple your hands, that you might have half your lung removed, that you could never cure it, that the drugs you have to take for it are nothing short of hideous. But I know it can't be good.

I linger just inside the door, near the sofa, trying to absorb as much information as I can. I must know it's going to change my life.

Gene just stands there, silently, one hand on June's shoulder.

Not that Gene says much even under normal circumstances. He doesn't come home from church and gossip about what the secretaries in the office have going on in their marriages or what the deacons are doing to screw up the church. He's a container. Strong and airtight.

The most I ever hear Gene say outside the pulpit comes during Monday night devotions—the one we have at home, not the one at church (that's on Wednesdays and it's called Bible study, not devotions). After dinner he sits in his olive green upholstered rocker and we gather around. He says some stuff about the Lord, or maybe reads some of the Bible, or tells a story about Jonah, or Noah, or Moses, or some other guy who'll have a ton of children named after him come the late 1990s. Then he prays. We know it's praying time because he always bows his head and says, "Let us pray."

Also, Gene's a busy guy—he's got a whole congregation to deal with. Hundreds of people! All of them getting baptized, getting confirmed, getting married, having babies, getting sick, and dying. In that order. Because of his huge responsibilities at church, Gene and I don't come into all that much direct contact unless I'm in big trouble. And then he's a kind, gentle, patient teacher who usually offers me some version of what Jesus would have done, which is never ever what I just did. That's because Jesus doesn't steal candy, play with matches, or forget to take his Ritalin.

But within the family, Gene communicates primarily through his presence, which is like a color or a tone—impossible to describe but completely tangible. When he's in the room, you can feel it. And it's comforting.

So when he says to June, "The Lord is going to get us through this," I know he's just taken all that energy, his presence, the color and the tone, and distilled it into nine words.

The Lord is going to get us through this.

I'M DEFINITELY GONNA NEED A LORD. Because me and my new caseworker Ralph Timmons just parked in front of an uninspired two-story tract home in a place tragironically named New Hope. It's a split-level ranch, a type of construction (architecture is too fancy a word) I have never seen before. I will come to dislike split-levels for the rest of my life, and this house is why.

The Werners are professional foster parents, which means they do it for the money. They've got a gang of foster kids up in here: a twelve- or thirteen-year-old boy with a slight menace to him; a kid with cystic fibrosis who sleeps in a plastic tent; another girl a bit older than me who tells me she's "an Israelite." Her name is Laurie and she's obviously the favorite here, probably because she's part of the permanent collection; the rest of us are on loan. There's also an older teenage girl whose name I never get but who listens obsessively to Cat Stevens's *Tea for the Tillerman*.

This is a halfway house for me. A transition between the Ericsons' house and my dad's, where I will be going on June 7. That is sixty-four days from today. (I have already counted.) I guess social workers think it's a bad idea to have you just go straight from wherever you've been for the past four and a half years to wherever it is you're going next. Probably because all the tears and shock and grief might bum the new people out. Better to get all that out of the way with some family who is never going to see you again.

Things at the Werners' are different than things at the Ericsons'. For starters, they only give you half a Popsicle. I react to this with surprise and, I'll admit, maybe a hint of indignation, which does not strike Mrs. Werner as particularly gracious or appreciative. I don't know exactly what I just said to make her mad, but her jaw is set hard. Apparently she prefers her foster kids gracious and appreciative. And who wouldn't?

There's another problem. They use this soap called Irish Spring, and it smells really strong, like kelly green. Neon kelly green. At the Ericsons', we used Ivory. It smells like white. And it floats. If you also take into account that there are no trees and no sidewalks in this awful suburb, and I am the only brown person at school, things are not really off to a great start.

My social worker, Ralph, checks in on me every week or so. He is low-key to the point of dolefulness, with a sad, stuffed-animal quality about him. At least he's nice, but I prefer my old social worker, Constance Ryan, who smiled a lot and took me shopping.

"How's it going there, Tracy?" Ralph drones. His cadence is steady and even, and he overenunciates, like perfectly formed letters on a piece of lined elementary school practice paper. If he hadn't gone into social work, Ralph probably would have made a halfway decent third-grade teacher. Or activities coordinator at a nursing home.

I don't have a lot of patience with Ralph's questions. He means well, but there's not a whole lot he can do about my situation and we both know it. "I'm fine," I answer perfunctorily.

"Good." Pause. Beat. "Good."

Ralph is observing me very closely, which makes me nervous. I'd rather that he not see how they're giving me only half a Popsicle or how I am crying my eyes out every night to "Diamond Girl" by Seals and Crofts.

No one talks about the Ericsons. The Werners have given me stern warnings not to try to contact June or Gene. I think they are hoping that I will just forget about them.

Ralph turns to Mrs. Werner and does some social working. "How's she doing with her medication?" He means me. And my Ritalin.

"Okay, I guess," Mrs. Werner says in her scratchy Virginia Slims voice. "It doesn't really seem to help all that much. Her teacher says she can't sit still." Mrs. Werner says this so matter-of-factly, I'm starting to think she's a bitch. Doesn't she know that eight days ago I had a mom and a dad and brothers and sisters and a best friend named Carrie and a Girl Scout troop? That I'd just sung the solo in the children's choir at church? And that seven days ago it was all gone? But I don't say anything. "Maybe she needs a higher dose," Mrs. Werner offers.

Ralph speaks up in my defense. Slowly. "Well. There's definitely an adjustment period any time a child goes into a new home. Let's see how she's doing in a couple of weeks." He turns to me. "Tracy, let's see if you can listen better to your teacher, okay?"

I'm thinking, *Love to, mean it,* but I just stare at the clock and swing my legs back and forth wildly. Ralph is looking at me again. I feel obliged to speak, to either stop him from looking at me or break the tension, I can't tell which. Probably both.

"Can I get a dog when I go to my dad's house?" It's the only thing I can think of to say. In the time since June told me I was leaving, I have added a dog to the very short list of two reasons that leaving the Ericsons isn't going to suck as bad as it obviously already does. This list—the dog and the pierced ears—is pretty much the only thing keeping me going right now.

Ralph smiles. It's a kindly smile, but maybe it's a brokenhearted smile, too. "We'll have to see about that."

"My dad said I could." This is meaningless, as Ralph and I both know my dad would lie to god. "Can I get my ears pierced, then?"

"We'll see." Ralph, who has been taking notes in my file, places it back into his attaché, which he snaps shut. My stomach sinks. Ralph is kind of useless, but I feel better when he's here. Like I'm not alone. "Time for me to get going," he says. He places a hand on my narrow shoulder. "I'll see you soon, Tracy. Be good for the Werners."

Mrs. Werner and Ralph have a little exchange sotto voce at the front door. I can't hear exactly what they're saying, but from their body language and facial expressions, I know that Mrs. Werner is not too hopeful about me, and Ralph is not too hopeful about Mrs. Werner.

But the situation, in the scheme of things down at the Hennepin County Welfare Department, is not that bad. I'm not getting hit, and I am getting fed. That's probably considered a rousing success. And, really, you can't hope for a lot more from a place you're only going to live in for sixty-four days.

MY NEW HOME PAUL'S LOFT is spectacular. You open the door into a small foyer, then walk down a long, long narrow hallway, one wall of which is painted acid green. When you reach the end of the hall there's this dramatic reveal: a whole floor of an old converted bank building, maybe three thousand square feet in all, looking exactly like something out of an interior design magazine. There are three huge sets of plate-glass windows across the front, with neat period hardware that makes them swing open wide into the room. The ceilings are tall enough for a trampoline. The floors are a beautiful polished concrete and the walls a mixture of wallboard and exposed concrete and brick. There are several massive paintings, which give the place the feel of an art gallery. And outside the window is a view of Los Angeles's two tallest buildings, made of dark blue glass that gleams in the night light.

There's a word in the advertising business for this sort of thing: "aspirational." It means you see it, and you want to be it. Boy, do I want to be it.

The moment we are inside the loft everything shifts into another, sexier, gear. If there was little to say before, now there is nothing. He backs me up against the kitchen counter and starts kissing me. There is something so powerful about him. He dominates me—it's not overt, it's energetic—and I am willing to submit to him like I've never been willing to submit to a man before.

The make-out session moves from the kitchen counter, to the other kitchen counter, to the exposed brick wall. *Uh-oh.* I am in trouble here and I know it. It is everything I can do to A) keep my clothes on, and B) leave, which is not a problem I usually have.

"I have to go," I say, barely. For a second I wonder what his reaction is going to be. Does he want me? Or does he just want me right now? It's going to say a lot about his intentions.

"Okay," he says sweetly. "I don't want to, but . . . I'll let you go." His voice is affectionate, and he's touching my face like he already loves me. He kisses me a little bit more, just enough so that it's not an overly abrupt ending. Then he takes me by the hand like a polite schoolboy.

"I will see you to the door," he says, smiling. I smile back.

We walk down the long hallway and kiss as we ride the elevator to the front door.

"I shall see you soon," he says as I get into my car. He gives me one last, unforgettable kiss and I start the engine, forcing myself to be aware of every move necessary to get the car going, like a pilot running through a checklist. Because all I can really think about is him.

I float home thinking, *That is the best second date I've ever had.*

Five

I Love You,

Now Meet Your New Mom

IT'S PROBABLY JUST AS WELL I'm not a minister's daughter anymore. Because this outfit Daddy bought me is hot. I've never worn anything this hot, probably because the Ericsons don't really do sexy. It's superhot.

Man alive hot.

Daddy is taking me to the Cher concert tonight. That is, if I don't die of excitement on the way to the arena.

I'm wearing head-to-toe white. *White halter! White elephant bells! White clogs!* Daddy really knows how to dress a girl. The halter top shows off my bare back, tanned the color of fox fur, and even though there's nothing in the front to speak of at the moment, the plunging neckline absolutely promises that before you know it, there will be. My seersucker elephant bells are so wide I could pitch one of them into a tent. The bottom of the halter doesn't quite reach the top of the pants, so there's an alluring strip of abdomen peeking out whenever I move around, which is always. And on my feet are killer Swedish clogs—the near-certain genesis of a preference for high heels that I developed at the age of thirty-five, then avidly pursued into the gates of bone spurs and hammertoes.

Daddy's also wearing head-to-toe white—pants, shirt, and European-cut sport jacket—except for his two-inch platform shoes. Possibly the green ones. He has shaved, and cologned, and trimmed his mustache. He has stood before the bathroom mirror and carefully, obsessively, patted his medium-length Afro into absolute mathematical perfection. The Jet Propulsion Laboratory could probably do some calculations off that thing.

Together we are pretty much the perfect couple. Except for one thing: we're not alone on this date.

Yvonne is coming.

Yvonne is wearing white, too. Not like we are—her white is more like oyster bisque, and it has a print on it—but she tried. She's wearing a chiffon top-and-skirt combo that obviously didn't come from Dayton's or anywhere else at the Brookdale Mall.

"Do you like it?" she asks me in that obsequious way an adult who really really wants your approval talks to you.

"Sure," I say, underreacting. But the truth is, I really do like it. It's sensational.

"It's from Cartwright's," she says reverently. "I get a lot of clothes there."

Cartwright's is a place (it's safe to say) June Ericson has never stepped foot into, since they probably don't have much in a size sixteen. It's on the Nicollet Mall, and the clothes are hella expensive, and they're all "originals," which I'm guessing means you can wear them to the Cher concert and be reasonably assured that the only person who's going to be dressed better than you is Cher herself.

"Can I go to Cartwright's?" I ask hopefully.

Yvonne and Daddy laugh. "No," she says. "It's for grown-ups."

"I'll take you there when you're grown," Freddie chimes in. They look at each other and share some private, meaningful glance, and I'm not entirely sure that I like that.

The lights go down and the concert starts and even though our seats aren't terrible, it quickly becomes apparent that Cher is a lot more interesting on TV, where you can actually see her. The songs are better on TV, too, where they sound exactly the same as they do on the record, probably because on TV, they *are* the record. Live music is much less foreseeable—all those rambling instrumental interludes, and the occasional off-key vocals. I prefer to know what the song is going to do before it does it.

I start to get bored. Bored to a kid with ADD is like sleepy to a narcoleptic. Which is to say, normal. I get restless, begin shifting in my chair, and despite being in the presence of my Higher Power (Cher), I ask to leave. Matters are only made worse when Cher disappears backstage, leaving the crowd in the hands of the band and the backup singers. *Boooorrriingg.*

Daddy's no dummy. He knows Cher is changing outfits, and he seizes on the opportunity. "Let's go, little gyurl. I'm taking you to see Cher." He grabs my hand and pulls me down several flights of narrow concert-venue stairs, politely brushing past people standing in the aisles trying to get a better look at Chastity's mom.

"Excuse me," he says. "Pardon me. I beg your pardon. Excuse me." My dad's manners are as impeccable as his luxury socks.

I'm enjoying the burst of energy from the change in scenery and before I know it we're standing at the railing of a staircase that leads up to the back of the stage. There's a doorway at the top of the stairs, and through it you can see the asses of the guys playing guitar and the bobbing head of the drummer. Now this is a view! The part of me that loves—no, needs—to know how things work is fully engaged, which means I could stand here all night.

But then an invisible, but completely tangible *wave* of energy hits my right shoulder and forces me to turn my head away from the stage and toward whatever it is that created the molecular disturbance.

It's Cher.

Epic, legendary Cher—the one with the belly button and the Forever Tan, wearing a Native American costume of hip-grazing leather pants and a fringed and beaded halter. The whole thing is topped off with a feathered headdress so mighty and colossal it's breathtaking. I love Madonna, but damn! The sex. The outfits. The man toys. Bitch stole Cher's whole act. (Credit must be given, however, for Madonna's innovative addition of Catholic guilt.)

I am absolutely frozen in place, and here comes Cher, sweeping toward me, wielding that headdress. As she approaches the stairs it occurs to me that this moment is going to be over almost as quickly as it begins and I want badly to capture it, to keep it somehow, like I did Mrs. Jones. But there's no time for an autograph, and even if there was, the music for "Half-Breed" is already playing and Cher's got to go out there and sing. *Both sides were against me since the day I was boh-ohrn. . .*

So I reach out, just as Cher's hand grabs the hand railing to the metal grated staircase, and I touch her.

I touched Cher!

And like that, she is gone, and the band is in full swing, the pow-wow drum beating as hard as my heart. I look over at my dad, and he's looking at me too, and now it's us sharing a meaningful glance.

I frackin' touched her!

"Did you like that?" he asks me, and I nod my head.

"Man alive," I say. "That was *so* cool."

I still can't believe I'm here.

And my dad, he's got a look on his face that says he's proud of himself for getting his little girl, white elephant bells and all, so close to the stage that she could reach out and touch her hero.

PAUL CALLS ME THE NEXT MORNING. At noon. "Hello, hello," he chirps. This is what he says every time he answers the phone. It's even on his voice mail. *Hello, hello.* He says it so often, it should be written on his gravestone: *He said hello. Right after he said hello.*

"What are you doing?" he asks in a cartoon voice.

"Nothing!" I say way too fast. Actually, I'm hanging out with friends. We are waiting for a table at the 101 Coffee Shop, a place riddled with soon-to-be starlets and never-were rock stars. It freaks me out that I just heard myself tell a guy that I am doing "nothing" even when I am, in fact, actually busy. It's even more disturbing that it spilled out of my mouth before I had a chance to stop it. I guess it's better than saying what I meant, which is *Nothing I'm not willing to drop in a hot second to see you.*

"Meet me for lunch," he says. It's a command, not a question. What happened to the pathological politeness?

Who cares? I am hooked. If it wasn't the loft, or the kiss, or the story about his mom, or the sushi, or the flattery, or the fact that he made *me* come pick *him* up—all put together—it might have been any one of those things alone. In any case, I am gone. Done for.

"Lunch? Really?" My voice just turned coy. When I meet an irresistible force, I tend to become a movable object.

"I'm at Baja Fresh. At Hollywood and Vine." That's two minutes away.

"When?" I ask, kind of stupidly. He's just said *I'm at Baja Fresh.* What part of the present tense don't I understand?

"Right *now,* silly!" The doofus, with his giggly *hoo-hoo!* animation voice, is back.

"Okay," I say. I'm trying to stay playful. A part of me knows it is not the coolest thing in the world to be available on two minutes' notice, but something about this guy has me not even caring.

Six minutes later I am there.

Paul meets me at my car and the moment I step onto the curb, he leans me up against the passenger door and starts making out with me—with the force of a freight train. Or should I say an Obsession print ad? He's pressing the entire length of his body into mine, he's got my head cupped in his hands, and his lips are kissing mine—with perfect interplay between pressure, tongue, and release—the way I fantasized as a twelve-year-old girl a man would kiss me someday. *Someday has arrived, baby.* He's so completely sexual with me, it feels like I've never before been *wanted* by anyone. Or at least not wanted very badly. And in public! I'm imagining we must look so hot. I'm imagining I have the sexual power I've always suspected I possessed. I'm imagining other women must envy me for being so wanted.

By him.

What I'm *not* imagining is his gigantic boner. Is that *really* his dick on my *thigh*? How big is that thing, anyway?

We make out for the next hour—in the Baja Fresh line, while waiting for the food, during the meal, after the meal, and again once we get back to my car—which is all the time I have before I am scheduled to report to my TV news job.

The station is located just two blocks down Sunset Boulevard, so I stagger into work, drunk on adrenaline, oxytocin, and dopamine. I sit at my desk, struggling to write much in the way of TV news. I'm too gone even to tell Lisa to start shopping for a dress for the wedding.

This guy is going to be my next boyfriend.

YVONNE IS, APPARENTLY, going to be my next mom. No one has told her that I don't want a new mom—I liked my last mom just fine—and that even if I did want a new mom, I could certainly find someone with more qualifications than being my dad's chain-smoking girlfriend.

Yvonne also doesn't know that I phased out the position of My Mom the day I left the Ericsons, and I see no reason to tell her, because actually, I really like her. She's beautiful in a fierce Joan Crawford kind of way, with thick shoulder-length hair and wide-set eyes the color of the Swedish flag. She smokes Parliament cigarettes, thirty a day, swears whenever she wants to, and has a whole drawer full of sparkly cocktail rings. Even though she's always saying her hips are too wide and her ass is too flat, the truth is she's utterly glam and by pretty much any measure a total knockout.

And her house—her house is a seventies wet dream. Every room has its own custom wallpaper, "Special-ordered from Chicago," she says, and you can tell that's true because it's not like anything anybody has in the Ericson's neighborhood. (Nobody has anything like it in this area either, for that matter.) The living room walls are covered in a pattern of bluish-gray oversize fleurs-de-lys wallpaper—made all the more awesome because it's both mirrored *and* flocked.

The rest of the décor is straight out of *American Gangster:* a giant chrome Arco lamp shrugged sexily over the sleek maroon sofa like a studly guy moving in for the kill, and a pair of sumptuous almond-milk love seats separated by a coffee table wearing a glass top almost two inches thick.

It's tight.

But even without the house, I'd like Yvonne. She's like a really cool aunt who lets you ride in the front seat and drink soda at every meal. The one whose house you would run away to if your own parents got too parental on you.

When she's good, Yvonne is the most fun grown-up I've ever met—even more fun than my dad because she's a girl, which means she talks a lot more and the stuff she talks about is more interesting to me. Her kind of fun is very similar to my kind of fun—for example, she has a complete set of the *Encyclopaedia Britannica,* including the yearbooks.

That's major fun.

Our dining room is lined with shelves of books on every subject—philosophy, psychology, Eastern religion, art, music, and biographies. There are hardcovers of great contemporary literature: a Philip Roth, say, and Joan Didion, Truman Capote, and Tom Wolfe. But others are decidedly more grocery-store checkout line: Robin Cook, V. C. Andrews, and Stephen King. (There was even a romance novel phase—which lasted about as long as the vegetarianism.) And when I feel like putting a couple of notches on my "she's so mature for her age" belt, I can always find a *Looking for Mr. Goodbar* or pick up a *Cosmopolitan* magazine.

Yvonne is wicked smart. Worldly. Sophisticated, even, certainly by Minnesota standards. She is like a Pentium chip in a world of 256 megabytes. Moving in with her is like going to Yvonne School, a cross between a Chinese reeducation camp and one of those reality shows where they take someone from one world, like a Lutheran minister's family, and drop them smack-dab into another diametrically opposed world. Like a drug dealer's home. Yvonne talks to me like I'm a grown-up and gives me the full details on all kinds of things I've been wondering about—things June would never talk about, if she even knew they existed—and a lot of things I haven't.

"Liberace is gay as the day is long," Yvonne says to me one afternoon while watching *The Mike Douglas Show*. Liberace is doing his whole full-frontal piano thing, which I find fascinating, not just because I suspect I was a gay man in one of my past lives, but also because we didn't do pop culture at the Ericsons'. *The Lawrence Welk Show* doesn't count.

"Gay?" I ask. "What's gay?"

"See his outfit?"

"Uh-huh." I see it. How could I miss it? I love sequins.

"It means he has sex with men."

This could be shocking, but it isn't. Probably because I *already know* Liberace is gay. That is obvious, even to an 8.7-year-old. I just didn't know that there is a whole word dedicated to the concept of gay. And until Yvonne filled in the details for me, I didn't know what gay actually *did* to qualify it as gay. But the energy of gay—that, I know. Now I have a term for it.

Sometimes, Yvonne helpfully sets me straight on some of the things June and Gene taught me. Like the day I was telling her how Jesus rose up on a cloud and she looked at me, raised one of her long, thin, Bette Davis eyebrows, and said, "Tracy, you mean to tell me you *really* believe Jesus floated up into the sky? On a *cloud*?"

"Not into the sky," I correct her. "Into heaven."

Yvonne smiles and shakes her head. "Really?"

Suddenly, I'm not so sure. "Well, um . . . yeah."

"So let me get this straight. Jesus is just standing there. Preaching to the masses, people everywhere, listening to him preach. And suddenly he's hovering above everyone, on a cloud." Yvonne's not mocking me; she sounds more like a panelist on *Meet the Press*. "Think about it," she says. "That cloud sounds more like a magic carpet."

"But—" I stop. *Hmmmm*. Actually, now that I think about it, she sounds kind of . . . right.

"Doesn't make sense, does it?"

"I guess not," I say.

"You're way too smart for that stuff," Yvonne declares.

There go four and a half years of intense Christian indoctrination. *Poof!* Yvonne School is very effective.

Other times Yvonne just wants to talk. About random stuff. She only really has one girlfriend that I know of, and they don't hang out all that often. I think maybe Yvonne is glad to have me around, just to have some company.

"A lot of people mistake this for a Mercedes," Yvonne tells me one afternoon as we settle into her white Peugot sedan. It's a nice car—the seats are leather, so it smells good—but until this moment, my thoughts about cars have been limited to *big, small, convertible,* and *stick shift*. Those last two being very rare species not native to the Upper Midwest.

"What's a Mercedes?" I ask. Whatever it is, I like the sound of the word as it rolls out of my mouth.

"It's a German luxury car. They're the ones with the little peace sign on the hood?" Yvonne helpfully jogs my memory. "Rich people drive them."

I've seen those. Not very often, but I've seen them. From now on, I'm going to pay special attention. Maybe I'll start counting them, like the "slug-bug" game Betsy and I play in the car where we punch each other every time we see a Volkswagen bug.

"The Germans make the best cars, you know," Yvonne says. "And cameras. They're a very precise and logical people."

"Oh," I say. I have no idea why Yvonne's telling me all this, but I'm always up for some new information, so I listen attentively.

"Best engineers in the world," she goes on. "It's even in the language."

That I can relate to, since I took sixty-four days of German at that dull school I went to when I was living with the Werners. It was actually one of the more interesting parts of the curriculum.

Yvonne tools down Lyndale Avenue, elbow out the window, cigarette dangling between her fingers. We're going to Bachman's, the high-end nursery where Yvonne gets all her houseplants. She's got a thing for plants, and at least once a week we're scoping out some new philodendron or other. In fact, our trips to Bachman's are almost as much fun as our outings to Lake Calhoun. It's how we're bonding.

"My dad was German," she says. There's a hint of something in her voice. Sadness, maybe? No. It's more than that. Hurt, anger, and something else I can't really put my finger on. After a long pause, she adds, "I only met him once."

"Really?" Even at my age, I know the start of a good story when I hear one. "What happened?"

"He went to the war," she says matter-of-factly. "And he never came back."

Yvonne looks at me like *Did you get that? He never came back.* I get it, of course I get it. I had a couple of people never come back on me, too.

"Did he die?"

"Nope."

"How do you know?"

"Because one day, I was playing on my front steps and a man came walking up. He was tall and had blue eyes like mine. He looked at me and said, 'You're mine all right.' Then he went inside, talked to my mom for a few minutes, and left. I never saw him again."

I am comforted by hearing this, and though I don't have words for it yet, I know why. Because Yvonne is telling *my* story. She and I feel the same pain. I know exactly what it feels like to be a little girl wondering if she's ever going to see her dad again. What's even more interesting is that we're working it out *with the same man*! My dad. Okay, so Freddie is her boyfriend, and he's my father, but here we are, two chicks in the same car, living in the same house, dealing with the same lack of control over a man who can't or won't stop doing things we *know* will cause him to leave us. Again.

The only thing is . . . if we're both little girls who miss Daddy, which one of us is going to be the grown-up?

A COUPLE OF HOURS AFTER I get to work, Paul phones again. This makes me terribly happy. Not just because I really like him, but because it means I don't have to endure an excruciatingly long period of time not knowing if he's ever going to call me again. And by "excruciatingly long," I mean anything over two or three hours. I'm enough of an armchair marriage and family therapist to know that this is a classic sign of an attachment wound, but that doesn't make the fear that the other person will simply *disappear* any less real. Kind of like how statistics about the relative danger of automobiles have never kept me from hyperventilating on a plane.

"Hello, hello!" he crows.

"Hi!" I'm hoping I sound saucy.

"How's work?"

"Great!" Was that chipper? Casual? Fun?

"When are you done?"

Oh my god, I'm so glad you asked.

Casually: "Ten."

"You want to come over?"

"Sure."

"Doo-doo-dooooo!" He says it like the Imperial Margarine hat just popped onto the top of his head. "I can't wait."

"Me neither."

"When will you be here?"

"About ten twenty." News people can be excruciatingly exact about times. At least I didn't say 10:23.

"Perfect."

"Perfect."

"Oh," he says. "One last thing."

"What?" I say.

"Bring your toothbrush."

Ooooooh.

BETSY AND I ARE IN THE LIVING ROOM when the Yvonne school honeymoon ends. We're playing our homemade version of *The Price Is Right*—we've got "prizes" displayed left and right, and I'm pulling double duty as both Bob Barker *and* the legendary spokesmodel Janice. Betsy is the contestant—bidding on a glass and stainless-steel floor lamp. I know that without a proper look at the lamp Betsy's bid is going to suck, so I drag it a couple of feet across the hardwood floor to give her a better look. What I don't know, probably because I just moved into this place a couple of months ago, is that the smoked-glass globe containing the oversize halogen bulb is only *cradled* in its metal holder, not attached to it. So the moment it hits a snag on the hardwood floor, it bounces right out of its cradle and—

CRASH!

It's in fourteen million pieces, all of them special-ordered from Chicago, on the floor.

Yvonne—who is most likely smoking a Parliament cigarette (possibly while playing solitaire) at the black slate dining table with the matching Naugahyde chairs—calls out from the kitchen.

"*What was that?!*" She's not saying it out of curiosity either.

Betsy and I look at each other. We've been kids long enough to know we're in trouble when we break something, so we're fully expecting we're fucked; we just don't know how bad. When Yvonne comes around the corner, we see how bad.

Really bad.

There's this look on her face. Something about it is out of control, but in a way that neither Betsy nor I have ever seen before. (I know this because we still talk about it, and it's been thirty-five years now.) It's a little like the notes crazy people send to news anchors, where the letters and words are all off-kilter, and the emotional intensity seems way out of proportion to anything you would send to someone you only know on TV.

It's very scary.

As Yvonne surveys the extent of the damage to the lamp, her face draws dark and heartless in a way that makes you think about wicked stepmothers and wicked witches. And Doberman pinschers.

She turns to Betsy and says, "You better go home now." Apparently, whatever happens next is too terrible for a little girl from a nice family like Betsy's to witness.

Betsy and I have only been friends for a little while, but she shoots me a sympathetic look. This look will bond me to her for life. Because she is my only witness, the only living soul who knows what I saw that day in Yvonne's face, who knows what it really looks like and how indescribable it would be to anyone who has never seen it. She knows that Yvonne is much more than what she seems, that her good side is wonderful and that her dark side is lethal—not literally, but deadening in the sense that it robs you of any feeling that the world is a safe place in which to explore and play and create.

Betsy can corroborate my story.

She knows how important it is for me to watch my step, my words, my eye movement for anything that might provoke this reaction. She knows what I am dealing with.

Betsy quickly takes her long dishwater-blond hair, skinny arms, and Jack Purcelled feet and scurries out the front door, back to the much more sane and predictable benign neglect of her own home two doors down.

I, however, am stuck here.

After Betsy leaves, Yvonne rages on me for the first time.

"You little bitch." That's her opener. *You little bitch.* "Clean it up."

I am terrified. Because I have lived with a lot of people and have had more than a couple of moms, and no one has ever called me a bitch or looked at me in a way that scared me like this.

I go into the kitchen to get the broom. I'm crying. "I'm sorry!" I say.

"Well, that doesn't matter now, does it?" Yvonne is tracking me ruthlessly as I attempt to operate the broom and the dustpan. I never did much sweeping at the Ericsons'. "You just make sure you get every last piece of it up."

Or?

Or what?

How *does* someone make you fear for your life when you know they aren't actually going to kill you? Is it because the things they do and say to you make you want to die?

This is a question that never gets answered. Precisely because there is no belt, no fist, no nothing—just words, a glaring look, and an unsettling energy—I have no way to prove what Yvonne is doing to me. Even to myself. It doesn't sound "that bad." *Oh, so she called you a bitch, and now you're all upset? And she gave you a dirty look—what parent hasn't?*

Yvonne's violence is more like germ warfare; it happens at a cellular level—you get infected, but you're still able to walk around, and go to school, and have a paper route, and it's not until years later that you come to realize that you've still got whatever it is she gave you the day you broke the glass lamp. And it might even be killing you, in a way. It's definitely making you want to drink.

The genius of it is that the germ—the poison—is traceless. It leaves no marks. There are few signs. Which means if you lived next door to us, you wouldn't think to come and save me. Though a little voice would tell you not to befriend us, either.

After I sweep every single shard of glass into the dustpan and, through my paroxysms of tears, manage to get them into a garbage bag and out to the big trash cans in the driveway (all while being supervised by Goebbels), I am dismissed.

"Go to your room," Yvonne commands. I am happy to escape and to cry alone.

I STOPPED AT THE STORE and bought a toothbrush, which is now tucked into the outside pocket of my purse. I don't know what I am thinking. I'm certainly not ready to have sex with Paul. He hasn't even said anything about an actual relationship yet! I guess I just figure I can sleep over without having to confront the sex question. And if that doesn't work, I can leave before things get too hot and heavy. Practice setting boundaries, you know? I'm in therapy. I know how to do that.

Right.

But then I sit down on Paul's bed. Two minutes in that huge four-poster and all that is left of my "boundaries" is a pair of itty-bitty thong underwear. That's not much to have between you and a throbbing member worthy of a Magnum-size condom. Better come up with a quick Plan C.

"I have to say something," I venture, coming up for air.

"What?" he says. He's devouring me with the intensity of a grizzly bear in April.

"Just, um—" I put a hand to his chest to call a time out. "See, the thing is . . ." I hem. I haw. "The thing is . . ."

"What's the thing?" he asks, nibbling my pinky finger. He licks the tip, then slides the whole thing in his mouth.

Ohhhhhh myyyy gawddddd. "The thing is . . ."

I'm trying to tell him that I need to be in a relationship with him if I'm going to be having sex with him (after all, I am the marrying kind—for me to just sleep with a guy feels like going on one of those loop-de-loop roller coasters without bothering to wear the seat belt), but it's exceedingly difficult to form any kind of rational statement when you're starring in a foreplay scene worthy of *Nine ½ Weeks.*

"Go ahead . . . you can say anything," he coos in between nibbles. He's not toying with me exactly. It's more that he doesn't seem to know I'm trying to say something really important. Or maybe he thinks I'm trying to tell him something awful, like I have herpes—which I don't—and subconsciously, he doesn't want to hear it.

"Uh . . . Um . . . Ahhhh . . ." It's a struggle to locate some actual words. All my brain cells have taken up residence between my legs, leaving only the amygdala, or whatever part of the brain moans and groans, in charge. Finally, after a lot of effort, I manage something that comes pretty close to a coherent sentence. "Um. I don't know if I should 'go there' with you."

Once the words leave my mouth, you can feel it. He knows exactly what I'm talking about. After all, he's in his late thirties; he's not stupid. He stops nibbling.

I keep talking. Slowly.

"I mean, if I 'go there' with you, I'll get attached to you," I say quietly.

"Attached" is code for *I'll want a relationship, motherfucker,* without scaring the shit out of a guy. I have learned over the years to be unflinchingly honest with myself: there is no way in hell I am going to "just be friends" (with or without benefits) with a guy that I am this wet for. I need to get very very very real with myself, even if the only words I can muster are awkward and euphemistic. If not, I run the risk of having my heart broken, or at least trampled on, and it will have been something I, and only I, could have prevented.

I'm almost forty, and I finally get it: few guys will lie outright about not wanting to be my boyfriend, but tons of them will totally allow me to delude myself. It may not be entirely ethical for a guy to do this, but then, me being willing to delude myself isn't entirely honest, either.

On the other hand, I have found that a boundary, any boundary, even one as flimsy as a triangle of periwinkle-colored mesh on a Cosabella thong, will deter most men from sport-fucking me—but only if I am willing to say (in some way that is not super overly scarily direct) that I am the kind of girl who functions best in long-term relationships. Which is another, better way of saying that any sex we're having is only casual for one of us. If it appears to be casual for me, it's because I'm faking it.

"Okay, you," Paul says in that same sweetly affectionate tone of voice he used the other night. "I understand perfectly. With perfect"—he sweeps his top lip, just his top lip, against mine—"perfection." We drift off to sleep, and that's it for that discussion, maybe because it is four in the morning, but also because I think he gets it.

In the morning, we make out for a while, then go to the coffee place across the street. We order double Americanos and perform the choreography of fixing them up—I cream, you sugar; I sugar, you cream—in perfect sync. *We're so comfortable,* I think to myself, *no one watching would know we only just spent our first night together.* I want to be mistaken for his girlfriend.

It's almost time for me to go to work, so Paul walks me to my car. "Have a sweet, sweet day," he says as I unlock the door. Before I can get in, he tattoos me with another one of those soulful kisses, the ones that make me feel where he came from . . . and where he's going . . . and where I came from . . . and where he's taking me.

I climb into my car, besotted.

And as the keys in the ignition do their *ding, ding, ding,* I watch him walk away, still in his furry slippers, and I think to myself:

Jesus Christ, I'm in love.

Six

I Love You,
but I've Got Work to Do

THAT YEAR I HIT THE CHRISTMAS bonanza. After all, it wasn't just any Christmas. It was our first Christmas as a "family" and my dad was eager to be the best Mike Brady he could be to his daughter, Cindy, and his new wife, played by Sharon Stone in *Casino*. After four years in the joint (not to mention ripping me from the Ericsons' home), he had a lot of making up to do. A *lot* a lot.

Pretty much all I knew of Christmas—if you don't count the one I spent with Linda when we were robbed and all of our presents were stolen—came from the Ericsons, where the holiday was actually a spiritual affair. Okay, sure, I got an Easy-Bake Oven one year and a Barbie camper another, but the real party was down at Hope Lutheran, where the two blond children playing Joseph and Mary in the Nativity play were politely ignoring the fact that someone had made a terrible mistake and cast a biracial Baby Jesus. Me. On Christmas Eve we went to church, and on Christmas Day we went to church, and then Mrs. Ericson made a turkey with all the trimmings and somewhere in there we opened a couple of gifts, one of which was definitely going to be new pajamas. The big takeaway of the whole day: *Christ is born! The King has come! Rejoice!*

Not so in the McMillan household. In the McMillan household it's pretty much *Fuck the King! We're about to get PAID!*

Christmas is about *presents*.

"Are these all mine?" I say, eyeing the booty under the tree. It's like that old segment on the children's show *Wonderama,* where greedy kids go around grabbing gifts until either time runs out or they can't hold any more.

"All for my little gyurl," Daddy says proudly. I can see why he's happy. We haven't had a Christmas together since I wore diapers.

It's ridiculous with gifts under that tree. There are big ones. Little ones. Ones in between. More than you could ever use or want. If the Ericsons were the personification of what a New Age person would call Christ consciousness, my dad was pretty much the definition of anti–Christ consciousness. No, not like the devil. Like, materialist. Like, temporal. Like, Donald Trump. To my dad, god can be touched, tasted, worn, driven, and best of all, had sex with. Combine this with the need to atone for all those years of being gone, and you've got a pile of gifts bigger than Mount Sinai.

And it was a pile of surprising novelty and range, unless you consider that they were given by a man who painted a thousand square feet of hardwood floor in a blue, yellow, and orange psychedelic pattern for a party. Here is just a partial list: a rock polisher, a crystal radio set (never opened), a Baby Alive, a Barbie town house (my dad probably figured the Barbie and the girls could do some pretty lucrative "dating" out of that thing), a white Panasonic tape recorder I would use to conduct interviews with "Diana Ross" (played by me, of course), a pajama-and-robe set, and too many articles of clothing to mention. Thirty-eight in all.

After what seems like hours of ripping tape and paper, the mountain of presents dwindles to that one, final gift. I lean over to pick it up, but it's too heavy.

"Let me get that for you," my dad says, sliding it toward me. As it scrapes against the yellow swirl on the floor, the box makes one of those awful sliding sounds that usually make my skin crawl, but for once I don't care.

I get down on my knees, in prayer to the box. I can't believe it's all mine.

"Can you guess what it is?" Yvonne chimes in. This is one of her good days. When all the gerbils in her mind are working overtime to convince her that life with her recidivist new husband and his emotionally disturbed child is really just a disco version of *Leave It to Beaver.* I hope the gerbils are getting holiday pay.

Well, let's see. "It's not a bike," I say, stumped. I shake my head.

"Go ahead," Freddie says, eyes sparkling. "Open it."

I tear into the paper and open the box. Inside is a gift a nine-year-old girl could never, ever, have imagined. A perfect, glossy, seven-pound bowling ball. With my name engraved on it.

Tracy.

Looking at it, I know one thing with more certainty than I have ever known it before:

My daddy *does* love me.

PAUL NEVER CALLED. First two hours went by. Then four. Then a whole evening. Then a whole day. My anxiety starts like a coffee headache—at first a murmur I hope will subside, or go away completely, but instead it gets more and more insistent until it's a shout. At this point, it's a bullhorn.

I've been to enough therapy, read enough books, and been rejected by enough men to know that this is not what it seems to be. Oh, the racing heart is real. The sleeplessness is real. The feeling of abandonment is real. But like a ventriloquist who throws his voice into a creepy little puppet, none of this anxiety is coming from where it seems to be coming from, which is to say, Paul. It's *actually* coming from a time long ago and far away where a little girl without a mother is waiting for her dad to come get her—her dad who is probably out screwing some chick, or pimping some ho, or caught up in some other activity. Her dad, who could be anywhere, returning anytime. But even though *I know all that,* I could *swear* the puppet's talking.

Swear it.

And here's what the puppet is saying: *There is something wrong with you. You are not pretty enough, not smart enough, not well-bred enough, not skinny enough, not rich enough, and not sexy enough, not sexy enough, and definitely not sexy enough to be chosen. There are people who would love you, yeah, but not anyone you really, really want.*

I call up Siobhan, one of my most therapied, most yoga'd, most kooky, most spiritual girlfriends, and ask her for something, anything, to help me understand what's happening here. "What in hell is this guy thinking? He called me, like, twenty times in three days, and now—nothing!" I'm seriously confused.

"Dude, that sucks. But it's also really rad," she says in her born-and-raised-in-Berkeley voice.

"Rad," I repeat. Rad is not what I was thinking this was. "And why's that?"

"Because now you get to get free."

"Free," I say. "Keep going."

"Yeah. Think about it. This isn't a *new* feeling." She sucks in a huge breath because she's about to start giggling. Because this is so funny. And so rad. "This is how you've *always felt.*"

You know how some people can just string a few words together, words you've heard a thousand times before, but for some reason, this one time you hear them and you know what they mean and you know it's true? That's what's happening to me in this conversation.

This is how I've always felt.

She's right. I remember feeling pretty much exactly this way about Andy Weld, in second grade. He always wore this T-shirt with a happy face on it, which was ironic because he was definitely a future Zoloft user.

"You're just on a wheel, going over and over the same thoughts and feelings until you realize that they're an illusion. One day you just *see* it and then you're free." Siobhan puts a vocal flourish on the end of the sentence, the same one a game show host would use while explaining the rules to a new contestant. *Once you buy a prize, it's yours to keep!*

Oh, goody.

But wait, there's more. "You have to act like you personally invited every single person, place, or thing into your life so that you could see whatever part of the illusion it's showing you."

Huh?

I kind of get it.

Then I totally get it. If what Siobhan is saying is true—and I know it is—it turns cause-and-effect upside down. It means these feelings—of abandonment, anxiety, not-enough-ness—actually came *first,* and the men followed. Like maybe I'm conscripting them, at gunpoint, into my war against me. I stick a pistol in their ribs and say, "I need someone to prove to me that men will ultimately disappoint me. You're coming with me."

The guys I draft are the ones who already feel bad about themselves, already have mommy issues or daddy issues or whatever, who already can't believe they're worth being close to. So they abandon and feel guilty. And I get abandoned and feel worthless.

Perfect!

A nice guy isn't really a match for that. Unless he's a nice guy who feels bad about himself. In which case, I've been hired to play the abandoner. It's not that I don't love them. It's just that there's a script, and we have to stick to it.

I hang up with Siobhan glad to have some clarity. To understand what's going on.

Too bad it doesn't take this awful feeling away.

I HAVEN'T SEEN MUCH OF DADDY lately. He's a dashing figure, literally, on his way in or out all of the time. Mostly out.

Even though he's gone a lot, there are still signs of his presence. Like the spinach stain on the kitchen wall from the night he and Yvonne had that major blowout. Or my ill-behaved dog Stanley—50 percent German shepherd, 50 percent Siberian husky, 100 percent total nightmare—who'd be toast if my dad weren't here, because no one can stand him, not even me. Stanley is sweet, but he could do with some of my hyperactivity pills.

There are other indications that my dad's still here—like his friend Tina and her boyfriend Marvin (referred to by some as "a rat in a toilet"), who are upstairs living in my bed, where they've been hunkered down for the past three months. Tina is an unidentified associate of my dad's, or is it Marvin who is the associate? I don't know and it doesn't really matter. All I know is they never leave the room and they're *awfully* subdued.

When I ask Yvonne where my dad is, she says he's "at work." His job is obviously nothing like Betsy's dad's job. Betsy's dad walks down the street from the bus stop every night at precisely five-something carrying a briefcase and wearing a fedora. He works at Honeywell, where he's some kind of engineer.

My dad carries a briefcase and wears a hat and even works downtown, but it's just not the same thing.

Case in point. One night last week Yvonne and Freddie wake me up in the middle of the night. They pour me into the backseat of the car and we drive to one of those bad suburbs two tiers out—the kind populated with meth types and people who like aboveground pools.

We knock on the door, and it opens into a party. Not, like, a seventies party with Afros and hoop earrings and halter dresses. This was more like a Saturday-afternoon family barbecue where kids are running around, the women are klatching in the kitchen, and the men are off doing their (illegal, but the women don't—or don't want to—know) Men Things.

Except it's in the middle of the night.

There are probably a half dozen kids there, several right around my age. We quickly rustle up a competitive game of tag that—necessarily—takes place indoors. We run through the house, tagging each other, screaming, and having a generally fabulous time. No one has to tell me why that band Chicago is wondering if anybody really knows or cares what time it is. Gatherings like this are proof positive that time is just a number.

I'm barreling up the steps, hot on the heels of a sandy-haired girl with a voice that sounds like she's smoked one too many secondhand Marlboros, when I look to my left, into the master bedroom. The men must have heard us coming, because one of them is in the process of giving the door a nudge just strong enough to swing it shut. He doesn't seem *worried*. It's more like he's just being thorough. As if you were going to the bathroom with the door open and you heard someone on the stairs.

But he is too late. I see in there.

They are all holding balloons. Long, skinny ones. The kind used by street-fair clowns to make Jeff Koons–type dogs.

There are five guys, maybe six, and they are either sitting on or kneeling by the bed, arranged in the kind of classical tableaux you first encounter in Survey of Art History 101 during your freshman year in college. The wavy-haired dude nearest the door—a dead ringer for Oates of that band Hall and the Other Guy Who Is Not Hall—is holding a dangling, flaccid, green balloon. The other guys have them, too, and they're filling them with something—something that is apparently located in a pile in the middle of the bed, since that's where their attention is very intensely focused. My dad is the only guy standing, and he's apart from the rest of them. I guess that means he's the supervisor. I don't know if I'm seeing things, but I could swear there's a hat and a briefcase.

Then, in a split second, the door closes.

Suddenly I know where my dad is when he's not with me. He's out having birthday parties with men in bad suburbs in the middle of the night. Women, as a business, is over, replaced with "girl" (a street name for heroin), a substance of such towering profitability it moots even the easy money to be had in the sex trade. Not that woman-izing—the sport—wasn't in full effect. But that's not business; that's pleasure.

Not long after that, Tina and her rat-in-the-toilet boyfriend Marvin get out of my bed and go "live" somewhere else. I move back into my room, glad to be out of the guest bedroom, where the bed doesn't have a canopy and the wallpaper isn't a pretty Edwardian pale blue. As I'm exploring my new-old-new-again room, I find a saucer on top of the tall dresser, the one I don't often use. The saucer is lit-tered with a few grains of something that looks almost like salt and pepper, but darker and smaller. *That's heroin,* I say to myself. I don't really know how I know that.

But I know that it goes into balloons.

AFTER SIX DAYS, I CALL PAUL. This is a big deal because normally, I do not call men. Ever. I operate on the theory that men vote with their fingers—if they want you, they dial, and if they don't, they don't. I don't refuse to call men as part of a game. I do it be-cause when a guy doesn't call, he *is* communicating—the fact that he doesn't want to/can't/won't call. So why ring him up and make him say it out loud? That's just masochism for me and sadism for him. (Or is it sadism for me and masochism for him?) And then there's the fact that if the guy isn't highly motivated toward me now, how's he going to stick around when we get into our first fight? Better to just not start something I already know, deep down, he can't finish. You'd be hard-pressed to talk me out of this strategy, because it has worked ex-tremely well. My dating-to-living-together ratio is like 97.6 percent.

But this situation is different. Paul had called me so many times, and I had felt *such* a connection to him. I decide to break my rule. Just this once. I think long ahd hard before I pick up the phone. To clarify my intentions. Am I trying to get him to change his mind, to see how wonderful I am, to realize that he really wants to fall in love with me? No, I'm calling to act as if I am a girl you cannot just never call again—she'll think you got hit by a truck or something.

This is new for me. Usually, I think it's perfectly normal for someone to be your brand-new boyfriend one day and then fall off the face of the planet the next. *People change their minds about stuff all the time,* my warped thinking goes, *like deciding they don't want to be your mom anymore.*

Paul picks up the phone after one ring.

"Hello, hello?" Singsongy. Like nothing's at all the matter.

"Hey, it's Tracy."

Comic book noises. Lame excuse along the lines of *I know I haven't called.* Then: "I'm at the doctor's office."

"Really?"

"Yeah. This is embarrassing, but . . . I have a boil. On my leg."

"Oh," I say.

That's weird. First that you have a boil. Second that it's your conversation opener. When you haven't called me in six days. After leaving me with one of the most soulful kisses of my life and saying, *Have a sweet, sweet day.*

"How've you been?" he says.

Does he really want to know how I've been? Is he really asking me this? Like everything's normal?

"Good. I was wondering if you were okay." I pull over into the parking lot of Astroburger. Although I thought I would be more relaxed if I had the conversation while driving, this is taking more processor speed than I thought it would and I am unable to steer, accelerate, work the blinkers, and talk all at the same time.

"I'm good. I've been, uh, really busy," he says. Of course he has. That's what all guys who never call you again are: really, really busy.

"Oh. Okay." There you have it. There is nothing more to say. Why did I call this guy again? So much for my selfish exercise in contrary action. Good job wanting to practice acting like a girl who expects a man to love her. I'm totally a fool, and one who has read way too many self-help books, at that.

I'm about ready to hang up when Paul blurts out, "I just don't think we had any, uh, chemistry."

What?! This is terrible. The only thing worse than this would be if I slept with him, then ran into him at the grocery store the next day canoodling with another woman over a cart full of wine, and pasta, and very expensive olive oil.

Because "chemistry" is a code word for sexy. He rejected me because I wasn't sexy enough.

I knew it.

My heart starts beating. Here comes the team of wild puppets. Anxiety and shame wash over me.

I knew it! This is why I always get rejected by the men I really want. Because I'm not enough. There's always some girl/object just a little bit shinier, just a little bit juicier, who promises just a little bit more of a thrill. It's the same girl Freddie wants. The one they all want. And that girl isn't talking about "getting attached." She's going for it. Why can't I be that girl?

But then I remember what Siobhan said. *You have to act like you personally invited every single person, place, or thing into your life*—and I imagine myself holding a gun to Paul's head—*so that you could see whatever part of the illusion it's showing to you.* I struggle for a good thirty seconds to reconcile what Paul is telling me with the intensity of the time we spent together. *Could anybody fake that? Could they?!* Suddenly, I'm reminded of that old line "Who are you gonna believe, me *or* your own eyes?"

I felt your chemistry on my frackin' thigh, dude.

I'm going to believe my own eyes. I was there. I know what happened! It may sound elementary, but giving myself the authority to name my own truth *the* Truth is a quantum leap in evolution for me. It's like someone just installed a thousand megs of RAM in my brain, the cursor has stopped spinning, and pages are loading at lightning speed. I throw the transmission into "drive" and tear out of the parking lot headed for the 2 freeway.

Paul talks for the next four minutes straight—about how he had some initial concern over the exact nature of our chemistry, being sure that it included friendship but unsure if it went beyond that, and how he thought if he dated me at all he would probably have to marry me, and how he was "a silly goose" for not calling.

I listen.

To his contradictions and his paradoxes. To what he's saying and what he's not saying. But I have so much clarity about it—I may not know *why* he thinks we have no chemistry, but I do know it's absolutely not true. And I can also accept that to his mind, for the time being at least, it is. And I can let that difference in perception just *be*.

As I merge onto 134 East, this calm comes over me. And I hear myself do something I have never, in two-plus decades of dating, ever done. *I let him go.* Without anger, explanation, questions, or blame. Gracefully.

"Oh." I take a breath. "I understand," I say, and I really do. I understand that we each have a different truth and both are valid. I don't need to talk him into mine, because his version doesn't mean anything about me. It's just . . . his version. And that's it.

So now I'm all finished. Ready to hang up the phone. I tell him how nice it has been to meet him, how much I enjoyed our time together. "I wish all the very best things for you, Paul," I say. "It was lovely to meet you." I mean it, sincerely. "This is a small town. I'm sure I'll see you around sometime. Probably when I least expect it!" I'm light and playful.

There is stone silence on the other end of the line.

In the silence, I become acutely aware that this man has probably brushed off dozens of women in this exact manner, with this very line—*I just don't think we had chemistry*—and it's likely that not one of them responded by wishing him all the very best things.

"Okay," I say. Now it's me who's singsongy. "Take care," I finish. "Bye."

"Bye," he says, confused. "Bye-bye." He sounds like a little boy.

It's kind of hard to take the phone down from my ear and hang up. It feels like I'm letting go of the one man I've been looking for my whole life. But the second I do, this weird thought pops into my head:

That is who I really am.

EVER SINCE I SAW THE BALLOONS, I've been lying awake at night, listening for my dad to come home. And when he doesn't, which is often, my mind can't stop obsessing over and over about a single thought:

My dad's in jail.

I'm not exactly sure where I got this idea. Probably in the ether, where the collective unconscious of a household hovers disintegrated, weightless, and unseen. Eventually it is absorbed by the people who live there and is metabolized as fears, hopes, dreams, weight gain, headaches. Or maybe it's simpler than that—maybe it would have been obvious to anyone that my dad was on his way back to the penitentiary. I didn't have to be smarter than a fifth grader to suspect that.

In any case, it comes as no surprise, really, when one day Mrs. Turner, who lives on the corner of our block, knocks on our door to inquire about the article in the *Minneapolis Star* detailing my dad's arrest.

Yvonne opens the door. There stands Mrs. Turner in the small enclosed porch. She is not holding a casserole.

"Oh, hello." Forced smile. "I'm Susan Turner; my son Ronald goes to school with Tracy?"

Ronald is notable for his horn-rimmed glasses and not much else. (Not to disparage Ronald. For all I know he's an appellate court judge or something equally respectable by now.)

"Yes?" Yvonne isn't going to give this woman anything to work with.

"I saw the article," Mrs. Turner offers, hoping Yvonne will want to assuage her guilt for bringing ruin to the neighborhood by coughing up information without having to be asked directly. "In the newspaper?"

Mrs. Turner clearly has never met Yvonne. Because if she had, she would know that Yvonne has a special flat, dark gaze that is mostly awful but perfect for a situation like this one. And she doesn't hesitate to use it.

"Hmm," Yvonne replies. "I don't remember Tracy mentioning your son. What's his name?"

"Yes, well, she probably hasn't." Mrs. Turner is getting a little fidgety. Yvonne's gaze will do that to a sister. "His name is Ronald."

"Oh. Huh." Steely blue eyes. "Well, would you like to send Ronald down sometime? To play?" Yvonne can be such a scream when she wants to be.

From the look on Mrs. Turner's face, she would not like to send Ronald down to play sometime. She stands there in astonished silence.

"Well, it's nice to meet you, Susan. I've got to run." Yvonne shuts the door, leaving Mrs. Turner standing out there, wondering what just happened. Once she recovers the chutzpah that got her onto our doorstep in the first place, Mrs. Susan Turner turns and slinks back to her big house around the corner.

That's the last we ever see of her.

My secret is apparently out, but none of the kids are teasing me about it. In my new school I'm weird to begin with, so it's not as though my dad's transgressions are a threat to my social status. I have none to lose. My brand has pretty much become the Girl on Whom Jody Jeffs, the Queen Bee of Mrs. DiVito's Fourth-Grade Classroom, Proves Her Dominance. Jody does this by ordering her lieutenant, Pamela Vigen, to kick my ass every day. Just a single kick. What long blond hair and supermodel height alone couldn't do for Jody's social profile, a single kick to my ass could. Really, I should've been honored.

At home, the arrest and the trial are discussed ad infinitum but never openly. Instead, the name of my dad's lawyer becomes like a mantra—on a continuous loop of every third word in every last conversation. *Eisenberg* this. *Eisenberg* that. *Eisenberg* here. *Eisenberg* there. The name is not so much uttered as it is intoned. *Eisenberg* is being paid a lot of money to defend my dad. And *Eisenberg* will surely come through. Of this, Daddy seems very confident.

During the trial, I go to Betsy's house after school, while Yvonne sits in court. No one in Betsy's family (not even her boisterous older brother Randy, on whom I have a secret crush) says anything about why I am there, and I don't bring it up, either. And when Yvonne gets home from a long day listening to testimony, no one asks her how things are looking for my dad. No one really wants to know the answer.

Anyway, soon it becomes obvious how things are going. Badly. Because one day, it is just me and Yvonne in the house, and the next time I see my dad, I have just left the Cody Hotel.

Turns out not even *Eisenberg* could save him. But I'm sure Mrs. Turner is very relieved.

FIVE-POINT-FIVE WEEKS after I have my epiphany on the freeway, my phone rings. I just miss the call, but I recognize the number. Sort of. I'm certain I know who it belongs to, I'm just not quite sure from where. And even though I don't usually do this, I call back the number. Someone picks up on the first ring.

"Hello, hello?"

Oh, shit. It's him. That guy Paul. *I can't believe this. And BTW, what took you so long to call me?*

"Hi. You just called me." I make it a statement, not a question, because even though I already know it's him, I don't want him to know that I know. So I pretend I don't. It's kind of dishonest, yes, but I'm not sure why he's calling, and I'm not willing to give him that kind of power over me. Taking back my power was the *whole point* of my Freeway Epiphany.

"Hee-hee. I did." He sounds like a kid caught with his hand in the cookie jar. "I certainly did."

I smile like I do when we're all sitting around in TV news and someone asks what is, say, the capital of Bulgaria, and I say Sofia, and the other writers are dubious, but I just sit there while they debate (*Bucharest! Tallin! Bratislava!*), without saying a word. Finally someone will Google it and they look at me and see I'm still smiling that particular smile because I already know I'm right.

I smile like that.

Because I knew he would call me again. Those three days we spent together were probably the most powerful I have ever experienced with a man, and though I know there are times when two people can have wildly divergent perceptions of the same experience, I knew those three days weren't one of those times. If I had to surmise what happened—and I don't have to—I would say that Paul wasn't completely ready for what our connection was going to mean to his life, i.e., that it was going to change it completely. But that's really not my business.

All I know is I knew he would call me again, even if I didn't *know* that I knew. Until right now. So it's easy to be generous and act casual because mostly I'm just enjoying the confirmation that my intuition is excellent. And if that sounds just slightly bitchy and know-it-all-y, I suppose it's because it is.

"How've you been?" I say, but not like a know-it-all.

"Good. I just got done shooting a commercial. In Vancouver."

"Vancouver? I heard it's pretty there," I lob back.

"It's *bee-yoo-tiful*," he singsongs in his best Looney Tunes voice before slipping back into his management voice: "I'll have to take you sometime."

Here's what I want to say: *You'll have to take me sometime? Are you high? You told me we didn't have any chemistry!* But I don't say that, because if I do, this conversation will be over. And I don't want it to be over. It just started. Or restarted. So instead, I say, "What made you call me?" I'm a bit salty. Why pretend he hasn't called me in 5.5 weeks after a conversation where he in no uncertain terms gave me the brush-off? (Even if it *was* a lie.) My technique for getting straight answers is to ask straight questions.

"Huh?" Paul's got a technique, too. When he doesn't want to answer a direct question, he pretends he didn't hear it.

"Out of the blue like this. You called me out of the blue." I'm pressing, but just slightly.

"Oh, um, I had a dream about you last night." He's not saying it in a particularly suggestive manner, even though telling a girl you dreamed about her last night suggests you were lying in bed, naked or something, maybe even next to someone else, thinking about her.

"Was it a good dream? What happened?"

"I don't remember. I just know I woke up and thought, I have to call you."

"Really?" I'm going to allow myself to be flattered, just this once. "Huh."

Then it's Paul's turn to get really direct. "I think I made a mistake," he says, "and I want to see you again."

Hearing these words is a little like discovering exactly what you wanted under the Christmas tree. The red bike you almost didn't dare to hope for but did anyway? When it shows up, you have the sense that there really are forces for good in the universe—that not only does someone up there like you, but what you want for yourself is what it wants for you, too.

Still, I'm going to go slow. Sometimes the roads are icy and I wouldn't want to break something on this shiny red bike. Like my heart. "Why should I see you?" I ask.

"Because," he says.

"Because why?"

"Because you should."

Okay.

ONE NIGHT I AM LAYING in my canopy bed when Yvonne comes into my room. I should say first that I love every inch of this bed—the faux antiquing, the baroque style, the matching white organdy canopy, bedspread, pillow shams, and flounce. It is the biggest, best consolation prize for having to leave the Ericsons, right after my new pierced ears and the unruly Stanley.

Yvonne obviously has something important to say. "The Hennepin County Welfare people called," she begins, sitting on the edge of the bed.

"What did they say?" I am aware that the Hennepin County Welfare people do not call for no reason. They're like the IRS that way.

"Well," she starts, "since I am not your biological mom, and your dad and I aren't married, they called to inform me that you can't just live here indefinitely."

This is where I should be worried about having to move again, but for some reason I'm not.

"They did give you some options," she says.

Options? I love options. "What are they?" I ask. I've never been given options beyond "vanilla" or "chocolate." (Which is a cinch: vanilla.)

"Well"—Yvonne sounds very businesslike—"I can either marry your dad so I can formally adopt you, or you can go live at St. Joseph's."

St. Joseph's is an orphanage. Oh, excuse me. It's a "home for children."

"You mean St. Joseph's down past the freeway?" I've seen that building; it's on Forty-sixth Street. It looks like a rather large apartment building that got knocked up by a Catholic school. Four floors of red brick filled with kids who, like me, have swiped their metaphorical foster-care subway card to the point that there are no more rides left.

Yvonne nods her head. "That's the place." She looks at me, but there's no real question in her face. She's not talking about when I would leave, should I decide to leave. Or what life would be like at the orphanage. Or suggesting that we go down there and take a tour.

That's because there's no doubt in either one of our minds what my choice will be. I mean, how could there be? Have you seen this bedroom set? It's nicer than the most expensive one in the Sears catalog.

"Obviously, I am going to stay here," I declare. I sound a little bit snide, even. Not because I'm trying to be rude, but because if this were a Saturday Night Live skit, it would be hilarious, over-the-top satire to think that I'd even consider trading this bed for a bunk down at St. Joseph's.

Yvonne smiles. "Great," she says. Neither of us stops to ask how Yvonne, who can hardly figure out how to sign a permission slip or make a brown-bag lunch, is going to pull off this whole marriage-adoption-etc. thing.

A couple of weekends later, Freddie and Yvonne hightail it out to the MGM Grand in Las Vegas and elope.

And shortly after they return, my dad goes back to prison.

PAUL AND I MAKE A PLAN TO MEET two days later, at his place. It's good to wait a couple of days, because that gives me the time I need to do what I usually do in this situation—call about a thousand people to talk over the situation.

Historically, I bring my problems with love (if you can have a problem with a guy who's not actually calling you) to my various girlfriends, looking for answers. Every friend has her own point of view—a point of view for which she has been handpicked—so every phone call yields a different course of action. And they all sound so right! So right, I never choose. Sometimes I think I don't really want to make decisions. I just want to think about what decision I *might* make if I *were* going to make one. I'd rather just handicap the race than actually run in it.

I'm a pundit. In my own love life.

But as I sit alone with the prospect of getting together again with Paul, I begin to hear a voice that I've never really heard before. Or maybe I've heard it, but I was at a NASCAR race and couldn't quite make out what it was saying to me. Anyway, now that I've quieted down—maybe because of my age, or maybe because of the events with Paul thus far—I can hear this voice saying two things:

1. Seeing Paul is a decision I can never turn back from.
2. I know—with more certainty than I've ever known anything—that I *have* to do it.

Seven

I Love You,
but I'm Sick of Coming Here

I'M RIDING IN THE BACKSEAT of my Aunt Do's Mark V Lincoln Continental with my cousins Russell and Ray. We're on our way to see my dad in his new prison, counting drug money to pass the time.

"Eight hundred ninety-seven, eight hundred ninety-eight, eight hundred ninety-nine, *nine hundred*!" I'm hollering, but no one minds. We all love money.

At age twelve, I have never held this much money in my hand before. It's a big wad, about as thick as a volume of the World Book Encyclopedia—one of the less popular letters, like maybe "C." For "cool," because that's what money is. Or maybe "F," for "freedom."

After getting out of Leavenworth for a spell so brief it could more accurately be called a vacation (he took me to see *A Chorus Line;* all I could think was *When will this audition part be over and the show start?*), my dad got caught doing something or other, I'm not quite sure what. I heard something about a jewelry store, but there were never any details. This time they sent him to a medium-security prison in Terre Haute, Indiana, a town that brings to mind absolutely nothing. We should be there in a couple more hours.

Aunt Do (pronounced "due") is barely five feet one inch tall, but she deals drugs like a much larger person. DoDo, as we sometimes call her, is a cocaine dealer, who can't lift her arm above her shoulder because of the time she got shot. Aunt Do is way, and I mean *way*, fiercer than my dad. He's never been shot. I doubt he's even carried that much of a gun. Do did some time in a Texas prison, and since she got out a couple of years ago, she's been something of a presence in my life, buying me clothes, giving me money, and having me over to her house, where she smokes cigarettes and compulsively drinks Diet Pepsi.

Aunt Do also takes me to visit my dad, which is the only way I'm going to get there save hitchhiking, since Yvonne is finally *over* him.

That happened when Yvonne decided to sell the house, but my dad—who can even hustle from a prison cell—demanded $3,000 to sign the papers. (It's my fault he can even make such a demand. Minnesota is a community-property state, and they only got married because of me.) Yvonne was livid. She had bought that house herself, it was paid for, and my dad had never contributed, as she said on so many occasions, "one thin dime to it."

She held out. Furiously. Which worked, because we had just moved in with Yvonne's boyfriend—a kindly, older lawyer who used crutches due to a case of childhood polio—and his seventeen-year-old daughter, Stephanie, who took the whole bicentennial craze way too far by painting her bedroom walls red, white, and blue.

But the lawyer only lasted three months. One day I came home from school and Yvonne was standing in the living room, which was unusual because part of having a boyfriend was that she had gone back to school to finish her bachelor's degree, in Art History or something useless like that, so she was gone a lot of the time.

"Get your stuff, we're leaving," she said with the economy of a TV news writer. "Just take what you can fit into your suitcase."

"Can I take Popcorn?" Popcorn is my Siamese cat. He replaced Stanley, who died of distemper not long after my dad got arrested.

"Of *course*," she says, almost like the question was too stupid to ask. "Popcorn is part of the family." I guess the lawyer isn't, and neither is his daughter. We left them—and almost everything else—behind, including my beloved canopy bed.

Since then, we've been living in a twelve-by-fourteen-foot "apartment" in a rooming house with a communal bathroom (upstairs) in the third-worst neighborhood in town while we wait for my dad to drop his demands.

At school, I am a pigtailed pariah—a biracial late entry in an "integrated" junior high where the student body is made up of white kids from my old neighborhood and black kids from Aunt Do's neighborhood. All but a couple of the white girls have defriended me, the black girls like to beat me up, and I get a lot of D's. After school, I mostly shoplift at Sears and contemplate sneaking into the XXX theater at the end of the block. "Sucks" doesn't go anywhere near far enough in describing my life.

As the year drags on with no money because we can't sell the house, Yvonne's somewhat iffy grip on emotional stability is getting even iffier. She moves us into the attic of the rooming house, a groovy loftlike space whose only drawback is that it has no running water, which means we have to do dishes in the bathtub of the communal bathroom. (That is, when the Moonie or the ballet dancer isn't in there.)

My insomnia is getting worse, too—every night when I'm trying to fall asleep I am tortured by images from *Night of the Living Dead* and *The Texas Chainsaw Massacre*, a double feature that Stephanie took me to see at the drive-in when we were still living with the lawyer.

But the real monster is Yvonne's rage, which is consuming her more regularly than ever. You never know when it's going to appear either. One minute you're at Target buying toilet paper, and the next minute she's accusing you of things your child-mind could never think of, things she thinks you're doing to her, like trying to make her "look bad" in front of the other people in the checkout line.

"How dare you do that to me?" she says as we're walking out of the store.

I don't even know what I did. "What did I do?" I didn't do anything. But I know this tone of voice, and I know where this is going.

"Don't you pretend you don't know what I'm talking about," she hisses. We're still in the parking lot and there are people around, so she keeps her voice low. But it's still very threatening.

I have two choices now. I can argue about whether or not I did what she thinks I did, or I can just stop talking. Sometimes it's not worth trying to defend myself (it's not possible anyway), so I stare out the window the whole way home from Target, watching the street signs pass in alphabetical order. I comfort myself with the thought that the alphabet is absolutely stable. It never changes order suddenly. It never thinks you did something to it.

"Just *who* do you think you are?" Yvonne seethes. It's not really a question. It's more of a rhetorical statement that suggests I'm not worth the air I'm breathing. She's looking at me now, and I know that if I don't look back at her things will get even worse. But I don't want to look. Yvonne's eyes are belt straps with big buckles that she uses to hit you in ways no one will ever see. To look at her is to bleed.

"I don't think I'm anyone," I say weakly. I just want to be okay. "I'm sorry," I plead. "I didn't mean to do anything." I'm not sassy. I truly am sorry if I did something to make her look bad.

We ride the remaining quarter-mile in thick silence. Yvonne's method of retaliating for my crimes is to cut me off so completely—for a minute, an hour, or a day—that even though technically I am being fed and watered, it is as if I am all alone in a very small, dark room with very little air. Like solitary confinement.

We get home, the night ruined. It's hard to believe that just a half hour ago we were singing along to the Captain and Tenille in the music section. "You go think about what you've done," Yvonne says.

I go to my room. Thank god for Popcorn. He always comes around when the belt-eyes part is over and the banished part begins. At first, I'm scared and sweaty and I want to scream, but I can't, so instead, I plead silently with god, *Help me help me help me help me. How much longer, god, how much longer?*

On my knees, doubled over on the floor, rocking back and forth, I think to myself, *There is no way I can endure this much longer,* but I can, and I must. It's when I am left completely alone like this that the weight of my problem hits me: there is no one, *no one,* who can save me from her.

After god, I talk to Popcorn, in a whisper, because there are no doors in this attic—*You see what she's doing to me, don't you, Popcorn?*—and Popcorn blinks his blue Siamese eyes, cat Morse code for *Yes, I know, and I'm sorry, but hang in there, because this too, shall pass.*

Then I indulge in my recurring fantasy: that this is all a big test, like an episode of *Candid Camera,* and any minute someone—the host—is going to burst through the door and tell me it is over and I passed. No one ever does, though. And I know they never will.

But it still makes me feel better to think that they might.

IT ISN'T LONG BEFORE Yvonne tries to kick me out. The incident is ignited by the usual "fighting"—Yvonne indicts me for some supposed misdeed—but this time, things escalate to physical violence. Perhaps because I am in junior high and not just taking it the way I used to.

"I didn't do anything," I say back, with a hint of *you suck* in my voice.

My smart mouth is making Yvonne's eyes narrow. "I never should have adopted you," she sneers. "You ruined my life."

"Oh really? *I've* ruined *your* life?" I don't know where this is coming from. Puberty, probably. "Is that why you have no friends, *and* your mom *and* your sisters hardly speak to you?"

This is true. Yvonne is pretty hard-pressed to maintain a relationship. We do holidays with her family, but that's it, and it feels obligatory. Still, I shouldn't have said this. I know by now that saying the truth is the one unbreakable rule of living with Yvonne.

"You little *shit*." She pushes me to the floor and kicks me. With her Earth shoes. She's gotten physical with me before—a wooden spoon once, a slapped face here and there, some hair pulling, and once, a bar of *Tone* soap in my mouth—but never like this. Mercifully, she sticks to my midsection and it's over quickly.

"Get up off that floor and call your Aunt Do. Tell her to come get you right now," Yvonne spits. "You're going to live with her."

I'm scared. I don't want to have to call Aunt Do, and I don't want to leave really, and I'm crying, even though I'm also tapping into that place where none of this is even touching me.

"No!" I shout, refusing to move toward the phone. "I'm not going to call her."

Yvonne lifts her arm to me. *"You little bitch, you call her right now."* When Yvonne calls you a little bitch and tells you to do something, you just kind of have to do it. So I pick up the phone and start dialing.

My uncle Jimmie, my dad's brother and my September 12 birthday twin, picks up on the other end of the line. There are tears and snot in my voice. "My mom says I have to come live with Aunt Do," I say through the snot.

"Tracy?" Uncle Jimmie can't quite believe it's me. I've never before called them in a crisis. "Tracy? Are you okay?"

"My mom says I have to leave." I glance over at Yvonne. I never *ever* call her Mom, though I will refer to her as "my mom" to a third party. Never calling Yvonne Mom is how I preserve my sanity and remind myself, *At least she's not my mom.* I hold out on her like a POW, which makes sense since she's kind of like the Vietcong.

Uncle Jimmie says he'll be right over.

Twenty minutes later, he shows up on our doorstep. Like the

badly written domestic-violence scene that this is shaping up to be, Yvonne is light and matter-of-fact. And she plays down any trouble. "Oh, everything's okay," she says, like it was just a big misunderstanding. "I think maybe Tracy was overreacting a little bit. Huh, dear?" She's nodding at me to let me know that I'm supposed to nod at Uncle Jimmie.

"Right," I say to Uncle Jimmie. I nod. I know that "telling on" Yvonne is a bell that can never be unrung, and anyway, it's not my nature to make such a big decision in the heat of the moment. I'm more cautious, more calculated than that. Even at twelve. And then there's the fact that I don't think I want to live with Aunt Do. She's been shot! At least Yvonne is a known quantity.

So I send Uncle Jimmie home.

Yvonne takes a deep breath in victory. It's not really her win, though. It just comes down to one simple fact: I'd rather manage the devil I know than the devil with a gun and a Diet Pepsi.

THERE ARE STRANGE COINCIDENCES around Paul from the very beginning that give me the sense that the whole thing is ordained. Meant to be. And even though I know that sounds like something a teenage girl would say, I mean it. There are *signs*.

Even before our first meeting, I am dishing with my dear friend (also, crazily, named Tracy Renee) about Paul. "What does he look like?" she wants to know.

"He's supercute," I gush. "He has sandy-colored hair, blue eyes, a wide smile. He looks like Beck." I remember I have a picture of him on my computer. "Here, let me show you." I bring up the photo.

Tracy looks at him. Her huge green eyes grow even more huge (and more green) than they already are. "No. Way," she says ominously.

"What?!" I've never heard her use that particular tone of voice before. I'd think she slept with him, but he's just not her type.

"That guy lives in my building!"

"You're fucking kidding me."

"No. I'm not."

I know, of course, that Tracy lives in a loft downtown. And I know, of course, that Paul lives in a loft downtown. But it never occurred to me that they lived in *the same loft downtown*! Downtown is big. There are thousands of lofts downtown. I've never really believed in coincidences, but this is a lot to take in, even for me.

So you mean to tell me that the guy I fell in love with at first sight from a picture online lives in the very same building—technically, it will turn out to be a different building in the same complex, but still—*as one of my closest girlfriends?*

I just can't argue with that.

I'M SICK OF THIS. It only takes me two seconds inside the prison to realize it. (Or is it remember?) I'm sick of the guards, the guns, and the electronic doors. I'm sick of the waiting room, the vending machines, and my dad's perfectly shined shoes. I'm sick of the drive. I'm sick of the crappy hotels with the mossy pools. I'm sick of all of it.

Aunt Do, Russell, Ray, and I are waiting for my dad to come down from his cell. They chatter among themselves, excited to see my dad.

"How long's it been since you seen your father?" Aunt Do asks me.

"Three years." I'm guessing. All I know is it was some time before we moved in with the lawyer.

"How 'bout you, Ray-Ray?"

"*Long* time," Ray answers, shaking his head. "Since he went away to Leavenworth." You can tell Ray loves my dad. He's got that kind of loyalty where it doesn't matter what my dad did or how long he's been gone—Ray has the same level of respect for him.

Me, I've been indoctrinated with midwestern values, where you accord love and respect to a man relative to how "good" he is. And by "good," I mean does he not cheat, not lie, not hurt people, come home at night, earn a living, and replace your bike chain when it falls off? That's what gets my respect.

I'm contemplating this when my dad steps into the visiting room, beaming. We all jump up and hug him. He does that thing where he steps back to get a better look at me.

"What's that thing on your face, child?" My dad has my chin in his large brown hand and is examining a giant zit tucked into the fold between where my nose ends and my left cheek begins. "Is it a pimple?" He really wants to know. "That sucker's big."

I'm a teenager now, and my dad notices everything, so there's no lack of things to talk about on our visits. Besides my acne, he asks me about boys (they don't know I'm alive), school (I'm underperforming, as usual), and whether or not I can dance (I can, but not in front of anybody). There's still a sparkle in his eyes, but the usual fun energy between us isn't there. I don't know if it's him or me. Probably a little of both. I think prison is taking a toll on him; after all, it's been ten years since he first did time—he's in his early forties now. The old age of youth. Or is it the youth of old age?

We've lost a lot of time. In the past five years, Yvonne and I have moved four times and I've grown five inches, gotten my period, gotten drunk, bought my first ounce of weed, been to New York, had three paper routes, spent a year studying ballet at Minnesota Dance Theater, smoked pilfered Parliament cigarettes as often as possible, and become a regular every Sunday at the Roller Garden. And my dad wasn't there for any of it.

Moreover, there's no way to really connect anymore on these visits. When I was little, I used to sit on Freddie's lap, or we'd play Tic Tac Toe or Hangman, or he'd help me stay inside the lines of a *Mickey and Minnie* coloring book. It's actually easier to talk on the phone than it is to visit in person because on the phone there's no anxiety of having him stare at me, notice my zits, and gauge my reactions to everything.

I miss Leavenworth. It was a vintage prison, totally old-school—

the neoclassical gravitas of the building, the granite floors, and the tall ceilings. It's like the Harvard of the federal prison system! By comparison, these new prisons have the feel of a Denver megachurch, or maybe a steroidal Extended Stay America. There's carpet everywhere, and laminated furniture, and silk plants that are made of polyester.

It's just not the same.

We slog through some more polite conversation, notable much more for what it doesn't cover than for what it does. Many topics are off-limits, like what my dad did to get in here, how his being gone is affecting me and everybody else, how crazy Yvonne is getting, how she tried to kick me out, how our apartment has no running water, how bad school sucks, and how if he didn't want the $3,000 from Yvonne, none of this would be happening.

Instead we practice the fine art of saying nothing too much.

"How was the drive down?"

"Winter sure was long this year."

"Did you hear Cousin T. got popped? Yep. He's in a maximum in Ohio now."

We focus on the external and the mundane. We visit the vending machines and play a game of checkers. Mostly, it's just like any other normal American family gathering. Except it's happening in prison.

In what seems like just a few minutes, it's time to get back in the Lincoln Continental. My dad says good-bye to everyone else before me—we all tacitly understand that you have to save the best for last—which makes me nervous. I'm anxious about not giving "enough" of a good-bye—I know he has all these expectations for a meaningful farewell, or at least I imagine he does. But I'm also worried about what I'm going to feel when he hugs me. What if I feel something? What if I feel nothing? This is why I don't really like feelings. Because you can't, as they say, win for losing.

I spend these last few moments we have together pissed—pissed that I'm expected to fulfill some kind of pent-up need he has for connection, pissed that I'm now facing a six-hundred-mile ride home, pissed that I have to come here. After all, I didn't commit a crime.

So when it's finally my turn, I give my dad the hug. And vow never to come back here again.

PAUL CALLS ME THE MOMENT my shift ends. Six-oh-two P.M. It's the phone equivalent of standing outside the door of the TV station, waiting for me to come out. I take this as a good—not stalkerish—sign. It means he is just as excited to restart our relationship as I am.

I pick it up. "Hello?" I have no idea why I'm pretending I don't have caller ID.

"Hello, hello?" He sounds extra cute.

"Hi!" I'm smiling. He's totally with me. I can feel it. That whole messy business where he was too scared to start a relationship? History. Ancient history.

"When are you going to be here?" He wants it to be soon, I can tell.

"I'm just leaving work." I want it to be soon, too.

"Good. Hurry."

"I'll be right there."

I'm very calm as I drive down the 101. In the past six months, I've seriously taken up prayer (owing to last year's "nervous break-through"), and this is exactly the type of situation that calls for tapping into a higher power. I used to sneak around on god, hoping to get away with the occasional "freebie"—stuff I wanted that I knew-slash-suspected god didn't want *for* me—but those days are over. If it's not in my highest good, I don't want it. Prayer is where I put all that into words.

So I whisper to myself, "Dear Universe, I don't know why you made Paul call me again, but whatever it is you want me to do here, just tell me, and I'll do it. Because I don't have a clue. I mean, you and I both know there's no way in hell I'm going to be able to walk away from this guy, so if he's not right for me, please, *please* remove him from my life."

That sounds good. But then I figure I should throw in some kind of clause to cover unforeseeable contingencies. "And, god, whatever your will is for me, please make it *really big*, like billboard-size big, because I'm nearsighted. Thanks a lot."

I've heard that once you make a sincere prayer, you should consider everything that happens afterward to be part of the answer, so from now on, I really gotta pay attention.

A chill runs up my arms as I exit the elevator. *This is your home.* That's what the chill says. It reminds me of something I heard a spiritual guy say once, that you'll know when something is the truth because of the way it feels: not like you're getting new information, but like you *just remembered* something you've already known for a long time.

That's what this is like. As I walk down the long hallway to see Paul for the first time in 5.5 weeks, I remember what I knew the moment I saw his picture. This is my home.

WE FINALLY SOLD THE HOUSE (minus my dad's $3,000), and we're now living in a place Yvonne bought on the "good" side of Lake Harriet. Not that the other side was bad exactly, it was just a little less good.

My new school is loaded with middle-to-upper-middle-class teens sporting straight white teeth, alligator shirts, and Tretorn tennis shoes. I own none of these things. I haven't even *heard of* these things. Plus, I have a big gap between my front teeth.

I'm definitely bringing the fourteen-year-old awkward to Woodrow Wilson High. My skin is brown from a long summer spent mostly at Main Beach, my hair is puffy, and to put it frankly, I'm a tad peculiar. I'm full of non sequiturs, I bounce off the walls, and

I'm kooky, which isn't really charming until after one graduates from high school and moves to the part of town that used to be gay and is now home to people who purposely wear ugly glasses.

I take stock of what I have to offer in trade on some social standing and it's quickly apparent that barring a sudden run-in with a jar of hair relaxer (which probably would *change my life*) the only thing I really have going for me is that I possess a mean round-off and front handspring, and I can do the hell out of the splits. Add that to a voice that "carries" (as many a teacher has charitably put it), and I've got just one shot at high school happiness:

Cheerleading.

I'm pretty definitely an extrovert, but I also have a very pronounced timid streak that makes me pathologically afraid of asking for anything that I want. And auditioning is asking, right? (So is flirting. Another thing I am turning out to have trouble with.) The only thing I can get up the nerve to ask for is a job, but only as long as it's a job I don't actually want.

One of the girls in my homeroom, Mara "Call Me, Okay?" Moline, is a captain of the JV cheerleaders and, as such, is teaching the "clinics" for the upcoming tryouts. I don't know what possesses me, but I ask her about it.

I should backtrack a moment. When I got to Wilson, I was like a bedraggled refugee who'd been rejected by three other nations— junior high schools that were the rough equivalents of, say, Hungary or Poland or Greece—and had somehow landed in Denmark. On the one hand, I couldn't believe my luck. My new country was clean, and safe, and had a high standard of living. On the other hand, the Danish were all so blond! So beautiful! So well-bred!

And further, I had no idea how to speak Danish.

I had always had a popular streak in me, but once I got to Yvonne's, bad hairdos (pigtails) and emotional disturbances (a very special combination of anxiety and compulsive talking) had sent my social value plunging a good 50 percent or more. I needed some kind of rescue package.

One thing living in foster homes does for you is that you get a lot of fieldwork in the social sciences, and if you pay attention, you can apply it in ways that can make the difference between four years of social hell and three years of relatively fun weekends at keg parties plus one final year where you're totally over it. As a result, I looked around my homeroom and made a vow: *I'm going to figure out who the popular kids are at this school, and I'm going to be one of them.*

However (and it's a big however), high school popularity has a *scent* that absolutely *cannot be faked.* It's a supersecret formula no one in the world has ever cracked, although the Axe body spray people may kill the rest of us trying. Teenagers intuitively know how social status is to be accorded: to whom, how much, and what kind. A given individual can lose status but can never gain any *past a certain point.* Even dating the most popular boy (or girl) in school will only get you plus or minus a 20 percent differential. (Which you then lose when you break up.) Why? Because if you could gain any more from dating that person, they wouldn't want you in the first place.

In other words, there's nothing anyone can do to *make* themselves become popular. Otherwise everyone would be doing it—even the Goth kids who pretend they don't care.

I developed this theory during the first seven months of the 1978–79 school year, a time during which I was abjectly invisible, unless you were sitting behind my home-done "bubble" haircut during the science movie.

As I moved forward with my fieldwork, I saw that the only way to get popular was to somehow have the popular girls *ordain* you as a popular person. Obviously, this observation is not a huge break-through—anyone who's ever seen Alicia Silverstone remodel Brittany Murphy into a cute girl already knows this. But remember, *Clueless* was still seventeen years away from the multiplex when I hit Wilson.

It turns out I'm in luck. Mr. Harrington's homeroom is, for the class of 1982, a sort of popular-girl clearinghouse. In the same way South America churns out beauty queens, the last names beginning with the letters L through M tend, in my school, to produce bumper crops of girls who have that perfect combination of good looks (but not too good: too good is bad) and confidence that comes off as superiority and bitchiness to anyone in the theater department or the marching band. These girls are also incredibly centrist—so traditional they make Regis and Kelly look like members of a terrorist organization.

So homeroom is about location, location, location. Those fifteen minutes a day put me in the proximity of some of the most influential girls in school, and eventually, one or two of them decide to talk to me. Which is how Mara "Call Me, Okay?" Moline ends up answering my query about cheerleading by tryouts.

Of course, I balk.

"COME ON!! JUST DO IT!!" she cheers in her perpetually urgent way. "I'LL TEACH YOU EVERYTHING!!"

I hem and haw for a moment, fearful of actually letting it be known that I would even consider being a cheerleader. What if I fail? Then people would know I wanted to be a cheerleader but got rejected. That would be a fate more like social quadriplegia—where you get hit by a car but *don't* die. Besides, wasn't cheerleading for girls from nice families, with brothers who played football in the fall and hockey in the winter? I don't have a brother. I don't have a family! All I have is a mom, whom I don't call Mom, because she isn't really my mom, nor do I want her to be.

Not exactly cheerleader material. Especially in this place.

But cheerleading does have two things to recommend it: First, it is considered a sport, so the uniforms are provided by the school, free of charge. And I don't have money. But even more alluring is the bigger, more tantalizing carrot that cheerleading dangles. It could do for me what I don't have the power to do for myself, and that is *make me normal*. Or at least normal-like.

So the next day when Mara urges me again to try out for cheerleading, I see that she's really just thinking she wants to do for me what Alicia did for Brittany.

And I'm going to let her.

ALL WE DO ON THAT (SECOND) first date is walk Paul's dog around the block. That's it. The conversation is casual, as if the whole relationship is already in the bag so there's no need to spend a lot of time on courting rituals. (Maybe he got the arm chill, too? I'll have to ask him sometime, when we're eighty.) We've just skipped all that.

We talk about his trips to Vancouver and Buenos Aires to shoot commercials. We talk about the music I've been recording. We talk about dog poop.

He's not seductive, and I'm not anxious, and we are just being.

It's done already.

When we return to the loft, I lounge on the sofa and the setting sun streams in the window. I watch as the sky behind the Deloitte and Touche towers sinks from dusky mauve into midnight blue, like slipping deeper and deeper into a state of hypnosis, until the stars are out. It's a magical hour.

"So how did I end up here?" I ask. This is as close as I'm going to come to making Paul answer for what happened 5.5 weeks ago. It's one of those deals where possession is nine-tenths of the law. I'm here, and that's truer than anything else.

Paul tells me how he had a moment of clarity in Argentina. "I'm thirty-nine," he says. "I'm tired of going from job to job, woman to woman. I'm ready to settle down." He says he's made a decision to change his life. "I want a girlfriend. A partner. And when I thought about who I had dated that would be right for that"—he slows down now, like he's deciding whether or not to say exactly what he's thinking—"I thought about you."

Then he just comes right out and says it. "I want you to be my girlfriend."

Inside my chest, birds are singing, and fish are jumping, and all the animals in the forest are running around like they did in *Bambi* when the prince was born. This is a truly wonderful day.

Paul has a plan and he lays it out. "I want to commit, and you'll have to commit, too," he says. "We'll only date each other." I have no problem with that; in fact, it's pretty much my (second) first-date dream come true. "My hope is that we'll build a relationship and a life, and it will include your son, and my son, even though he lives in another state."

I'm good with that. So good with it, I hardly know what to say. Then I remember he once dated me for three days and just disappeared on me. Who's to say he's not going to do it again? I put it to him straight. "How do I know you're not going to just change your mind like you did before?"

He looks at me. This is a moment of truth. I'm scrutinizing his face, because whatever he says is going to be important, and I don't want to deceive myself into anything.

"You can trust me, Tracy," he says in that authoritative clipped way he has. "I've thought long and hard about this, and I know what I want."

"How do I know that?" I counter.

"Because I wouldn't have called you back."

And I don't say anything because that is exactly the right answer. If he didn't want me, want this, want us, he would have left well enough alone.

My fears laid to rest, the relationship is begun. All I have to do now is let it be there.

So, I do.

We make out for a little while and there's a different feeling between us. A little less heat—from, say, a blowtorch to an electrical fire—but a lot more warmth. Then it's time to leave. I have things to do, and besides, the deal is done. I can come back and get the keys tomorrow.

We kiss in the elevator all the way down the four floors to the lobby. It's a symbolic kiss—like getting married, or getting engaged—a promise of everything that's going to come from this day forward.

I get in my car and pinch myself.

As I drive back home, I consider how my life is going to change now that I've chosen a guy like Paul. A man, really. Until now, I've had a penchant for boy-men, and even though Paul has a boyish quality, there's no doubt that he is fully grown.

To start with, he thinks big. There's the movie project he's developing, with tens of thousands of dollars of his own money, because he believes, no, *assumes* it will succeed. It's about when, not if. By contrast, I'm accustomed to predicting failure, or at least limiting my expectations, as a way of buffering disappointment. And up till now, I've attracted men who did the same.

But Paul seems to think anything—actually everything—is possible.

Maybe because he went to Harvard, which, I'll admit, does impress me. (Just like it's supposed to.) He didn't even bring it up until our third or fourth conversation, and then he said it so casually—*"Oh, I'm a Harvard Man"*—like he was mocking it, but really he was invoking the power that the Ivy League holds, especially for those of us whose dads are in federal prison. This is America, and it's still a patriarchy where the man in your life—first your dad, and then very likely your husband—determines which spot on the Monopoly board you call home. With Paul I'm going to move from St. Charles Place to Pennsylvania Avenue, and I won't lie, I've always liked bright green.

For years I've lived solely on my TV news income, with no child support. (My child's dad is the farthest thing from a deadbeat, but because we have roughly the same earning power—and equal custody—we each simply maintain our own household.) I pull two or three shifts a week in what is essentially a news factory, turning real-life murders, fires, and water-skiing squirrels into thirty-second news sausages stuffed with mostly useless information.

Writing TV news is great—as far as shift work goes. The people are smart and nice, and the pay is good. It's also very flexible—if I suddenly get an urge to go to Paris, I can.

Not that I will. Because working three days a week in TV news doesn't offer the kind of money that would allow me to take vacations, buy a house, have regular spa days, or indulge myself in a thing (or two) from Prada—like many of my well-married (or well-divorced) peers. They are the grown-up versions of the girls with the Tretorns and the alligator shirts. And in many ways, I am still the girl who is with them but not of them.

But here is Paul, with the big paintings on the walls, and the high-thread-count sheets, and the $23 entrées. With the amazing apartment, the supersize sexuality, the long, thin fingers, the well-developed intellect, the serious talent, and the silly voices. With the eccentric spirit, the endearing smile, and the affectionate nature. With the love of politics, movies, conversation, art, and design. With the four-poster bed.

And he wants to give all that to me.

And I'm going to let him.

Eight

I Love You, Even
If You Already Have a Girlfriend

I NEVER EVEN THINK ABOUT my dad anymore. I haven't been to see him in a year, and to be honest, I don't miss him. It's not that he's dead, it's that I've buried him alive. Six feet under my fifteen-year-old "real" life, in which I am now a Wilson high school cheerleader. Yay!

The only time he really comes to mind is when I'm lying to my friends on the squad about him. It's not that I lie exactly—I'm very factual—I just omit the part about the prison.

What does your dad do?

He works in a barbershop. (At Sandstone federal prison.)

Where does your dad live?

He used to live in Indiana, but now he lives up north. (At Sandstone federal prison.)

Do you ever see your dad?

Not very often. He left when I was three. (To go to prison.)

Is your dad black?

Yeah. (In prison.)

Until about seventh or eighth grade, I was totally (compulsively?) open about my dad being in prison. It never quite occurred to me that anyone should think less of me because of him. Crime was his thing, not mine. But somewhere in there I must have picked up a facial microexpression or two that told me pubescent girls weren't terribly Christlike in their ability to accept the sick, lame, tired, and/or incarcerated. Which must be when I decided it was better just to hide that shit.

I follow the same policy with Yvonne. I tell as much of the truth as I think people can handle, carefully framing it in terms they can understand. That means rather than going into a lot of detail about just how, exactly, she ended up as my mother, I simply say she's my stepmom, who adopted me. I leave out any references to birth mothers, foster care, Lutheran ministers, or other colorful details that only beg more questions than I am willing to answer.

Having this kind of secret naturally makes me feel separate from the other kids. It's a tough choice: feel separate due to the stigma of having a parent in prison, or feel separate because there's a huge part of me that no one knows about—even my closest friends at school. It's kind of a no-brainer. This is high school; conform or die.

All I can say is thank god for Betsy and Dianne.

Somehow, Betsy and I have maintained BFF status, even through my moves. She still lives one door down from my old house, she still bites her nails, and she still has long, straight hair parted down the middle. She is a bulwark of stability in my peripatetic life.

Across the street and a few houses down from her lives Dianne, our third best friend. Dianne showed up in sixth grade, after returning from California, where her professor dad moved the family for a two-year sabbatical. Though all of us go to different schools (and have separate, other BFFs at those schools), the best-friend relationship the three of us have is—certainly for me, maybe for them as well—the most important one. Not least because I practically live with them, at least on the weekends.

It's a little like having a house in the Hamptons. I usually show up on Fridays after school and live with Betsy one night and Dianne the next. And, just like having a house in the Hamptons, it's the only time all week I really relax.

When I live at Betsy's and Dianne's, I get to be a normal kid: eat dinner at a table, be told to pipe down, and carry the groceries (eight bags!) in from the car. There are rules, and I like that. Not just for the kids; the adults have rules, too, which I also like, because it makes their behavior predictable. I know what makes Betsy's mother cross (munching cereal in the TV room and getting it all over the floor right after she vacuums); I know Betsy's dad will have a high-ball around five P.M., before the bridge club arrives; I know Dianne's mother will cook something weird for dinner, like curry, and I know her dad will be hunkered down in his home office, grading papers all weekend.

Betsy and Dianne (and their parents, and their brothers and sisters) know everything about me. They know I have an unstable mom who can't seem to keep the same job or the same address. They know I have a repeat offender for a dad. And they let me hang around anyway.

If I ever win an Oscar, I am totally going to thank them.

Both Betsy and Dianne also have older brothers—two for Betsy and one for Dianne—between the ages of sixteen and twenty-one. They're unaware of it, but these three boys are as close as I ever get to "men." In my "real" life, I only know girls: There's Yvonne and me, in a household where there's no dad, so the toilet seat is never up. There's Yvonne's mom, her mom's sister, and Yvonne's three sisters, who between them had five girls. The only guys at our family gatherings are Yvonne's sisters' husbands, and what can you say about them, except that they're outnumbered? Then there's me: a girly girl who likes fashion magazines and nail polish, gymnastics and ice skating, and talking. A lot of talking.

Boys are to me what fur is to violins—which is to say, completely unrelated.

I come into contact with some boys at school, but I don't know them on a personal level—like, none of them has ever said to me anything along the lines of "Hang on, I have to go to the bathroom," or "Man, my balls itch today," or "I can't believe the Vikings sucked so bad last night." They're mostly these strange unknowable creatures who can't see me unless they are making me the butt of a joke, like a couple of weeks ago when two of the hockey players threw me into Minnehaha Creek at a keg party.

So, these Betsy-and-Dianne-brother-people are *it* as far as understanding, researching, and/or relating to males. Which might explain why my skills are so lacking in this area.

On Sundays, one of Betsy's brothers, usually Randy, drives me back to wherever I am currently living, while Gerry Rafferty's "Baker Street" or Gary Wright's "Dream Weaver" plays on the radio. I'm always a little sad when Randy is driving me home, because it means I'm going back to the madness. Who doesn't wish they could live in the Hamptons all the time?

Even though Randy is a lot older—he must be, what, seventeen?— I relate to him. He is kind of like me: loud, boisterous, seriously energetic, maybe a little ADD. And his hair is kind of curly. I feel a little less crazy to know that even people who go to Catholic school and live in two-story houses with center-hall plans sometimes turn out like me. I mean, maybe not *as* bad as me, but still.

I'm pretty sure Randy relates to me, too, because sometimes he actually talks to me about stuff on the ride home. Stuff like my life and the wacky people in it. Stuff most people are afraid to ask me about.

"How's your dad?" Randy doesn't wait for an answer before firing off a follow-up. "You still see him?"

"Sometimes."

"He's still in prison?"

"Yeah."

"Man . . ." Randy trails off. You kind of get that he's considering what it would be like to be in prison, or what it would be like if your dad was in prison, and you can tell that he's not feeling pity, he's feeling a mixture of *That would be a wild adventure* and *That would totally suck.*

I like the way Randy asks me questions—curious, not sympathetic. He's amused and maybe a teensy bit fascinated by my interesting story, and it makes him treat me if not exactly like an equal, at least like someone who might be an equal someday. That's more than I can say for most boys I know.

Dianne's older brother Tommy, sixteen, is a different story. He seems to regard all three of us—Betsy, Dianne, and me—like David Letterman regards some of his guests. He thinks we're silly, when he bothers to think of us at all.

Mostly he hangs out upstairs in his attic bedroom, which is just like Greg Brady's, except less groovy. When he does interact with us, it's something like this:

"How many times are you gonna play that stupid song?"

Tommy is shouting at us down two flights of stairs because we have the song "The Groove Line" by Heatwave on repeat. We're playing Choreography, a game where we make up dance moves to a song until we can't stand to listen to it anymore. Unfortunately for him, Tommy gets sick of the song way before we do.

"Shut up!" Dianne shouts back good-naturedly. Dianne is always good-natured. She's got a Sandra Bullock–like quality: she's strong, funny, and pretty all at the same time. Guys love her. Years later, when I have her senior picture hanging on the corkboard in my very first college dorm room, guys will, almost to a man, ask in hushed awe, "Who's *that*?" That's Dianne, the girl who's showing the rest of us how easy life is when you just allow it to be.

Tommy appears on the staircase to watch us go through our paces. You would think we were in a Bob Fosse show. *"What* are you guys doing?"

"We're dancing. Don't bug us," Dianne says. She knows how to handle boys in general and Tommy in particular. Of the three of us, Dianne is the one who will have the first period, get the first real kiss, and birth the first baby. (I, however, will walk down the first aisle. On a boat. But I digress.)

Dianne pushes the button on the cassette player, and we take it from the top of the chorus. Again. The singer's raging falsetto squeezes through the tiny speakers.

I'm busting my little moves, feeling pretty good, when Tommy, who's still watching, says a word I've never heard before.

"Are you guys gonna do this act at the homecoming talent show? Because Tracy can be the Token."

All three of us look up at him. We don't know what he's talking about.

"The what?"

"The Token. You *know*." He says it like we're terribly uninformed. "The Token?"

"Tommy," Dianne says, rolling her eyes, "leave us alone." She knows that whatever he means, it can't be good.

"No, I want to know," I say, grinning. I have a tendency to smile when I know I'm being made fun of. Intuitively, I already know what Tommy is talking about. There's an invisible energy that happens when race comes up. An energy that by kindergarten, I knew well.

"The Token," he repeats. "The only black person."

For two seconds we're all reminded that, at any moment, I can be shamed in this particular way—by being set apart—and whoever is with me can be shamed by association. But Dianne is an alpha girl and as such, she does not just let folks go around trying to shame her.

"Tommy, go away!" Dianne's not offended so much as she's bored with her older brother's attempts to make fun of her and her friends.

I feel bad. I know Tommy's not a racist. (Dianne's family is probably the most progressive on the block.) He's just being the oldest brother, and is therefore wayyyy above us, in the manner of super-smart, privileged Baby Boomer men (think indie film directors or intellectual rock stars, like, say, the guy in the band Pavement). They place themselves above other people without having any idea they're doing it. They don't mean to. If I had red hair, Tommy would probably be making fun of me for that.

But I also have a deeper awareness—that the exchange has touched on how people of Tommy's particular caste (Future Obama-Voting White Guys: The Teen Years) view people of my particular caste . . . as the Other.

And because I'm fourteen and starting to become obsessed with boys—Future Obama-Voting White Guys in particular—I'm wondering if this means that no one is ever going to date me.

I STILL CAN'T BELIEVE PAUL picked me. I didn't used to be attractive to men like him. And now I know why: I'm way better at wielding sexual energy these days. After years of playing it down (out of fear, in order to be taken seriously at work, or because I simply found male sexual attention more of a nuisance than flattering), I finally tapped into my sexual power, and as it turns out, I have considerable stores. It is almost as if my mother, the thousand-dollar-a-night hooker, and my dad, the hypnotic pimping Svengali, had been throwing money into a sort of sexual A-game trust fund that I suddenly decided to cash in when I hit my midthirties.

I peg the beginning of the transformation, interestingly, to the adventure of childbirth. I read somewhere that birthing, if you think about it, is actually the last stop on the sex train, and I agree. It's the end of the line—the logical conclusion of the passionate kiss or even the flirtatious glance. And if you've ever gone through twenty hours of unmedicated labor and pushing, you totally know what I mean: when that baby pops out, it's a release bigger than if the Beatles somehow came out with a brand-new album. And you are panting really hard, too.

At the risk of sounding truly weird, I would go even further. I think the actual process of carrying the growing baby inside me, and then the physical intensity of giving birth, had the consequence of rearranging all sorts of energy patterns I'd been carrying in my sexual organs up till then. Something like a balloon angioplasty, where they blow up the balloon in your artery in order to push back all the old stuff that's accumulated in there and is blocking the flow. Maybe this is why a lot of women become a lot "hotter" after motherhood?

Just a theory.

So I pinpoint the moment of my transition—from a maiden who trills and giggles to a full-throated woman who possesses herself as a sexual being—to that Saturday night in early April 1997 that I spent in labor, in an overflow room in the Woodland Hills Kaiser hospital, swearing I was going to die if I had to endure another three-minute contraction.

Instead, a beautiful baby was born and in the process I was *reborn*. As someone who could finally get the guy she wanted.

I HAVE BOOBS NOW. Big ones, apparently, that fill out my cheerleading uniform in such a way that I have suddenly come to the attention of the boys. Not the boys in my grade—I am like a little sister to them, and a black little sister, at that—but the senior boys, who, at age seventeen or eighteen, have possibly grown familiar with the standard chicken-noodle-soup type of girl on offer at Wilson and are now becoming curious as to what a skinny little bowl of gumbo might taste like.

The closest I have come so far to having a boyfriend is this kid named Chris, a tall, thin, quiet runner lacking the temperament (read: not an asshole) to hang with the alpha males. Like me, Chris is an only child without a dad at home. We've been "flirting" (can you flirt without making eye contact or speaking?) since ninth grade, and by sophomore year I finally worked up the nerve to invite him to the girl-ask-boy formal dance. (I wore floor-length sea-foam green polyester with spaghetti straps and a matching shawl.) I consider the night a success, even though at the end, the two of us were way too frightened to kiss good night. We waved instead.

But since I got my nickname, things have been different.

It was given to me by Bobby Quinn, hockey player and best all-around dum-dum. Bobby is a cute guy with big brown eyes, puffy lips, and hair that is as pretty as any girl's. He's also a senior. I can only guess that he sits behind me in tenth-grade social studies because he flunked it the first time around and needs the class in order to graduate. Academically speaking, Bobby is definitely not the sharpest skate on the ice.

Soon after the term begins, Bobby starts paying attention to me, talking and joking with me and often drawing the ire of the teacher. Like I need any help with that! Talking, joking, and drawing the ire of the teacher is pretty much my *major*. Or it would be if you had to declare a major in high school.

Not long after that, he starts calling me at home. I'm not even sure how he got my phone number. But one day after school, I pick up my blue princess phone and hear his bored, thuggish voice.

"Hey. It's Bobby."

"Who?!"

"Bobby, stupid. From social studies."

WTF? Why is Bobby Quinn calling me? "Wow, okay—"

He cuts me off. "What are you doing?"

"Nothing . . ." I sound like a kid. "What are *you* doing?!"

"Calling you."

"[*giggle*]"

"So what's going on tonight? Are there any stupid sophomore parties to go to?"

And so on . . .

I don't think much of these calls. It would never occur to me that one of the most popular boys in school would like me or consider me attractive. And the truth is, he doesn't like me or consider me attractive, at least not in a girlfriend way.

However, he definitely likes my boobs. And he definitely considers them attractive.

Which brings me around to my nickname. One day, just some random Tuesday or Wednesday, Bobby makes a silly pun on my last name, and it just . . . sticks. And now it *is* my name, at least as far as the boys are concerned. The girls never use it. In fact, they never even *refer* to it. So what is it? (I know you're dying to know.)

Stack-Millan.

Clever, huh? Just like Mack-Millan, but with a side order of sexual objectification.

Bobby Quinn says it *once* and, like that theory where all the monkeys on an island suddenly know how to peel a banana once the hundredth monkey does (maybe because that monkey was an athlete other guys looked up to?), soon every boy in school is calling me Stack-Millan.

Or Stack for short.

Or Stacks. I guess for plural.

They yell it down the hall, toss it casually around in conversation, and use it to refer to me when talking to a third party, as in, "It wasn't me talking, Mr. Harrington, it was Stack." When they say it they laugh a little, but it doesn't really seem mean-spirited. Eventually, it becomes completely normal.

And here's the scary part: I like it. I'm flattered. Kind of tickled. A little honored, even. But mostly I'm just happy to be noticed. My new name constitutes my arrival in the minds of the boys in school. Until Bobby Quinn "made" me, I didn't exist for them, lacking as I do feathered hair, or a twin sister, or a big house on Lake Harriet. I've been virtually invisible! But the whole Stack-Millan thing has been a game changer. Now the boys acknowledge me in the hall with a nod, occasionally even call me by name (*Stack-Millan, what'd you get on the test?*), and generally treat me like a human being. (Funny paradox that in order to be treated like a human being I had to be objectified . . .)

Not for a moment do I consider the name offensive. But even if I did, I probably wouldn't act offended. Because mere weeks after Bobby Quinn ordains me as a sexually desirable girl, the unbelievable happens:

I get my first boyfriend.

THERE IS ONLY ONE PROBLEM with my new boyfriend, Scott: he has a girlfriend. Actually, it isn't really a problem. At least for me. In fact—and this is really sad to say—it doesn't even *occur* to me that this might be a problem, because as Jen famously said about Brad, I seem to be missing a sensitivity chip.

(Aside #1: Here is my important personal observation about missing sensitivity chips: If you're missing one, *you don't know you're missing it*! Seriously. You just think you're *really, really happy*. And by happy I mean having a feeling of invincibility identical to the one you get after snorting two giant rails.)

(Aside #2: Let me just take this moment, before going one word farther, to say to Scott's girlfriend—you know who you are—that I am deeply, deeply sorry. I was selfish and uncaring, and I know I caused harm to you. I say this with the understanding that the only way to ensure that I never, ever repeat that behavior again is to take full responsibility for it, and I do. I hope you can forgive me. And if it makes you feel any better, I definitely *did* get what I had coming to me, and karma definitely *was* a bitch. So there.)

Back to my love affair.

It starts out all innocent. Under Bobby Quinn's expert tutelage, I have now learned how to flip the flirtational puck back to a guy who shoots it toward me, so when Scott starts some low-level conversating, I am able to hit my talking points with a new confidence and flair.

Sophomores, juniors, and seniors are routinely mixed together in the English department, and Scott sits one row over and three seats back in Ms. Cameron's Shakespeare class. One day, as the class is reading *A Midsummer Night's Dream* aloud, I feel a tap on my shoulder. It's the kid behind me, handing me a folded-up piece of paper with my name on it.

Tracy.

It's from Scott. And here's what he's written inside:

> You know how your fake mom is totally abusive, how you hurt so bad all the time that you've randomly pierced your own ears three times on one side and four times on the other just so, for one moment, the pain on the outside matches the pain on the inside, and how you think life sucks and no one loves you and you might as well just end it all?
>
> Well, those days are over.
>
> xo, Scott.

No, it didn't really say that. But it might as well have. Because as I unfold that note, harp-playing cherubs drop from the sky, flowers burst into bloom, and the ulcerous throb I've developed over the past year in the pit of my stomach suddenly goes away.

All because *he* wants *me*.

Never mind that he's a liar and a cheat. (He's cheating on his girlfriend by being with me, and lying to her about it.) Or that now that he's my boyfriend, it means I am, too. All that matters is that he likes me and that means everything is going to be okay.

PAUL'S HOTEL ROOM is probably the nicest I've ever stayed in. It's on the thirty-second floor, with floor-to-ceiling windows and staggering views of English Bay. We are in Vancouver, where Paul is on a job and I am being treated like a movie star. He brought me with him, just like he said he would the day we got back together.

That makes me so happy.

We've been here for two days, holed up in a hotel suite, making love in a hotel bed, on hotel-bed sheets, wearing fluffy five-star bathrobes, ordering wonderful somethings every night from room service.

I love all this luxury, but not just for its own sake. What is really blowing my mind is that everything I could possibly ever want or need—within reason—is here for me. This is the feeling I've been looking for my whole life. A feeling I haven't had since my dad bought me Slim Jims *and* Pixy Stix. I don't say it to him, but in this one way, Paul is teaching me my true worth. Where I have always seen myself as a sort of Little Match Girl, a tattered princess who sleeps on a futon/manger on the floor, drives a fifteen-year-old car, and hoards her money because she is sure to run out someday (and *soon*), Paul represents a shift in my consciousness.

With him (not because of him), I am getting to experience myself as someone who is very well taken care of, rich even, who naturally attracts everything she needs. Not too long ago, I would have scoffed at this idea. I would have rejected some bright shiny version of myself as silly and bourgeois, possibly even dull. I would have looked down my raggedy hipster nose at myself, I would have called myself a sellout, I would have compared me—unfavorably—to some kind of biracial Reese Witherspoon–type character.

But now that I have had the guts to stop hating what I don't have (and despising those who have it), I can see that it's pretty awesome. Bright, shiny, clean, whole . . . these are things I'm now claiming to be, and I'm acting as if I *already am*. All I do is simply acknowledge what's in front of me and allow it to be more real than the past, with its huge hurts and tragic disappointments.

This is more difficult than it sounds.

To me, struggle feels like reality. Easy feels like cheating. It feels temporary, too. And so what if it is? As I walk along the Vancouver waterfront, listening to Paul's iPod, living a version of the life I've always wished I had, I've decided that, at least for now, I'm going to enjoy it.

SCOTT DOESN'T REALLY LOOK like my type. I am attracted to light-haired, light-eyed depressive romantics—in the tarot, they are the men signified by the Prince of Cups. Scott is more the Pentacles type: noted for their very dark, almost pitch-black hair; dark, penetrating eyes; and thick build. But he possesses the two things I like the most: a sharp mind and a sense of humor. He also has a fine singing voice and the gift of gab. Of course, the *very* most important thing about him is that he likes me, and he has let it be known that I can have him if I want him.

By the end of the week, we are in love.

But not with each other!

I am in love with the way he whisks me around in his mom's forest green Pontiac, and takes me out to eat at the Brothers Deli on Fiftieth and France, and drops me off at five and picks me up at nine thirty from my job at the Southdale Mall. And he is in love with how needy I am (even though I think I'm hiding it) and how that makes me put him way high up on a pedestal, even though he's kind of chubby, and his dad divorced his mom and lives in another state, and even though—especially even though—he was only second-string on the hockey team.

We don't know that the feeling of falling we are experiencing is really the sensation of diving headlong into the hole inside another person. Or that the feeling of fullness is less like fulfillment than it is like Thanksgiving dinner—so much goodness at first you feel sick, and then you want a nap, and then it wears off. And then you want more.

But who's thinking about *that*?

Not me. Because Scott took me to the Rose Garden and now we are making out on the top of a hill. I've never made out before. His tongue feels strange inside my mouth, but I pretend like I know what I am doing, because I don't want him to know that no one has ever wanted me before him.

I'm sort of sure I like making out, but I can't be completely certain, because all that sexual energy is a little overwhelming for me—like when, for a practical joke, Betsy and I would flip on every single knob and button in the Dodge Duster so when Betsy's mom turned the key in the ignition the radio would go on full blast, the windshield wipers would start swiping, and the blinkers would blink their asses off, all at the same time.

There are things you just don't know about making out until you do it, things no one could ever tell you, like what it feels like to have someone kiss your neck right below your ear or the goodness of having someone's entire body pressed into yours. To be so enveloped by another person—now I get it; only babies get to feel this!

(Which reminds me—I've always thought it seems kind of unfair that you have to wait eighteen years to sleep with another person. That you get to have plenty of human contact up to, say, the age of two or three, and then you're just, like, *cut off* until you round up your first boyfriend. No wonder teen sex is such a big deal!)

I am just becoming accustomed to the level of sensory overload in our make-out session when Scott slides his right hand under my shirt. I've never had someone's hand under my shirt (but over my bra), so I'm not prepared for the strong voice that begins, almost immediately, to talk to me:

Any farther and you'll be sorry.

"What?" (Looking around for source of voice) "I'll be sorry? Who is this?"

This is you speaking.

"Me? I'm not speaking. I'm making out."

Not "you" exactly. Just part of you.

(Sassy voice) "Really . . . Which part? Let me guess, you must be the obnoxious Tracy everyone keeps telling me about."

You're funny. Really. Look, you created me. So you can either listen or not. I'm part of your programming.

"Programming . . ."

The programming you got growing up in this medium-size city of mostly Scandinavian immigrants in a decidedly liberal but still very midwestern state.

"Oh. *That* programming. What do you want? I'm making out."

You know what I want. I want what's best for you.

"What's best for me . . ." (Bored teenage expression) "And that is . . . ?"

To not *destroy your reputation, first of all.*

"*What* reputation?"

What reputation? (Bored grown-up expression) *Please. Don't be naïve. Every girl has a reputation. Good, bad, warm, hot, boring, needy, easy, hard.*

"Jesus. Leave me alone. I'm just trying to make out with a guy."

Just making out? You know better than most fifteen-year-olds that nothing is ever as simple as "just" doing whatever it is you are thinking you're going to do. Like your dad "just" dealt drugs. Like your grandma "just" gave you up. The word "just" is a red flag. It means you're about to start deluding yourself.

"Wow! Who gave you this phone number?"

This is about what kind of girl you want to be. What kind of boy you want to attract. And how you want to be treated. It's all up to you, sweets.

"What are you, my mom?"

You don't have a mom. Remember?

"Nice."

That's why you have me.

"What are you trying to say? Just say it. Because if I keep listening to you instead of acting like I'm super-duper into making out, he's going to think I'm boring. And I like him. He wants to be my boyfriend. Even though he already has a girlfriend. But, whatever."

Here's the deal: You're already a little too goofy, a little too black, a little too poor. What you don't need now is to be a little too slutty. So keep him out of your pants, for now.

"Do I always have to think so much about everything?"

Only if you want to stay off Section 8.

"That's a really mean thing to say."

You're gonna thank me later.

"Good-bye."

Peace out, sister. Oh, and you'll be hearing from me again.

"Good-bye."

STANLEY PARK FEELS LIKE the greenest, quietest, most amazing sacred space I've ever been in—a kind of nature church. Paul and I have spent the day walking all over Vancouver, and we've ended up here, in the jewel of the city, surrounded by acres of evergreens. We aren't saying much as we walk, which is unusual for us. Normally we keep up a steady stream of patter about politics, movies, art, architecture, economics, pop culture, ourselves, the past, and/or the future. We don't really debate the topics as much as we each take turns making observations that the other one then riffs off of.

Sometimes I notice that Paul doesn't really ask me much about my deepest interior life, and I notice he doesn't really talk about his, either. He tends to gambol along on the surface of things. (The three exceptions to this are the topics of his baby's mama, his first wife, and his dad, which get him all riled up.) This worries me sometimes, but in the scheme of things, it doesn't seem like all that big a deal, so I don't bother to question it. To be honest, I don't want to rock the boat. This is a good boat. I like it. I want to keep it afloat.

Besides, here, in the middle of this forest, there are no words. What we are and what we have is distilled down to its very essence.

"I love you," he says to me.

"I love you, too," I say back. Actually, it goes way beyond love. I feel like he is my karma, my destiny. I know how that sounds, but maybe because I'm a mom now and I believe in miracles because I gave birth to one, or maybe because I'm getting older, or maybe just because I feel more comfortable living in my truth instead of needing to be taken "seriously" all the time, I dare to say what I'm really thinking: "You know what?"

"What?"

"I feel like I came across time to meet you." It's true. I've been wanting to say that for a while but didn't find the courage until right this moment.

"Really?" Paul likes this. He likes that I am willing to be vulnerable, that I don't live in my defenses. I love that he doesn't think I'm weird.

We stop in the middle of this fantastical clearing—really, it's like something out of *The Lord of the Rings*—and we kiss, no, we *kiss,* and in my mind there is one of those cameras that reels around in circles, enveloping us in the moment, blurring everything out but this kiss, in this moment, in this forest.

And that's when I know: *I'm going to marry this man.*

It is done like *pi*. There may be a thousand million places after the decimal point still to be discovered, and those places may be surprising or difficult or happy or wonderful. But the numbers are already there waiting for us. We are going to be together.

Nine

I Love You,

but I Think I Can Do Better

A WEEK BEFORE MY HIGH SCHOOL graduation, I get
a call from Daddy. It's a surprise, because I haven't talked to him in
maybe eighteen months. I'm not sure exactly when his phone calls
stopped coming. Probably after I told him I considered him nothing
more than a sire.

Teenagers.

Daddy has two reasons for calling. 1) He's out of prison again.
2) He wants to come to my high school graduation.

My responses are 1) Oh. 2) Fuck no.

"Absolutely not." I say firmly. "I do not want you there."

I know it is selfish. But I just cannot imagine spending the final
two hours of my high school career taking my dad around to meet
my friends, their parents, and my teachers. Not after all this time.
Not after successfully convincing them that I am a girl who only
barely knows her dad, the guy who divorced her "stepmom" when
I was three. They all think he works in a barbershop in northern
Minnesota. They've never stopped to wonder aloud whether there are
anywhere near enough black men north of the forty-fourth parallel
to warrant a whole career in African-American hair care, and it's way
too late to start explaining all that now.

"Tracy Renee," my dad says, trying to reason with me, "this is a very important day in your life. You're starting down the road to adulthood."

"Exactly," I counter. "Which is why you won't be there. You can't just show up at the end of a thirteen-year journey and clap! You've never even been to a parent-teacher conference! Yvonne might be a meanie sometimes, but at least she's done that much."

Daddy's not giving up easily though. "I should be there to see my baby gyurl in her cap and gown, getting her diploma." He says it sweetly, trying to prevail upon me in a fatherly, sentimental way. I'm not giving an inch.

"No." I say. "No way."

If this conversation were a piece of film, like a preview in a movie theater, and if you were able to slow the film all the way down, super-duper slow, you would see—subliminally inserted in between the frames, like the words "buy popcorn," "eat hot dogs"—that this is actually the first time in my life I have been in a position of power with my dad, the first time I've ever been able to deny him what he wants. And I'm running with it.

"Tracy Renee"—he's impatient now—"come on."

"Don't beg. You're not coming." (Like many young women, I sometimes have *no idea* how bitchy I sound. I think I sound smart. And authoritative.) Then I add, just to make myself perfectly clear: "And by the way, I really don't want you calling me. I gotta go."

I hang up. I feel good. Like I'm not going to let him push me around. Like I'm doing "what's best for me"—even though it will be years of therapy before I learn that verbiage—instead of making Daddy happy. I'm downright proud of myself.

For all I know he came anyway. There must have been a thousand people there. He could easily have chilled out way in the back and gone unseen. And it's not as though, as I walked up to the podium to accept my little piece of paper, I was wondering if my dad was out there, watching.

No. Sitting in that chair, listening to all the good kids imagine their very bright futures, I had the same feeling I always have at this kind of thing.

This whole charade is for normal people.

PAUL IS AT THE WHEEL. His elderly hound is hunkered down in the backseat of the Land Rover. I am riding shotgun, white paper coffee cup in my hand. It's one of those crystalline Los Angeles mornings—bright, bright blue and thriving yellow—the kind half the world moves here for. We're on our way to the dog park. It's a magnificent day, and it just started.

I fish around in the center console, looking for a piece of gum. There isn't any, but I do come across an innocent-looking ticket stub from my favorite movie theater in Los Angeles, the Arclight. The movie is *Van Helsing*. Dated a little over a month ago, 5/7/04. An afternoon show. Four o'clock in the afternoon. It's not a movie we saw together—I'm not the *Van Helsing* type—but I don't really think much of it.

(You go looking for A and find B.)

Until later. I am driving on the 134 freeway again (I take that freeway a *lot*), actually on my way to Paul's loft, when it hits me.

May 7: Wait. *May 7??!*

Paul was supposedly out of town that weekend, visiting his young son in another state. In fact, he called me from that state. To say how much he loved me!

BEGIN FLASHBACK

INT. NEWSROOM—DAY

Tracy is supposed to be writing news, but Paul, her boyfriend of two months, is calling for the fourth time that morning.

He sounds especially ardent.

PAUL

I miss you.

TRACY

I miss you, too.

PAUL

I love you sooooo much.

TRACY

(giggles, embarrassed)

I love you, too.

PAUL

I can't wait to see you.

TRACY

When are you back?

PAUL

Uh, late Saturday night. But you won't see me until Sunday. Because
I'll be really late. But then when I do see you . . .

TRACY

(giggle)

PAUL

I can't wait.

TRACY

Me neither.

END FLASHBACK

So, wait. That was, let's see, a Friday. I remember specifically, because I work on Tuesdays, Thursdays, and Fridays. And Friday was
May 6. And he was supposedly calling from Texas. And he wasn't
going to be home until "late Saturday night . . ."

Random clues start springing out of the recesses of my mind, fast and furious. Like:

- He had a new haircut when I saw him on Sunday.
- Who would get a British rocker haircut in Texas?
- No one. That's who.

My heart starts beating like I've just happened upon a dead body. *I need to see that ticket stub again.* Maybe I got it wrong. Maybe it didn't say May 7. Maybe it said May 17! *I have got to see that ticket stub again.* I can't even begin to think about what that ticket stub means, I can only think about confirming what it says.

I formulate a plan. While in the parking garage, I will simply retrieve the ticket stub from his car and look at it. That way, I will know before I go into the loft, before I see him, if he has lied to me, and I will be able to confront him with facts. Exactly what I would say in such a confrontation isn't clear. But I need facts. I know that much.

Why I would even consider speaking to Paul if the ticket stub *does* turn out to be a smoking gun isn't quite clear, either. I can only guess that the ticket stub is part of my whole once-in-a-lifetime attempt to get my most hard-core childhood wounds to surface. A hundred-year flood of childhood trauma. Then it makes perfect sense.

How this is part of the answer to my prayer is another thing. The only thing I am sure of: I am apparently hell-bent on a healing.

I SHOULD MENTION that we've moved in with Yvonne's new boyfriend, a harmless dolt several years younger than she is. His name is Frank and he's a plumber—far from rich, but a decent earner—whom she met during her brief-but-life-changing bowling league phase.

They've been together for nine months now, my entire senior year, but poor Frank still has *no* idea what just hit him. And even if he figures it out soon—and it doesn't look like he's going to—it will be too late. They are planning to get married this summer.

Take, for example, this fancy apartment building we've moved into. We've already lived here—with Yvonne's *last* boyfriend, the lawyer!

But that's our little secret.

"Don't you *dare* tell Frank we used to live here," Yvonne says, mustering her best forties movie star menace.

"I *won't*. Jeez." I roll my eyes contemptuously. I'm bored and impatient with Yvonne's drama. I just don't have the energy. What am I gonna do, tell Frank that four years ago we lived on the eighth floor (we're now on the third) with the lawyer, the one who was wonderfully sweet hearted but looked like a troll? The guy we just moved out on one day, while he was at work?

The whole chapter was so brief, I don't think that lady in the management office even recognizes me.

There is another thing I'm not allowed to tell Frank: that Yvonne actually married my black dad before adopting me. I'm guessing this is because Frank hails from an area where miscegenation is considered quite downmarket, and Yvonne doesn't want her new man to think less of her—or worse, reject her. I'm not sure where Frank thinks I came from. Perhaps Yvonne told him she found me in the rushes along the edge of the Mississippi River.

Whatever.

My life is too busy for me to care much about that stuff. I'm seventeen and, by some miracle, about to go off to college. All I do in this apartment is sleep, change clothes, and occasionally fuck my boyfriend on the couch late at night, after Yvonne and Frank have gone to bed. And I'm getting tired of doing even *that*.

I've been with Scott more than two years now—his only girlfriend for a year. His other relationship ended when the girl finally found out what the whole rest of the school already knew and forced him to choose between the two of us. He chose me, probably because I made him.

Scott has really stabilized my life—to the point where I got almost all A's this year. I feel better than I have since I lived with the Ericsons. Yvonne's ups and downs don't affect me as much, since I can always call Scott and he will immediately come whisk me away. Scott basically drives me to work, feeds me, buys me stuff, and has sex with me. If I were giving him money, he would be my pimp.

It's also probably no coincidence that Scott's arrival was followed closely by Frank's. Without me around all the time, Yvonne suddenly discovered she was lonely and needed a boyfriend. Or maybe she needed someone to serve as the focal point for all the personality quirks that make it so difficult to be so close to her. Either way, I'm glad Frank's here, because that shit is exhausting

I can't believe I am counting the days until I'm gone.

Free at last.

Free at last.

I FIND PAUL'S CAR in the parking lot, but it's locked. *Shit.* I really want to know what's on that ticket before facing Paul. I force myself upstairs, rubbery with adrenaline. I methodically make my way up the elevator. Down the long labyrinth of a hallway—this way, that way, this way again. Into the loft. Down the long interior hallway. All this walking is giving me time to contemplate the fact that I don't really need to see the ticket. I already know the answer.

Paul has a big smile for me as I round the corner into the living room, but the second I come into view, his face falls. He knows instantly that something is off. Of course. Liars are wildly perceptive. It's part of the skill set.

"Are you okay?" He stands up from behind his desk and makes his way toward me. He is wearing his short-sleeved plaid Dolce and Gabbana shirt, the one he says he wears on first dates, probably because we are going to a nice dinner tonight at a French bistro in Los Feliz.

I don't say anything. I just look at him.

I look so closely, I can see—I mean, actually *witness*—his whole mien shifting. His eyes blink more slowly. His muscles poise. His mouth narrows and thins. He's like a color-changing animal sensing the presence of mortal danger.

"What's up?" He says it like a question, but really it's a challenge. It gives him time to rapidly flip through his misdeeds, trying to figure out which one I know about.

Sharp yellow afternoon light bounces off the blue skyscrapers that tower outside the window. Paul stands there, staring at me. He wants an answer. And I can see he's afraid.

"Nothing," I say lightly. I've managed to scrub any hint of defensiveness out of my voice, out of my posture. Twenty-eight years fold in on themselves, and it's like I'm standing in front of Yvonne, where survival means hiding any sign of my real thoughts, feelings, deeds. Not just hiding them and then after four or five seconds revealing the truth so we can laugh about how funny that was. Hiding them like I'm in a war movie and the soldiers really *will* kill me if they know I stole the loaf of bread.

Paul's expression shifts again. He's walking toward me. Almost like he's in a trance. Or maybe it's me who's in a trance, because somehow, I know exactly what happens next.

Sex.

LESS THAN AN HOUR LATER, I am standing in front of the passenger door, waiting for Paul to unlock it. I'm calm now, my brain awash in sex opiates. It no longer seems so god-awfully important to get my hands on that movie ticket, though I am curious, in an almost abstract way, as to what it says.

Perhaps that is how I am suddenly able to turn in a performance that would be Oscar-worthy—if they gave Oscars for lying to your boyfriend in order to find out if he is lying to you.

"I need something to spit this gum into," I announce. I'm careful to say this exactly as if it were true, as if I have simply been chewing a piece of gum that I am now finished with—not as if I've planned ahead of time by putting a piece of gum into my mouth in order to have one to spit out. All so I could have a plausible reason to do as I am doing now and rummage through the center console of the car. I casually retrieve the ticket.

May 7, 2004. Four o'clock in the afternoon. *Van Helsing.*

He's a liar.

(But I already knew that, didn't I? I probably knew it the moment I met him.)

It occurs to me that I need to make absolutely sure that it was Paul himself who saw the movie, and that (for example) the ticket didn't belong to, say, a friend who borrowed the car and then left the ticket stub in the center console. So I ask a simple question:

"How was *Van Helsing*?"

I query just like I am making polite conversation. I can hear my voice coming out of my throat, and even I can't believe how casual I sound. I forgot I knew how to lie so well.

"Bad," Paul replies. He doesn't know he's stepped right into my carefully laid trap. He probably forgot that he lied about being out of town that weekend. He undoubtedly never suspected that I am even craftier than he is. "Actually, it wasn't bad," he clarifies. "It was just boring. I don't know what's worse."

Neither do I, and I don't care. I'm too busy thinking about my next move. What do I do now that I know Paul lied to me? I wonder what exactly it is he lied about? Deep down I don't think he's fucking another woman, but at the same time, deep down I know there is another woman mixed up somewhere in this story.

It is confusing. But only if I try to make sense of it with my left brain.

Because one thing is immediately, abundantly clear. My right brain has already informed me that I have no intention of leaving this man.

And I know that is seriously fucked up.

I'VE DECIDED TO STOP HAVING SEX with Scott. I'm not really sure why. I suddenly just "got sick" of it. I feel like sex is everywhere—on billboards, in magazines, in movies—and there's this intense pressure to be having it all the time. I don't like the pressure.

It's been a year since I lost my virginity to Scott. I made the decision to go all the way like I make all my decisions: I thought about it, considered all my options, and calculated the best course of action. It was time. After all, we'd been together a year, he definitely loved me, and I had to lose it to *someone*. Might as well have been him. And to top it off, he and his main girlfriend were clearly on the verge of breaking up.

It finally happened one night at a Minnesota Kicks soccer game. Actually, we never even made it to our seats inside the stadium— probably as a result of the two Big Gulp–size cocktails I'd had of rum and Tahitian Treat. Instead of watching the game, we turn the tailgate party into heavy-duty canoodling in the car. One thing leads to another pretty quick.

"I have an idea," Scott whispers to me as he turns the key in the ignition of the forest green Pontiac.

"Wha?" I am perilously close to retching. I am a lightweight who can totally hold her liquor. Once I've thrown up.

"Yeah," he says. "This is a great idea."

I manage to open one eye wide enough to see Scott's face. He looks even more like a Cheshire cat than usual. He also looks a little frightened. Part of me already knows what's about to happen—like how people on the news say they definitely knew their assailant was planning to kill them—but the Good Girl part of me feels it would be unseemly to be "okay" with losing my virginity, so I force myself to pretend that I'm too drunk to know what's going on.

In four minutes we have pulled into the parking lot of a Motel 8. "Wait here," Scott says. He's going to take care of everything. I like that about Scott. He disappears into the lobby.

If I were writing this as an episode of a 1980s teen drama, Scott's absence would be the moment where I reflect on my life as a little girl and my impending transition to full-fledged womanhood. There would be some sort of montage with shots of me on a swing, me blowing out birthday candles, and me getting my very first kiss, set to the sweeping emotion of a big dumb song like, say, "Endless Love" or some shit.

But it's not. It's really just me, with my head lolling around on the headrest, hoping that I don't throw up or chicken out before I get to become "a woman."

Scott is back in a jiffy, and next thing I know he is guiding me down a brightly lit hallway. "How *mush* was this room?" I slur. I am very concerned with how much money this little rite of passage is going to cost.

"Forty-two dollars."

Let's see, that will come to, oh, seven dollars a minute.

Everything between the moment the door opens and the keen pain between my legs is a blur.

Fluorescent lights. Thin sheets. Kissing. Fumbling. Scott's nervous. He doesn't want to seem like he doesn't know what he's doing. I don't want to embarrass him. I'll just pretend I don't notice. Uh-oh. Awkward. Really awkward. God, this is kind of weir— Shit. What was THAT? Wow, is that it? Is that what it feels like? That's not at all what I thought it would be like. Weird. I wonder if I'm bleeding. Aren't you supposed to bleed the first time? Was that my hymen? I didn't feel anything break. Wow, Scott is kind of embarrassing himself. He's, like, grunting! This hurts, kind of. I wonder how long it takes. Just curious. This isn't like bad really, but I wouldn't really call it good, either. And it's certainly nothing like those

Foreigner songs. Scott's speeding up. Oh. Wait a minute. I think he's going to—

Wow. That was quick.

SO AFTER A YEAR OF THAT, more or less, except in the backseat of the green Pontiac or downstairs in the basement in Scott's brother's old twin bed, I've just decided to stop. I simply don't like sex all that much. Maybe if I had orgasms from it, it would be different. Maybe if it was more like masturbation. But it's not. The thing I like most about sex is how it makes me feel that my boyfriend loves me. But now that we've been together for two years, I already know he loves me, so I don't really need to have the sex anymore. Right?

"I'll give you blow jobs, though," I offer him. Generously.

Scott doesn't have the temerity to get angry at my abrupt decision to cut him off. He'll take the blow jobs. I think we both know that I'm very willing to just walk away from the relationship entirely if he doesn't.

Unfortunately, abstinence isn't having the intended effect. I wanted it to help me shake the feeling that everyone else is getting something out of sex that I am somehow failing to get. Madonna is the face of this feeling—when she urges me to be like a slut, but be one like a virgin? To wield sexual power like it's a big giant bag of money or drugs? To measure myself by how many people want to have sex with me? It makes me want to rebel.

Years from now I will make the connection between my feelings about sex and the fact that I spent the first three years of my life steeped in the energy of people who trade sex for a living. But right now, I hate this idea that my sexuality is my worth. Not only because it feels hopelessly archaic, like I'm some slave girl or a geisha, even if I'm a well-paid, well-dressed, well-regarded geisha. But also (mostly) because I feel I don't measure up.

And I don't really feel like trying to.

MAYBE THERE'S ANOTHER reason I don't want to have sex with Scott. Because I've met a new guy. In a bar, one of those places with peanut shells all over the floor. My friend Christie and I started frequenting the place a couple of months ago, after hearing that they don't ask for IDs. We go on Tuesdays and Thursdays, when drinks are cheap.

The drinking age in Minnesota is nineteen. We are only seventeen, but it takes little more than a warm smile and a short skirt to make up the two years in between. Sometimes I wear my sweatshirt falling off my shoulder just like that girl in *Flashdance*. (I haven't seen the movie yet, but people tell me I look like her. I wish.) As an insurance policy, I have a fake ID, but I'd rather not use it, since it's kind of really obvious that someone took a razor blade and sliced off the "4" in 1964 and used superglue to replace it with a "2."

I drink gin and sours. Many of them. One night I counted. I drank eight gin and sours between seven forty-five and closing time. That's a lot of gin and sours.

Good thing I'm not paying for them.

That's because—as a second insurance policy—I've made friends with the bartender. His name is Ken (everyone calls him Kenny), and he's really sweet. He has thin medium-brown hair and medium-blue eyes. His skin tone is medium too and so is his height. In fact, he is medium in pretty much every way, at least externally.

Internally, he's one of the more interesting guys you'll meet in a place like Minneapolis. He's twenty-six (about to turn twenty-seven), has traveled all over the world, and has a black belt in some random martial art the exact name of which I can't recall. He's got a degree in international studies and in two weeks he's going back to the University of Minnesota for an MBA. He's all kinds of smart. He also keeps the gin and sours coming.

I am kind of dazzled by him.

I think he likes me, too. The past couple of times we've been at the bar, he's asked Christie and me to stay late after the bar closes and hang out. We turn the music way up and sit in the booths and drink cocktails. I dance around and I can tell Kenny likes watching me. Cham, the Cambodian dish boy, hangs out with us, and so does Bonnie, the waitress, and a couple of the kitchen guys, too. We all play Ms. Pac-Man with quarters Kenny gets from the cash register behind the bar.

Last Thursday something unexpected happened. Kenny and I were cozied up in one of the back booths, marveling that we'd gone to rival high schools (I carefully avoided saying how many years apart) and had at one time belonged to the same church congregation. (That was during Yvonne's Lutheran period.) I hadn't been feeling any particular sexual chemistry (not that I would have, since heavy sexual chemistry tended to overwhelm me, hence the need for all those gin and sours) but suddenly there he was, kissing me.

And he has amazing, cushy lips.

It's *a lot* different kissing a guy who's twenty-six (about to turn twenty-seven) than kissing the fumbling twenty-year-old I've been dealing with. Kenny has got skills—*Subtlety! Nuance! Technique!*—obviously cultivated over years of experience. I'm pleasantly surprised, and where I think I opened this night merely interested in him, now I am downright smitten.

Meanwhile, Christie has hit it off with one of the cooks. She has just emerged from the kitchen looking disheveled. "He's gonna give me a ride home," she announces. "Is that okay? I mean, can you get home okay?"

Christie is a bold girl. Usually, this particular girl-girl transaction—where you have to figure out how to bail on your friend to leave with a guy, without looking (or feeling) like a slut—has an element of slight shame to it. Not for Christie. She looks at me. I look at her. She looks at the cook. I look at Kenny.

"I'll give you a ride home," Kenny offers. He is a real man, taking charge of the situation like that. "No problem at all."

"Really? It's not that far away," I say. He's already agreed to drive me, but I still feel the need to talk him into it, I guess because I automatically consider myself a pain in the ass. "Just on the other side of Lake Harriet."

"I know where you live. You went to Wilson, right? I went to Grant, remember?" he says, tapping the tip of my nose. "It's absolutely no problem. I'd love to do it." He smiles, and it's so warm, and so—what?—*loving,* I just know I'm in perfectly good hands with this guy. He's like Scott, in that he clearly wants to take care of me, except he's better. Way better.

Christie takes off with the cook, and soon it is Kenny and me alone. We make out for a while, and I'm really enjoying it. I feel grown-up, sophisticated. Like I'm finally hanging out with My Type of People.

My mouth is starting to get stubble-burned when Kenny stops kissing me and checks his watch. "What time is it? I've got to get you home."

"It's okay. I'm fine."

"Don't you still live with your parents?" He's very thoughtful. But obviously his idea of parents and my idea of parents are two totally different ideas.

"It's not like that," I reassure him. "I can come home anytime I want."

It's 3:52 in the morning. "Okay," he says, sliding out of the booth. "We'll stop off at my house for a quick nap and then I'll take you home. How does that sound?"

It sounds like he's opening the door to having sex with me. But I don't say that. That would make me sound young and silly.

And I want him to think I'm nineteen.

I WAS HOPING SCOTT would just die a natural death, but it's turning out that a natural death is just as painful as an unnatural one. At least for him. I'm in college now, having the time of my life.

I'm going to St. Cloud State University, widely known as the biggest party school in the state, but that's not why I'm here. I chose it because it accepted me. And it's cheap. If the state of Minnesota didn't make it so easy—no letters of recommendation necessary, no personal essay, and it's not very competitive—I wouldn't be here.

So far my studies are going well. It turns out I am much better at college than I ever was at high school. I am getting all A's! This is a miracle, seeing as how I drink a lot of gin and sours. Like, every night. Unless it's not a miracle and the gin and sours are *responsible* for my new, improved academic performance. Actually, that sounds more like it.

Anyway, everything is great except for Scott, who is gasping for breath, though he doesn't seem to know it. I just don't have the courage to break up with him. I know that he will not take it well. It's not that he will yell at me or cry, it's that I will feel responsible for giving him pain and I really, really don't want to inflict pain on anyone. It seems easier to just let circumstances do the dirty work for me—just go off to college and let the relationship drift away.

Unfortunately, Scott's not allowing that to happen. The phone rings in my dorm room every night, and it's him, calling to make sure I'm still in a relationship with him.

"How's my Trace-Face?" he coos. Trace-Face is his nickname for me. It's a sweet nickname. Much better than Stack-Millan. But hearing it makes me feel bad. Guilty. Scott really does love me. How do you leave someone who really, truly loves you just because someone better came along?

"I'm fine," I say. There are six boys and girls in my dorm room playing Quarters. With gin. "How are *you?*"

"I'm okay." He sounds needy. He wants something from me that we both know I can never give him. "Good news! I'm coming to see you."

"This weekend?" *There go my plans for Saturday night.*

"Tomorrow!" He thinks this is a wonderful surprise. I think it is a bummer. "I have the next two days off from work."

Scott has this crazy job where he sprays pesticides on people's lawns to kill crabgrass. This being Minnesota, business drops off substantially come September. When it snows. (Just kidding. It won't snow until Halloween. Though I hear global warming is changing all that.) "*And* your birthday's almost here."

It's true. My birthday is really soon.

I wave the party out of my room, since it's obvious Scott's going to need more extensive servicing tonight. The boys and girls reluctantly get up, en masse, and head to Heather's place, two doors down. I mouth the words *I'll be there in a minute* and shut the door behind them. I'm sad to see them go. We were having such fun.

"I thought I could drive up and give you your birthday gift in person," he says.

Ugh. "You don't have to do that!" I'm hoping I sound thoughtful, like I don't want Scott to go to all the trouble. Not uninviting, like I would dread his visit.

"No, I want to. I have something special for you," he says. "You're going to love it."

Probably not, I think to myself. Whatever it is, it will make me feel worse than I already do.

The next day Scott shows up on my doorstep with his own stereo, a very fancy (for the early eighties) Technics setup that includes a turntable, cassette deck, radio/tuner thingy, and speakers. I am . . . pleased. And guilty.

"Oh my god. It's great." I try to sound excited, but in my heart I've already written him a dear-John letter and mailed it—by Pony Express. It's just going to take a few weeks to get there.

That night I have mercy sex with Scott, in the bottom bunk of the bed I share with my roommate Penny, a farm girl–slash–homecoming queen whose feathered-hair game is seriously world-class. Penny is staying with her boyfriend tonight, so she is spared the pain of listening to a long-term teenage relationship in its death throes.

It's the last time Scott and I will be together, and as usual, it kind of sucks.

On my eighteenth birthday, I come home from class to find a bouquet of flowers on the doorstep of my dorm room. Pink roses. The card says: *Happy Birthday!* It is signed, *Kenny*.

I can't believe it. I haven't heard from Kenny since the second weekend in August, before I came to St. Cloud. I thought it was over. We had that one cool night where we made out in his bed as the sun came up. But since then, we'd both had major life changes—he returned to school, and I started college. I thought he'd forgotten about me. But apparently not.

It's official now. Scott is toast.

Not because I don't love him, I do, in this one way. But I've always suspected I could do better—not in terms of looks or money; I don't seriously care about those things. But in terms of being with someone who is more interesting, more challenging, and who is going more in the direction I see myself going in life—a better overall match. The flowers are proof positive that I can.

Actually, they're proof that I already have.

I WAIT FOUR MINUTES before confronting Paul about the movie ticket. I pick up the ticket stub and, still in character, pretend like a thought just occurred to me. "Wait a minute. This ticket says May seventh. Isn't that when you were out of town visiting your son?"

I watch Paul's face carefully. It betrays *nothing*, which should scare the bejesus out of me, but it doesn't. Probably because I'm a hunter right now, closing in on a big ol' moose.

"Hmm. I don't remember." He shrugs.

No way am I letting him off. "Yeah! I remember it now," I say, not breaking character. "You called me on Sunday morning. It was Mother's Day. That was the eighth. And you said you got home late the night before. Wait. I can show you." I lean over and start rummaging through my purse. "I have my calendar right here."

I can feel tension coming from Paul's direction, but I don't stop. There is a small part of me, the part of me that is always observing myself, that can't believe I am putting the screws to him like this. I know myself as a person who doesn't have the balls to confront people directly in this way. It's pretty much the entire reason I've spent my TV news career behind the scenes rather than sticking microphones into people's faces.

I produce my date book, a ratty old thing I got at Sav-On. "Right. See here? The seventh was a Saturday. I have it marked down—Paul returns, Sunday the eighth."

I turn my full face toward him. I wait for a response. He's staring straight ahead, at the road. I can see his chest heaving up and down. He knows he's caught.

"Are you sure? Huh. Well, I must have made a mistake." He's giving me one last chance to back off forever and allow things to go back to "normal." Whatever that is.

I'm not taking it.

"It's not a mistake," I insist. "It says right here—"

He cuts me off. "Okay." His voice is taut, metallic. He takes a big breath. The decision to tell the truth ripples across the muscles in his face. "I lied."

I'm kind of surprised he just admitted it like this. I guess I expected him to defend himself to the death. Like Yvonne would have. Instead, he flipped. And quick, too. Maybe he's not so bad after all.

"Oh, Paul." Now I'm momentarily flooded with this weird compassion for him. I see that he is scared. That this is how he has survived his life. That he grew up in a world where being truthful put you in danger. I get it. I get it. I get it.

I grew up like that, too.

"You don't have to lie to me," I say calmly.

He looks at me distrustfully. He doesn't believe me, but at the same time, he does. His expression shifts to contrite. "I'm sorry. It's just that when I come back from seeing my kid, I have to spend a couple of days decompressing. It just affects me so much."

This should raise a red flag—and it does. But I'm so eager to forgive him, it's a red flag only about the size of one you might find floating in an overpriced fruity cocktail at TGI Friday's. So instead of continuing my interrogation, I forgive him.

"It's okay," I say. For some reason, I feel more concern for him than I do worry for myself.

"I just can't deal with people." He looks stricken. "I'm sorry." His eyes are sad. He sincerely feels terrible.

"You can tell me anything, you know," I offer.

"I know," he says.

We look at each other. He has an expression of gratitude on his face—that I'm going to let him off the hook. That I'm not going to leave because he was just doing what comes naturally to him. *It doesn't mean I don't love you,* his eyes say.

Which, weirdly, I know.

It doesn't feel crazy to just go to the restaurant and eat coq au vin and profiteroles and let something that happened two months ago just be in the past. Because I'm hell-bent on healing.

Remember?

Ten

I Love You,
and I'm Leaving You Anyway

I GET DRUNK ON THE PLANE. There is some kind of delay taking off—we sit parked for an hour on the runway—and to make up for it, the airline offers us free drinks all the way to Minneapolis. So, I drink. And smoke—Benson and Hedges Menthol Light 100s. It's only a two-and-a-half-hour flight, but I nevertheless manage to make a pretty good-size dent in my liver. I'm twenty-two, though, so no worries. I'm still immortal.

My dad meets me at the airport. This is our second or third visit since getting back in touch a couple of years ago. That's when I, bored with my life as a teenage housewife, called him one day, pretty much on a whim. I just dialed his number, and he answered! I think I was more startled to hear his voice than he was to hear mine. But after two seconds, it was like we'd been playing Crazy Eights at Leavenworth just yesterday.

We've never talked too much about the years in between. About how Yvonne finally kicked me out for good (though she says I "left") after my freshman year at St. Cloud, and how I couch-surfed all summer at Betsy's and Dianne's (special thanks to their moms, Bev and Lois—lifesavers), and worked three jobs to save enough money to move into a little two-bedroom with this really troubled girl whose boyfriend ended up getting shot by a guy outside a club (he lived). Or about how I got pregnant on my nineteenth birthday, had an abortion, fell into a depression, dropped out of college, started smoking pot all day long, and only got out of it when Kenny got his big job in San Francisco and I begged, I mean down-on-my-knees *begged*, him to take me along. Or even how I married Kenny later that year in a ceremony on a yacht sailing around San Francisco Bay, wearing a satin dove-gray vintage dress with pearl-pink shoes, and how at the end of the cruise I said to a guest, "Well, it's all over," and she shocked me by replying, "No, dear, it's just *begun!*" and how that's when I knew that the marriage would probably fail. Or how a year after that, Kenny's job transferred him to Salt Lake City, of all places, which is how I ended up in Utah.

My dad doesn't say a lot about those years either, though he did tell me how he'd spotted me a couple of times downtown when he was still driving a taxi, so at least he didn't have to worry that I was dead. I didn't mention it, but I had seen him, too. One time I got on the Grand Avenue bus at Thirty-eighth Street, and out of the corner of my eye I saw him sitting near the very back. It was during my New Wave phase, and I had on black velvet capri pants and white majorette boots. I remember being a little distressed that my dad was going to think of me as the kind of girl who wears white majorette boots around town. I slipped into the first open seat, a blistering heat rising in my face, pretending I hadn't seen him and hoping he hadn't seen me. I mean, what was I going to do? Have a big dumb reunion with my dad whom I haven't seen or talked to in four years *on the bus*?!

Right.

But these days, we're quite chummy. Not to sound weird, but being a daughter to Freddie is an awful lot like being a girlfriend to any other guy. You laugh, and swear, and talk about life and love and relationships. It wasn't hard to get used to Freddie being back in my life, because not that much really changed. We talk on the phone and visit once or twice a year, just like we always have. Except now when we visit, there are no guards.

On this trip, I am traveling alone, and the plan is for me to stay at his house not far from the University of Minnesota. Usually I come to Minneapolis with Kenny and stay with his parents or his brother. But marriage has been feeling especially confining lately, and Kenny and I both decided a trip alone might alleviate my boredom and do me some good.

"Hey, little gyurl!" My dad gives me one of those giant hugs he does. Then he puts his hands on my shoulders and holds me away from him, so he can get a better look at me. As usual, he notices *everything*, and he feels free to coach me if he thinks he can bring my game up some. His favorite pointers regard my posture and my outfit. This time I pass the preliminary round and head straight for the semifinals. "Lookin' good," he compliments me. "I like those pants you got on."

"Thanks!" I'm all smiles. I want approval, so I'm glad he's giving it.

Besides, I've learned my lessons well. If you want to make it as a pimp's daughter, you *must* know how to dress. It is imperative to develop a personal style that gets you admiration and—even more important—envy. A cute outfit every day of the week is essential. And that includes smart and/or whimsical accessories. You will never catch the female offspring of a pimp dashing out to the grocery store wearing sweatpants, no makeup, and a pair of Ugg boots. Uh-uh. We are held to a *higher standard*. It's part of the legacy. The downside is that you never *really* feel that you measure up underneath the clothes, underneath the skin. The upside is that your dad likes to shop as much as you do.

We jump into Freddie's two-door Mercedes sedan and head north on 35W, past Fort Snelling. Off in the distance I can see the big red-and-white-checkered water tower I tried to climb when I was twelve. I was never much for taking stupid physical risks, preferring the more calculated kind that I'd get from a new drug, or venturing off to a new part of town, or meeting a prospective new boyfriend. But I guess the screwdrivers must have had an effect on me, because out of nowhere I hear myself ask Freddie, "Where does Linda live these days?"

That's right, Linda, my birth mother—whom I last laid eyes on the day she came to Yvonne's to sign the adoption papers that would essentially *give me up* to her chief rival for my dad's love. The image in my mind is of Linda, kind of heavy-set and undecorated (these were her lesbian years), sitting in the sunroom, talking rationally with Yvonne, as I watched from two rooms away. She didn't feel at all like my mother. I don't even remember saying good-bye.

"Linda?" My dad always says her name with a fondness, like he's reliving what it feels like to be young and in love. He was still (relatively) innocent when they met. He hadn't even been to prison yet. "Last I heard she was living over on the north side. She calls me sometimes. I give her money. She's good right now, I think."

"Good right now" means sober. Linda's life has two channels: "drinking" and "not drinking." When she's sober, she's a halfway decent welfare mom. When she drinks, she gives her children away. I am aware that she and my dad have maintained some type of loose contact with each other. Since he's been out of prison he has turned into something like an uncle to three of her four remaining children, all of whom carry the McMillan last name, for no apparent reason other than because Linda uses it; it's the one name they all have in common. But until this very moment, it has never occurred to me to want to see her.

"You want to see Linda?" my dad asks. "I know where she lives."

Maybe it's the alcohol, maybe it's just time, but suddenly I am ready. "Yeah," I say. "Let's go see her."

I NEVER DO FIND OUT exactly what happened during Paul's lost weekend. But my "decision" to love him despite his lie has an interesting effect on our relationship. We are closer than ever.

It makes sense, if you think about it. Now we are truly joined in an unspoken, powerful agreement, a covenant. We are both putting the relationship above something—anything, everything—even the truth.

It's not just me. It's him, too. Because if he didn't value me, value the relationship, he wouldn't even bother to lie. He'd just say what he did and let me leave if I wanted to. But he doesn't want me to leave. Won't allow me to leave.

We're bonded together now.

Paul wants us to move in. He kind of backed into the discussion today, as he was packing for a two-week trip to Chicago, and I was getting ready to go pick up my son from school.

"I'm thinking of painting this room," he says. "Green." He kisses me deeply. "What do you think of green?"

"I like green." I'm always very agreeable with Paul. Where I used to be wildly argumentative with men (like with Scott, or my dad, or Kenny), now I'm much more subdued. You know how in the gay world there are tops and bottoms? Well, I used to be a top, and then I met Paul.

"Are you sure? I want you to like it." This is one of those times when Paul sounds very vulnerable. It makes me love him. "It's really important that you like it."

"Green is fine. Really. Do what you like, I'm sure I'll love it." He's getting at something, and I think I know what, but I don't want to be the first one to say it.

"Do you think Sam would like it?" Sam is my seven-year-old son. It always warms my heart to hear Paul mention his name. Somewhere deep inside, it triggers the hope that I could be the mother in a family unit.

"Yeah. He loves green." I smile quizzically. Wow, is this going where I think it's going? I don't want to get my hopes up, but then again, I already know.

He kisses me again. It's another one of those moments where I feel so connected to him. "I want you guys to move in."

He looks at me. He really means it.

"Really?" I smile bashfully. My heart is just wide, wide open. It's hard to believe that the person I want—this person I love like I've never loved any man before—actually wants me in return. "Wow." And he cares about Sam, too.

"Do you want to?" he asks.

"Yeah, I want to!"

We kiss. We gaze. I can feel the heat starting.

"So, you will?"

"I will," I say. "I totally will."

It is decided that when Paul gets back from Chicago, we will make it official. In the meantime, I will house-sit while he's gone, taking care of the dog and living in this place that's not only beautiful but has central air-conditioning.

I love my new life.

FREDDIE PARKS IN FRONT of a large rental property in a tough African-American neighborhood. I feel out of place—I've always had some sort of invisible sign on my forehead that says MY MOM IS WHITE, MY FRIENDS ARE WHITE, AND EVERY GUY I'VE EVER KISSED IS WHITE—and I look out of place, too, enough that an older lady next door offers assistance, asking, "Can I help you?" She's not being nosy, she can just tell I'm not from around here.

My dad answers for me. "We're looking for Linda?"

"Linda? Oh, she moved," the lady offers. "She's over on Knox, I think. Somewhere over there." She waves her hand in the general direction of Knox Avenue.

"Why, thank you," my dad replies, pouring on his customary oozy charm. "This is Linda's daughter. Tracy." He gestures toward me. I've never been introduced as Linda's daughter before. "Linda's oldest."

"You don't say?" She has that black-lady sass, but not over-the-top like you hear on TV. It's more like the language equivalent of a creative color combination or a unique hairdo. "Well, good luck," the lady says, and she means it. Minnesotans are seriously the nicest people. Even in the tough neighborhoods.

We get back in the car and stop at a pay phone outside of a Qwik Mart. I call directory assistance and ask the operator for a listing for Linda McMillan. She gives me one. Just like that. It's a bit disconcerting to discover that one of my life's central mysteries and core losses could have been (re)solved by calling directory assistance. It's like, *I could have had a V8!* Except in my case, I could have had a mom. Not to be maudlin.

I fish the dime out of the coin return and drop it back into the slot. I dial. It rings. This whole thing is unfolding so smoothly, it's happening before I can even get an opinion about it. Then she answers. My heart stops. It's really her.

"Is this Linda?" Wrong thing to say. She'll probably think I'm a bill collector.

"Oh, my god, baby! How are you?"

Wait, she just sounded like she recognized me. Is that possible? "It's Tracy," I say. She's probably mistaken me for someone else.

"I know, baby. How *are* you?" Her tone is one of concern, like I just ran a very long race or maybe got into a minor, but still unsettling, car accident.

"You really know it's me?" I can't get over this.

"Of course! Oh, baby, I've missed you so much." I'm struck by her voice. It's kind of raspy, and even though she's only said, like, six words, there's a clarity to her, an intelligence that I recognize. As my own. "And your sisters, they miss you, too."

Um, now she's weirding me out. But I pretend I'm cool. "Hey, my dad and I are at the Quik Mart on . . ." I look up to see where we are. "I don't know, somewhere near you—"

"Come on over!" She says it way too fast. I'm not ready.

She rattles off the address. There's something slightly unstable in her voice. You know when you can tell over the phone that someone's just a little crazy? That's how she sounds. Too much familiar. Not enough wary. And what's with saying my sisters miss me? I don't even *know* these people.

One time, when I was thirteen, Linda called me, drunk, and told me she loved me, and missed me, and that I had a sister, "who loves you, too," she said. I didn't think much of it at the time, but now it's making a little more sense. Linda's been thinking I'm still part of her family all this time! Even though I was living with some other mom in some other part of town.

Linda's clearly delusional.

WE PULL UP OUTSIDE the house about two minutes later. There are three kids with their faces pressed up against the screen door, filled with expectation. You can tell from their expressions that I am not a stranger to them like they are to me. As my dad and I get out of the car and walk toward the door, they bound outside and crowd around us. I am thinking this must be what it feels like to be Tom Cruise. On vacation in a developing country. I am also starting to sober up really fast.

We walk into the house, the lower unit of one of those big old Minneapolis duplexes built in the 1920s. Inside it's way tidier than I would have expected—apparently this is the difference between Sober Linda and Drinking Linda. Sober Linda seems to be an okay gal.

She even cooks. There she is now, standing at the stove, stirring something in a pot.

"Come on in! I'm making spaghetti," she practically bellows. "You hungry?"

God, no.

She's tallish, with dark brown hair and a thick middle. An apple, not a pear. Her thick glasses make her eyes look smaller than they actually are, which explains my extreme nearsightedness. *I hope I don't look like her,* I think uncharitably.

There are probably fifteen feet between us when I walk in, and she doesn't move toward me or put the wooden spoon down. It seems she'd rather just "view" me as I cross the living room, following timidly behind my dad. She's got a huge, almost embarrassed smile on her face and is looking at me a way no one has ever looked at me before in my life—including my dad on visiting days in prison. (And that's some major scrutiny.) "Wow. You are stunning" is what she says when she finally speaks. "Just stunning."

She's regarding me like a painting or a statue—an object, unreal. Her eyes are supercurious and superhungry; she really can't see enough of me. "Wow," she keeps saying. "Wow." After she stares some more, she puts a hand on Freddie's forearm. "Freddie, you believe we made this girl? She's really somethin', isn't she?" Her teeth are kind of screwy and she's got a lisp.

I have a lisp.

She gives me a hug, and it's awkward, especially because my mind keeps saying, *Oh my god, dude, this is your fucking MOM!* over and over and it's making the whole encounter just a little bit more strange than it already is, if that's even possible. All the while I'm experiencing this other indescribable sensation—a floating, vibrating, liquidy feeling that I can't quite name.

She motions to the couch, and I sit, prattling on a little about the plane ride. I'm both remarkably comfortable and terribly uneasy at the same time.

The kids are checking me out. One girl is draped on the end of the sofa, the other, smaller one clutching her leg. Another plays with a doll on the floor, not making eye contact. They're making me a little nervous. "Kids, this is your sister Tracy," Linda says. They look at me like I'm some kind of alien princess.

She continues, "They know all about you. We even drove by that place you used to live in with Yvonne a couple of times . . ." She struggles to recall. "Where was it you were living?"

Let's see, that could have been any one of a number of locations. I give her the name of the street we lived on the longest.

"Was that the big place over near Lake Harriet?"

"Yeah."

"That was it." She nods, impressed, and I know why. The area is one of the best in Minneapolis. To them, it must have looked like we were rich. "Yvonne had you living in that fancy neighborhood. She always *was* like that," Linda snipes.

In her eyes is the glint of the love triangle between them, and it strikes me how dramatic it must have been for Linda to give her first-born child to Yvonne, who stole her man.

I glance over at Freddie, who wears a relaxed smile, as if he doesn't know what Linda's talking about, as if he had nothing to do with any of this. I'm sure in his mind, these particular ladies, like ladies in general, just naturally found themselves competing for his affections.

God, these people are crazy. I need a cigarette.

"Meet your sisters, Gina and Carrie." Linda points at a ten-year-old girl who looks to be half–something ethnic and a three-year-old who's all white. "And that's your other sister, Kayla." The sullen-looking girl with dark hair has already got reform school written all over her.

My dad makes some conversation. "Tracy just got off the plane from Salt Lake City."

"*Salt Lake City?!*" Linda hollers. "Is that where you're living now?"

I nod my head. "I moved there with my husband, Kenny."

"And you're married? Wow." She's staring at me again, and when I take notice, she doesn't even bother to look away. "You really are stunning," she repeats. She's really annoying, but I kind of like her, too.

It hits me then, about this feeling I'm getting from her. It's novel and warm and familiar and nice and trusting. I *know* her, that's what it is, I *know* her. *Shit.*

It's mother love.

I've never felt that before. Actual love from your actual mother. Not a foster mother or a mother substitute, but the real live woman who carried you in her womb. The voice you heard in utero. The vadge you squeezed out of. My mind struggles to calculate the seven hundred and one permutations of meaning here. *She loves me. She still loves me? She always did love me. She never didn't love me. She . . .*

Oh. I get it.

She loved me, and she left me anyway.

MY DAD AND I DON'T say another word about visiting Linda. There is nothing really to say. It happened; end of story. The key to being in a superdysfunctional family is that everybody acts like everything is normal. Because, in this paradoxical way, *everything* is normal. Which is to say, *nothing* is abnormal. Nothing. Even when your dad the former pimp takes you to see your mom the former prostitute whom you haven't seen since she gave you away to your other mom, the one who is barrels of fun except for when she isn't. Not even that.

Which is also why it isn't too strange when, later that night, my dad and I do some cocaine together.

It happens innocently enough. I inform my dad that I have a big party to go to, and I will be partaking in some, um, extracurriculars, and that if he could, well, hook me up, I would greatly appreciate it. No big deal.

He gives me that amused look he gives me sometimes. Like he thinks I'm cute and he thinks I'm outrageous at the same time. "Do you use drugs?" There's no judgment. He's asking the same way you'd ask, "Do you like apples?" Like, just curious.

"Yeah. Of course."

"Really? Which ones?"

"Cocaine, ecstasy, and marijuana. A lot of marijuana." He doesn't react, so I blather on about the party. "It's in a big warehouse downtown. And it would be extra-fun if there was something . . . extra." I give him my best version of winsome.

I can see from his face that he's actually considering helping me out. Which emboldens me further. "You must know where to get some coke. Don't you?"

"I do."

"So, will you help me?"

There's no answer, which I immediately construe as a maybe. Time to take my arguments to the next, unassailable, level. I appeal to his logic, and naturally, his fatherly concern.

"Besides, if you don't help me, I'll just end up going to a guy on the street, or buy it at the party, and you know it would be all stepped-on with baby laxative or god knows what."

Bam!

Two hours later, I'm waiting in the car. I'm already dressed for the party, in my favorite black vintage minidress with the rhinestone "diamond" trim. With my post–*Purple Rain* haircut, my eggplant lipstick, and my arm full of bangles, I'm feeling ready to get my velvet rope on. When my dad comes out the back door of the small suburban house where we're scoring, I know my night is complete.

"Let's see it," I demand excitedly even before he's started the car.

"Gyurl! You can wait a minute." He bats my hands away like so many mosquitoes. We decide to drive a couple of blocks away so we don't make it so screamingly obvious that we just bought some drugs by looking at them right there in the guy's driveway.

We pull over in a small empty parking lot down by the Mississippi River. I'm trying to contain my glee, and doing a pretty good job of it, too. I don't want my dad to suddenly change his mind because he thinks my desire for it goes beyond recreational. He pulls out a small two-inch-square bundle. "Now you're sure you can handle this?" he asks.

"Of course, I've done it millions of times." Which is true. I've been doing coke since I was eighteen. It hasn't gotten out of control—yet—but it certainly could. And probably will.

"Millions of times? With who?" It occurs to me that this type of questioning is routine in most parent-child relationships, but it centers on things like driving the car, not doing drugs.

I'm impatient. "All kinds of people," I argue. "Friends. People. Kenny. Everybody."

"*Kenny* does cocaine?" My husband Kenny is the picture of law-abiding, rule-following good sense. Especially compared to Freddie. From looking at him, you'd never think Kenny would do drugs or cheat on his taxes. And he never *would* cheat on his taxes.

"Not like I do, but he has," I say. Which is true. However, Kenny is just a tourist in the party world, always with a round-trip ticket. Me, my mom, my dad—we're more like one-way people. We go there and have to hitchhike back. If we make it back at all.

"Let's just have a look at this," Freddie says, retrieving the small white packet from his coat pocket.

"How much is there?" I'm wondering exactly how much fun is on offer tonight. Freddie opens it and I lean in to get a better look. "It looks like a lot."

"A gram," he says. "And it looks good, too. Quality. Not like that bad shit you'da probably gotten off the street."

"See, I told you." I want him to know what a good dad he was to make sure I didn't get the crap coke.

We peer at the tablespoon or so of white powder gathered at the bottom of the shiny paper envelope, then look at each other. No one has to say a word.

He goes first.

So maybe it isn't exactly a *normal* thing to do, but it doesn't seem like that big a deal, either. After all, it's been a really eventful day. And besides, normal is relative.

* * *

IT IS CHRISTMAS EVE, and I'm back in Salt Lake City. I have a terrible cold, my nose is stuffy, and I'm achy and feverish. I rarely get sick, but I think all the partying I've been doing lately has finally taken its toll.

Or maybe it's because I am driving to the airport to pick up Kenny, whose wife I have been for 2.5 years now. He is coming to take me "home" to San Antonio, Texas, where he has been living for the past two months, since his job with the big Fortune 500 company transferred him again. I have managed to stay in Salt Lake by giving the excuse that I really wanted to finish my term at the university. Which I did, barely.

I've been pursuing a very busy nightclub schedule in Kenny's absence. Between Tuesday nights at the gay bar, Thursdays and Saturdays at the Twelve Oaks, and Fridays at the Dead Goat, I haven't had a lot of time for such diversions as Print Reporting 201 and Principles of Mass Communication 206. I even got some B's. And that's not like me.

But that's not my real problem. My real problem is that I am clutching the steering wheel so hard my knuckles are white. Repeating over and over to myself: *You can do it—stay married—you said you would. You can do it—stay married—you said you would. You can do it—stay married—you said you would.*

Obviously, I don't really think I can do it, or I wouldn't even say this to myself once, much less a hundred times over and over, the whole way to Salt Lake International.

Making things much worse is the fact that last night, I had sex with someone else. This is the first time I've ever cheated on Kenny, though I've been obsessing about it for a while and have come very close a number of times. I knew I was in trouble when I started to get insane crushes on every Spanish TA I had. How many Mormon returned missionaries can I get the hots for? Apparently one every quarter. Something about their super-repressed sexuality is wildly attractive to me. Probably because it's a lot like my own.

The guy I had sex with isn't a Mormon. But he probably used to be. He's the lead singer and guitarist in a band that plays at this bar I frequent. His name is JT and his band plays old Stones covers, like "Under My Thumb." I wish I could say JT's band is good, but they're really only average or slightly below average. Still, even though JT will come to have a potbelly and (yes!) drive a Salt Lake City bus before the eighties are out, at the moment, I think he's unbelievably hot.

In my defense, I had sex with JT for a very specific reason. I wanted to find out if there was something wrong with me, sexually. (For the record, I'm still unsure.) In the four and a half years I have been with Kenny, I have had an orgasm just once. Right at the very beginning of the relationship, by accident. Since Kenny and I got married, we have averaged sex about once a month. I'm obsessed with sex, but only with men other than my husband. With Kenny, I only do it when I can't take the guilt of not doing it anymore.

You'd think maybe I was just a person with a low sex drive, but ever since we moved to Salt Lake, I can't stop fantasizing about guys. Besides the Spanish TAs, there is the guy in my anthropology class; there is a guy named William, who took my name and number down on his driver's license; and there is the platinum blond Depeche Mode type I fell in love-at-first-sight with at Anthropology Guy's *wedding*. Which I actually took Kenny to. *Then* there was JT. And we've only been here a year and two months.

I didn't have all these crushes in San Francisco. Which, on second thought, shouldn't surprise me.

Then there's my sex life with myself, which is very, very active. I've been masturbating ever since I can remember—from at least the age of three. But despite being supercharged on the inside, I am apparently frigid on the outside. Kenny, being a very kind and considerate Minnesotan, has never mentioned this to me. I, having been raised pretty much in a barn, would like to talk about it all the time. The conversations always go something like this:

ME (lying in bed, staring at the ceiling):
Don't you think it's weird that we don't have sex?

HIM: Not really.

ME: Why not?!! [Or more accurately, "WHY NOT???!!!"]

HIM: Because. I don't. I'm tired. Let's go to sleep.

[Long pause while I can't let it go]

ME: I think there's something wrong with me.

HIM: You're fine. You think too much.

ME: But I *want* to have sex. Don't you *want* to want to have sex?

HIM: Go to sleep.

What I don't say is that not only do I want to want to have sex but I eventually will, whether it's with Kenny or someone else.

JT was just in the wrong place at the right time.

And now, the time is up. I have arrived at the airport, and Kenny is standing there, waiting at the curb. In his grown-up man coat, holding his briefcase. With his thinning hair and his full lips and his soft eyes. He is the smartest man I have ever met, funny and wry, and he is a great, great friend. I could never, ever be bored talking to him.

You can do it—stay married. *You said you would.*

IT IS SURPRISINGLY EASY to live in denial. All you really need is a good imagination and a compulsive behavior to practice, something you can do over and over again that serves as the shortcut, like the ladders in Chutes and Ladders—something that skips you right past the truth whenever it vexingly pops up.

For Paul and me, that thing is sex. Every day.

Rain, shine, at home, away—I could count on one hand the days we have missed—sex is the thing that smooths over every rough edge, metabolizes every fight, and contains our every lie, self-delusion, shadow, fear, and hope.

There is nothing too fancy about it, either, and that is part of the appeal. We do it in bed, almost always, and in pretty much exactly the same sequence—him on top, me on top, I come, he comes, and then we both immediately fall asleep. There is a ritualistic quality to it, not like devil worship, but like the British take tea or the Chinese do dim sum. I find it a relief that we know exactly what we like and that we do that; there is no need to perform, no demonstrations of prowess, no sexual equivalent of ordering the sea urchin just to prove how adventurous we are.

It is the antithesis of sex between brand-new partners, who run through a repertoire of moves hoping to find a winner or two in there somewhere. Something that will bring the new partner back for more, if you want them to, or at least make you feel like you could pass for second runner-up in a Megan Fox pageant.

Sometimes I wonder what will happen when we move to the next stage of our relationship, the stage where we no longer have sex every twenty-four hours, but so far, at least, that hasn't happened. To be honest, I'm scared the whole thing will fall apart. Couples don't *have* to run out of sexual desire for each other, do they?

But that thought is subsumed into the moment it becomes nine thirty and I crawl into our huge four-poster California king–size bed, and before I even have my contact lenses out of my eyes he is reaching for me. There is a comfort, a security, in being wanted like this: so durably, so regularly.

I can almost convince myself it will last forever.

But not quite.

Because trying to hold the whole truth and nothing but the truth from one's awareness is sort of like trying to hold a (very large) beach ball underwater. It seems easy at first—see, nothing to it!—but soon it becomes clear that the air inside the ball is exerting a pressure *every second of every day* and I, being only human, cannot do *anything* every second of every day, much less apply constant counterpressure to a very large beach ball. Invariably I become hungry, or bored, or angry, or tired, and the next thing I know—*pop!*—the beach ball is right up in my face.

Then I do the "chutes" part of Chutes and Ladders.

Chutes suck.

KENNY WOULD NEVER LEAVE ME. Never. This unspeakable truth is the central fact of our relationship. It's the reason we don't have sex but stay married. It's the reason I smoke pot from the moment I wake up until the hour before bedtime. It is, if I am honest, the reason I chose him.

What it means, of course, is that it will be I who must leave him.

When we get home from the airport, Kenny gives me my Christmas present, a Pentax single-lens reflex camera. It is one of the most expensive gifts I have ever been given. Until I married Kenny I was poor, working three jobs; I was so scared about money. That's how it is when you don't have parents. You start to think like Evel Knievel. Any slight miscalculation could lead to dire consequences. Kenny took me away from all that.

But I still didn't have a gift for him. All I had were excuses:

I had my finals up until the day before yesterday.

I had to work.

I didn't know what you wanted.

I figured I would get something in San Antonio.

It's not that I am thoughtless and heartless and selfish. (Although I am certainly self-centered.) It's more that I have always had trouble with gift giving in general. It just requires a level of planning and execution that I am rarely capable of.

The only time I am able to successfully gift-give is if I have *just* fallen in love with you, say, sometime in the last six months. Then my need to ensure that you will continue to love me will supersede my inability to think much past this afternoon.

But what I really can't handle about giving gifts is the emotional part. If I bought Kenny a gift, it would mean that I wanted Kenny. That I was *loving* Kenny. But I can't stop wanting to *leave* Kenny. How could I leave Kenny and buy him a Christmas gift at the same time? Wouldn't that be, like, lying? Somewhere in my distorted sense of integrity, I know I can't give Kenny the impression that he can expect another year out of me when I'm having trouble coming up with another week.

The moving to San Antonio "plan" included us spending the night in the apartment where I've been subletting a room (now *there's* a story—involving doing lines in a nightclub bathroom with a crazy chick who needed a roommate), then getting in the car the next morning and starting the 1,438-mile drive to San Antonio. But after I open the camera it somehow seems more right to just pack my stuff into the car and take off now.

I am getting sicker by the hour, so I lie on the sofa while Kenny loads everything into the Subaru. I have only a few boxes and a single futon that can just be rolled up and stuffed into the trunk. Antonia, the girl from the nightclub bathroom, is out of town, so I just lock up and, unceremoniously, we drive off.

Good-bye, Salt Lake.

It is a beautiful night for driving. The moon is full and huge and it's throwing the towering peaks of the Wasatch Front into silhouette against the night sky. I have come to really love Utah, and as we travel south on Interstate 15, I try to "feel" this part of my life come to an end. But I can't, really. We stop in American Fork and spend the night. It's more than a little forlorn, listening to the sound of the trucks on the interstate bleeding through the cheap walls and windows.

The next morning is one of those glorious Zion days, with the snow-capped mountains and the intense saturation of the blue sky. Perfect for getting high. I pull out a film canister where I have stashed a large bud of sinsemilla that JT gave me. Kenny is known to partake of some good weed, and nothing goes better with a road trip than a joint. Probably some of the greatest fun we've ever had together was driving from Minneapolis cross-country when we moved to San Francisco. Hard to believe that was less than three years ago.

In minutes we are burning one down. "I got this from a friend of mine," I say as I roll a flawless little pinner joint. I like them slim because I'm a lightweight, and my rolling technique is unsurpassed. "He's in a band?" I half-swallow the words, because I'm busy sucking in the smoke.

Kenny glances at me but doesn't really respond, which isn't unusual. Most people would call Kenny "laid-back" but that's not completely accurate. Really he just doesn't react to things. It's like a defense mechanism. If you don't know him well, he seems relaxed, but if you do, he seems removed, even arrogant or superior. In any case, I'm ignoring him ignoring me.

"His name is JT. We got to be good friends over the past couple of months."

Kenny still isn't saying anything so I keep talking. It's almost like that's my job in this marriage, to keep the conversation going. Probably so neither of us notices how lonely we are.

"He's great. I think you'd like him." I can feel a thousand little urges popping words right into my mouth. It's like I'm dying to just come right out and tell Kenny I fucked this guy last night. I want him to know that I'm guilty and I'm a liar, because I'm from Minnesota so I hate lying, and if I just tell him the truth I won't be a liar anymore. Twenty-four hours of lying is about all I can take.

I also want to tell him so he'll finally be disgusted enough with me to leave me. Because I resent the fact that Kenny is making me do the leaving. That he doesn't have the balls to do what we both know needs to be done. Especially when it's so obviously the right thing to do.

"Yeah?" is all he says. Just "yeah." Like *Uh-huh, everything's cool, you're not trying to tell me anything, there's nothing to see here, folks, so just keep driving* "yeah." The sad truth is that I could probably tell him all about JT and even *that* wouldn't make him leave.

"Yeah." I inhale sharply again and hold my breath. "He's in this band. They're really good friends with Robin." Robin is (was) my best friend in Salt Lake, the one I go out with, drink with, do drugs with, and blame for everything I can't or won't admit to. I've been hanging out with her constantly, but I probably won't really miss her.

I pass the joint back to Kenny and he takes a hit off of it. What he doesn't do is say anything.

It's just as well. My high is coming on now. For the first twenty minutes, it's like having a halo all over my body. I feel more alive, more perceptive, and nicely, finally, at one with the sky and the mountains and the road. I love this feeling. Kenny loves this feeling too, not as much as I do, but he loves it. Especially, though, Kenny and I love this feeling as a pair. It's when we feel the most "together."

Kenny pops a cassette tape into the deck. It's Prince, which reminds us of home. My favorite one: *Dirty Mind*. The thoughts about JT recede into the background as Prince tells me that morning, noon, and night he'll give me head. I imagine being Prince's girlfriend. With him I would be who I *really* am. I am sure of it.

Neither Kenny nor I mention that it's Christmas. Anyway, out here, in the middle of nowhere, it's just Wednesday.

THAT NIGHT WE HAVE SEX. I lie there without making a sound. Afterward I turn over and pull the worn motel blanket up around my shoulders. For the first time in years, I cry. Not some big major dramatic cry, but I squeeze out a few tears. Which never happens. I am so numb from my daily pot habit, and the neural bridge to the neighborhood where I keep my tears washed out a long time ago, maybe around tenth grade, that even when I want to cry I can't. I'm quiet, so Kenny doesn't even notice I'm crying. He wouldn't want to notice even if he could hear me. Some old part of me has awakened, a part that has been asleep for a long, long, long time.

I know I have to go.

When my eyes open the next morning, the room is empty. I immediately turn on the TV. I don't want to be alone. The news anchors are talking about the second-biggest shopping day of the year. I'm going to be returning something today, too. Something that never quite fit.

I wait for Kenny. A few minutes pass and I start to worry. Where is he? It hits me that maybe he knows I'm leaving—did he "hear" my thoughts somehow?—and he's beaten me to the punch. I throw on some clothes and run down the motel stairs. The car is still there. I'm relieved. I don't want to stay, but I don't want him to leave.

Barefoot, I walk across the parking lot to the truck stop café. Kenny is eating breakfast, alone. He's always been an early riser; it's part of his normalness. He was probably just letting me sleep in. He's so considerate; he was raised so well. I love that he still opens doors for me. But that's not enough of a reason to stay married. He sees me and smiles, but right away it fades. He knows something is not all the way right.

Fifteen minutes later we are on the road again. It's cool, and gray, and flat. I have said hardly a word, unusual for me. He has said hardly a word, either. After a long, long ripple of highway, I cannot stand it anymore.

"I think we should get a divorce."

There. I said it. I am shocked at how "done" it already sounds. The words only just came out of my mouth! This is where I learn that the words are the last part of the truth that comes to pass. Even if I wanted to, there is no way to take them back. The words are only symbols for an energy, a knowledge, an understanding, that has been there for months. Probably it was there the day we married. Maybe it's been there since we met.

"Should I turn the car around?" he says. Perfect acceptance. He is so graceful, Kenny.

We are in Albuquerque, 622 miles from where we started. Five hundred forty-three to go. It will take almost as long to reach San Antonio as it will to get back to Salt Lake.

"No," I say. "We'll need the rest of the drive to work out the details."

And with that, my first marriage is over.

IT'S SWELTERINGLY HOT IN CHICAGO. After a few days apart, we couldn't stand it anymore so Paul bought me a ticket to fly out for a few days. I arrived early this morning on the red-eye from Los Angeles. I am so excited to see him.

Paul is directing a music video for an old friend of his who manages a British pop star. Actually, she isn't quite a star, she's more of a pop asteroid. But she's trying to take things to the next level and since Paul wasn't working on anything else, he's volunteered to make a video that will help her do that. He's either so nice that way or so codependent that way. But I don't really care since I've never really experienced Chicago and I'm going to have a great time just hanging out, all expenses paid.

We are staying in an adorable (and empty, except for us) bed and breakfast. The owners are loaning us the room as a favor to Paul's friend, and we are happily taking them up on it. I don't even feel guilty that there are no other guests here, which is probably just because it's a Monday.

After sex, Paul and I walk to a cute coffee place down the street. It's been a week since I've seen him, and it's nice just to be back in his presence. I'm a softer, more subdued person around him. I'm not totally sure why this is, but I guess that it has something to do with the fact that he is quite manly and dominating. He has a big voice and hair on his chest, and for whatever reason, he brings out the submissive in me. The most interesting thing is how much I like it.

"You know what we need for this video?" he says.

"What?"

"One of those backdrops with a forest of trees. You know, it's like a giant photograph? Totally cheesy seventies," he says excitedly.

"I remember those!"

"Can you call around and see if you can find one? You should be able to get one from a professional photo-supply store."

"Sure," I say. "I can do that." Feminism be damned, again.

I'm a strong woman who is used to being the dominant partner in my relationships. How many boyfriends have accused me of being domineering? The same number who have said what a great lawyer I would have made. Which is to say, all of them. My last boyfriend left me over it, in fact. To be honest, I've always felt guilty about my need-slash-tendency to wear the pants in a relationship, and it's kind of a relief to be with a man who is *no way in hell* going to let me boss him around.

Paul and I spend the day side by side, carrying out a zillion little tasks related to the shoot. We are never better than when we are traveling or when we have a project to focus on, and now we're doing both. It's heaven. By the end of the day, there's a sense of being totally in sync, totally connected. Even the pop asteroid notices, and she's completely self-involved.

"You guys are so good together," she says.

We look at each other and smile. It's true. We are really good together. People say it about us all the time.

As dusk settles in, the skies open up into the kind of torrential downpour that never happens in the summer in Southern California. Where the heat and the humidity build up into such a stifling thickness that there is no way out but thunder and lightning and rain. It's glorious.

Paul and I are just getting out of the car when the clouds burst, but rather than running inside we stand there, embracing each other while the warm water washes down. It's similar to that moment in Stanley Park; we really feel as one.

After a long kiss—there's so much *steam* between us—he looks at me. For a long time.

Oh, my god. He's gonna ask me to marry him.

Then he does.

He says, "Do you ever think of getting married again?"

All I can do is nod for a couple of seconds. I don't really want to say anything, because it might break this feeling and this feeling is so pure and perfect. I used to be afraid of this kind of intensity—the sheer force of actually getting what you want. It makes me understand why most people never have their dreams come true. They're afraid. Of this. Finally, I am able to speak. "Yeah, I do," I say.

He looks at me for a long moment. "Will you marry me?" He says it with the emphasis on "me," not "marry."

I can't believe I'm hearing these words. I know that sounds absurd since I've already been married twice before. But the first time, I never really was *proposed* to in the classic sense of the word. Marriage was more of a decision we arrived at together. And then only at my urging. The second time I did hear the actual words, but it wasn't like this! I was pregnant, so it felt like it was something he had to do.

This feels like my life has finally landed where it was supposed to be all along. *This* is what I imagined as a girl it would feel like to hear those words. Like the most handsome, most talented, richest, best man in the land has just chosen me to come live in the castle.

Any doubts I have, about Paul, about myself, about the serious challenges we are already facing as a couple, are immediately wiped from my mind. Not as in forgotten-about wiped. As in the-universe-will-find-a-way-to-resolve-those-problems-for-us wiped. Because I'm still considering everything that happens after my prayer part of the answer to my prayer.

Which leaves me with only one thing to say:

Yes.

Eleven

I Love You, Even
Though I Just Told You to Go

I THINK MY DAD IS DOING crime again. I can tell by the tone of his voice. We've been close ever since we reconciled in my college years—he gave me money from time to time when I really needed it, and one time he even drove all the way out to Salt Lake to visit me (and ended up on a sort-of date with one of my friends; don't ask me how). I've come to know him very, very well, even though I'm living in Portland, Oregon, now and most of our relationship is carried out on the phone.

But I'll wager we do more "relating" over the phone than many family members do in a whole season's worth of Tuesday-night debates over who should be the next American Idol. Maybe because we can't be duped (or distracted) by facial expressions, or fashion choices, or whatever's going on in the room. Like blind people whose ability to listen is heightened beyond the normal range, we listen between the (over the?) lines. We lean in really close.

Over the phone.

And now I'm hearing some things, between the lines, that I don't want to hear. My dad's been dropping definite hints that he's back in the game. It's almost like he *wants* me to know.

"How's everything?" I ask him.

"Yeah, well. Good." He says "good" like he's considered it and he's come to the conclusion that "good" is a true answer—at least for the time being. "I got a couple of things going on. Nothing major."

I know what "things going on" means—it means some kind of criminal activity—and I find it alarming. But we're on the phone, so there's only so much I can say. In case the FBI is listening.

"You know you can't just think you're just gonna just do . . . *whatever* . . . and just . . ." I search for words that will communicate what I mean—"commit crimes and *not* go to jail"—but without incriminating him. In case the FBI is listening. "And just be *fine,*" I say, putting a heavy emphasis on the word "fine." "If you know what I mean."

"I know what you mean, little gyurl," my dad says reassuringly. "Don't you worry about me; I know what I'm doing."

Now I'm really worried. My heart rate is climbing like that of a white person on Mount Everest, and I have a terrible spinning sensation. Because if my dad says he knows what he's doing, then that means he's done it before. And if he's done it before, then one thing is for sure: it didn't turn out well.

"You know they'll catch you, right? You *know* they'll catch you. That's what they do! The whole system is set up to catch you." Fuck incrimination. I don't care if the FBI *is* listening. Freddie needs to understand that there is no way he's going to get away with anything. It just doesn't work like that. The FBI can play this tape in court for all I care . . .

BEGIN FLASH-FORWARD

INT. COURTROOM—DAY
The PROSECUTOR (early forties, a Sam Shepard type—except with good teeth) produces an audiocassette tape like it's the proverbial smoking gun.

PROSECUTOR
I'd like to play this tape for the jury, Your Honor. On it, you will

hear the defendant's daughter [he nods toward me, played by
Halle Berry] implicate him in the crimes he's been accused of.

(The prosecutor hands the tape to an ASSISTANT D.A. [a comely, ambitious
late twenties woman], who loads it into a tape deck and presses "play.")

TRACY'S VOICE

*You know they'll catch you, right? You know they'll catch you. That's what
they do! The whole system is set up to catch you. They never rest. They just
wait, watching, for you to do whatever it is that you always do, and then
when you take your eye off the ball for one second, BOOM! They're right there.
Isn't that how it works? You know that's how it works. Admit it!*

FREDDIE'S VOICE

*Now, now, little gyurl. Your dad is smarter than that. Maybe they could get
me back then . . . but I'm a smart fellow and I've learned what I needed to
know to stay one step ahead. Besides, if you know the right people, it doesn't
matter what you're doing . . .*

END FLASH-FORWARD

I can't stand talking to my dad when he gets delusional. When he
insists that everything's going to turn out fine, that he's got it all under
control, that he's going to outsmart the Drug Enforcement Agency.
But there's nothing I can do about it. I can't stop him from thinking
what he thinks, even if I know it's bullshit. If he was here, sitting in
front of me, I would probably start making arguments—pulling out
different facts, bringing forth examples of past behavior—trying to
make him see that there is no way in hell he's going to get away with
any significant criminal enterprise. He's too much a recidivist, and
the police are too constant a presence. It is plainly obvious to any out-
sider that if you commit crimes for long enough, you *will eventually
get caught*. It's like being in a Las Vegas casino or shopping at Whole
Foods. If you stay in there long enough, you *will end up broke*.

Period.

The conversation is over. I see the writing on the wall. And there's nothing I can do about it. I hang up and call my friends. It's Saturday night and three hours from now, if I drink enough, I'll have forgotten all about this.

I'VE BEEN IN PORTLAND almost two years. I came here with my now ex-boyfriend Michael after a long postgraduation stint on the sofa, which involved a lot of frustration and many ounces of weed. Michael is one of the best friends I've ever had, but our relationship was pretty much doomed from the very beginning.

Two words: He's. Gay.

I'm not even mad he didn't figure it out sooner, because without him I'd probably still be getting baked on Almond Street. And I had to get out of Salt Lake. Going to college there is one thing—you're kind of insulated from the fact that you're not Mormon—but as soon as you get out into the world (i.e., try to find a job) it becomes terribly apparent that you smoke, and drink, and in my case, are divorced and are having sex outside of marriage. (With a hasn't-quite-figured-it-out gay guy, no less.) This puts you at a marked employment disadvantage since there are plenty of other candidates for the same job who don't, won't, haven't been, and never would. (Or are and don't know it.)

"Let's move," I say one day.

"Where?"

"I don't care, anywhere!"

"Well, it needs to be somewhere I can get a job." Michael is right. Especially since he's the only person in this relationship who's working right now.

"Where can you get a job?"

"Not Los Angeles. They don't really hire out of Salt Lake. Somewhere smaller."

Michael works as a television promos producer (*"Coming up tonight at eleven . . . something that's not half as interesting as I'm trying to make it sound!"*) and the television business is organized by market size—generally the bigger the city, the harder it is to get a job and the more experience you need. If we could go somewhere that he could get a job *and* I could use my brand-new broadcast journalism degree . . . Well, that would be ideal.

"I hate San Diego. Too Republican. Too military," I say.

"I love San Francisco," Michael says. "But it's still too big."

"What about the Pacific Northwest?"

"I've never been there."

"Me neither."

"How about Seattle?"

"Edward lives there." Edward is an old flame of mine who also had a bro-mance with Michael. (It was the eighties. Everyone was a little bit bi.) It's a sore subject.

"Well, then. How about Portland?"

"I've never been there."

"Me neither."

"I heard it's nice."

"Me too."

"Okay, then. Portland it is."

Minutes later, it seems, we are rumbling over the Hawthorne Bridge in our white Chevrolet Caprice Classic, packed to the gills, our two cats furiously shedding fur in the backseat.

"So. This is Portland!" I say. It feels just like when Kenny and I drove into Salt Lake. I moved there sight-unseen, too.

"It looks like Mr. Rogers's neighborhood," Michael deadpans.

It really does. It has the cutest little train system, and an adorable downtown, and quaint little mountainy hills to the west. When it's not raining, there are rainbows, and sunsets, and pine trees everywhere. What you can't see is the chicken-fried steak and the level of gun ownership. I thought Portland was going to be all hippies in

Birkenstocks, but those hippies are just the blue chocolate chips in a very, very red cookie. Here, I am a black person again, whereas in Salt Lake, I was just a non-Mormon.

After six months of floundering, I finally land a job in TV news. It's not that I wanted to work in TV. What I really wanted was a job that would allow me to smoke cigarettes, chat, and drink heavily at posh cocktail parties . . . you know, exploit my *real* talents. But no one pays you to do that. (Not in 1991. 2008? Different story.) So television it is.

I get hired to work as an associate producer on a light news program called *First at Four*. My big break comes just three months into the job. I am at home one night, stoned, watching *Twin Peaks,* when the phone rings. It's the five o'clock newscast producer, Sid.

"You're going to produce the *Four* tomorrow," he informs me excitedly. News people love having news.

"What?!" I'm not sure I am hearing him correctly. Marijuana has a slight hallucinogenic effect that messes with my hearing. It's why music sounds so good when you're high.

Sid drops his voice. "Gary"—he's talking about the *First at Four* show producer—"had an emergency. He's going to be out for the next month. You're going to have to jump in and take over the show. Starting tomorrow. But don't worry, I'm going to help you."

"Wow. Okay."

Eighteen months later, I'm a newscast producer. I'm responsible for every aspect of the show—fifty-nine minutes and thirty seconds of airtime every day—where I decide on the order of the stories, I write all the lead-ins (*"Two people are dead after a big fire in northeast Portland tonight; reporter Joe Blow is there now with all the details. Joe?"*), and I take all the blame when the news anchors get pissed off. I'm not really cut out for this kind of work—for one thing, I'm not the most detail-oriented person and this job is a *festival* of details—but most nights I manage to slide into home base. Barely.

The news business has awakened my inner adrenaline junkie.

Live television is filled with risk—you're working against outrageous deadlines, and it's all do or die, or at least it seems to be, since if you miss your slot or make factual errors you're certain to be fired sooner than later. This is the kind of risk I can enjoy taking, where the hair on the back of my neck stands on end every single day but I'm never actually in any physical danger.

As my star rises at work, it begins to fall at home. Michael and I settle into a narcotic routine of work and television and marijuana, with weekend binges at the bar and the disco. People ask me if I am going to marry him and—gay notwithstanding—I know I never will. It's hard to pinpoint why, but I guess the simplest answer is he's just way too committed to me for me to commit to him. There is something I have always been looking for in a man that I still haven't found yet.

(Daddy.)

And so, I leave Michael.

Then he comes out of the closet. Which makes me feel a lot better about leaving him.

MY NEW BOYFRIEND LOOKS like a movie star. His name is Brandon and his eyes are enormous splashes of blue sky, his hair is dark-dark-dark and tousled, his mouth is out of a fairy tale. He looks exactly like a thicker, more masculine Rob Lowe, but he hates it when people say that. He prefers to think he resembles Ray Liotta. Probably because he wants to be a gangster. Come to think of it, he looks way more like Snow White.

We meet when I look across a room—okay, a bar—and see the most amazing creature staring at me. Him. Looking like a supersexy satyr.

Is he staring at me?

Normally, receiving the amount of pure sexual attention Brandon is directing at me would send me scurrying away, but I guess all the therapy I've had in the two months since Michael and I broke up is working, because I find myself doing the unthinkable. Walking across the room to talk to him.

"Hey." He says it quickly but suggestively. He nods his head a little, then smiles r-e-a-l-l-y wide, showing a mouth full of perfect teeth the approximate size and shape of pieces of Dentyne Ice. "I'm Brandon."

He's wearing a leather motorcycle jacket, holding a motorcycle helmet, so it's safe to say he rides a motorcycle. For a moment, we just look at each other. He shifts his weight from his left foot to his right, tapping his right heel on his left toe as he does it. I take this to mean he can dance.

"What's your name?" His voice is slightly raspy but not quite as deep as the motorcycle jacket would suggest.

"Tracy." I offer my hand to him. We shake. It's intense. We make conversation, but it's not that great. (Why is it that the guys you have the powerful sexual connection to are the guys with not that much to say?) The high point is when he tells me he's always figured he would die by the age of twenty-three. Which, I guess, means he's not twenty-three yet.

"How old *are* you?" I ask, laughing.

"Twenty-one."

Oh boy. "Insurance tables say if a guy lives past his twenty-third birthday, he is statistically likely to live out his natural life," I say. This is the kind of thing you end up talking about in bars when you work in TV news. Not such sexy banter.

Who cares what he says in return? All that matters is that he's taking my number and telling me he's going to use it. "Call you tomorrow," he says, in a way that makes me know he will.

Later that night, on the way home, my friend Beth says, "I would never, ever date Brandon."

I think to myself: *Me neither. But I'm going to anyway.*

By the end of our first date, he's looking at me like he's already in love.

"I had a great time with you tonight," he says softly. We've had a lot to drink and I am lying on my bed with my eyes closed because there's nowhere else in this apartment to sit. Not that I could hold myself up even if there was. Although I'm halfway passed out, I can hear in his voice how much he already needs me. He's not all defended like so many other guys. Maybe because he's only twenty-one. He's probably never even had his heart broken yet.

Brandon leans over and kisses me. *Whoa.* I swoon, but I try to stay cool. (I'm nearly twenty-seven. I *am* all defended.) I've never been kissed like that.

This is exactly the kind of sexual connection I've been studiously avoiding. I mean, my last boyfriend was *gay.* Gay guys don't kiss you like that. My boyfriend before that was a philosophy major. Intellectuals don't kiss you like that. My boyfriend before that was my husband. Husbands don't kiss you like that. My boyfriend before that was in high school. High school boys don't kiss you like that.

You know who kisses you like that? Guys who ride motorcycles, who are way too young, and who, when you lose track of them at the nightclub, turn out to be dancing in the go-go cage. On your first date.

That's who.

BRANDON AND I MOVE IN after twenty-nine days. We don't really mean to. It happens after he and his gun-toting, Mohawk-sporting, Aryan Nation–looking roommate get evicted from their house because of Portland's skyrocketing real estate market. The plan is for Brandon to come stay with me until he can find another place to rent. Of course, he never leaves.

Which is totally fine, since if he lives with me, I know he'll always come back, sooner or later. Which is probably the only way I would risk giving myself so completely to someone. I am truly, madly, deeply, and sexually in love with Brandon. It's the first time in my life I'm not withholding anything.

Not even orgasms.

I've noticed that the moment you stop doing something you realize exactly why you were doing it. Or in this case, the moment I *started* doing something I realized exactly why I *hadn't* been. It wasn't that I didn't have orgasms because I was frigid. It was that I was refusing. Refusing to let go. Refusing to let a man have an effect on me. Refusing to be vulnerable. Refusing to be with someone completely. Refusing to lose control.

And I'm not in control of Brandon. Not in control of him. Not in control with him. Not in control of any of it. *So* not in control.

It's not that Brandon is a bad guy. He's not at all. In fact, for a twenty-one-year-old, he's surprisingly mature. He works as the head chef and kitchen manager at an upscale Asian-fusion bistro downtown. It's one of those places that has an open kitchen with a bar around it, which is good, because it would be a crying shame to waste Brandon's face in some dungeon in the back. Like a lot of chefs, Brandon has mad sex appeal. A fair number of single women come to eat at the bar (no doubt to watch him work), and he always makes them feel good by smiling at them while he cooks. I tease him that if he can't fuck them, at least he can feed them. It's pretty much the same thing.

But this is the first relationship I've ever had that has sex at its core. Being with someone I want this bad feels dangerous to me. Maybe because the men I am superattracted to carry a lot of my dad's sexual energy, and I know all too well what that means. They'll abandon me. Somehow or other.

Until Brandon, all my relationships have made *sense*—they involved good guys, with nice jobs and bright futures, sensible choices, the lot of them. I have selected every partner against a set of very rational criteria. Is he going to "fit" my life? Is he going to be nice to me? Is he never, ever going to leave?

Sexual compatibility was fifth or sixth on my list of qualifications. In fact, it was an *anti*-qualification. I have a theory that you can tell who's having the least sex (or is secretly gay) by who has the most stable relationship. Passion is very destabilizing. And stability has, until now, been the most important quality I looked for in a man. My inner foster child demanded it.

But besides his regular job, nothing about Brandon is a concession to my inner foster child. And she's none too pleased about it. Because Brandon does a lot of stuff that scares the living shit out of her. Like drink. Way too much. And disappear, sometimes for hours. And worst of all, Brandon flirts. Ceaselessly. With women, men, children, and mailboxes. Then my inner foster child freaks out and I have to talk her back into the relationship. The conversation goes something like this:

I can't take this anymore!

"It's not that bad," I say to her. The grown-up me likes Brandon. I especially like the sexual freedom I'm experiencing and I don't want to have to give it up. I know he's not actually going to cheat on me, and I wish the little girl in me would just calm the fuck down so I could enjoy him. But that little girl gets kind of hysterical.

It is that bad! Did you see him last night? I thought we were just going to go play pool and have a beer and the next thing you know, he had jumped into a car with that guy Demetrios and they were taking off across the Burnside Bridge! I was really scared! I didn't know where he was going or when he was going to come back!

"I know. It sucked," I say sympathetically. "But he doesn't mean anything bad by it. He really doesn't. Anyway, once we caught up to them, everything was fine."

I don't want to have to catch up with them! And who's this fucking Demetrios, anyway? We're Brandon's girlfriend! He's supposed to be taking care of us. Not running off with some idiot because he's all drunk.

"You know he loves you. Us."

That's what he says. But what about when he was talking to that chick from the ice cream shop? You could tell she liked him, and he was going along with it! We walk down Twenty-third Avenue and it seems like he's had sex with every pretty girl we see. I don't even like going out with him anymore.

"That's just how Brandon is. He would never cheat on you. You know that." I say this emphatically. It's definitely true.

Maybe. Okay, all right, yes. But it sucks. I'm scared!

"He always comes home," I remind her.

So? I'm scared . . . I think we should break up with him.

"No. I mean, no. You can't do that."

Why not?!

"Because."

Because why? There are other guys out there. Nice guys. Who aren't scary.

"Because I said so."

That's not a reason.

"Okay," I say. "Because I want him."

And that's what it comes down to. Big Me doesn't really care if Little Me is terrified by Brandon's behavior. Big Me wants him, and what Big Me wants, Big Me gets.

IT SUCKS TO WANT A MAN in particular, which is the way I want Paul. It's fine to *want* a man. And it's fine to be *particular.* But you have to keep the "want" and the "particular" far away from each other. Preferably not even in the same sentence. Definitely not in the same man.

I must have known this intuitively because up until Paul, I'd managed to pretty much sidestep all desire for a specific man—one single man whom I needed above all others, one single man for whom I couldn't substitute some other single man. This is how I stayed safe.

Brandon would have been the exception. But I always knew I didn't want to marry him. He was too motorcycle-y and too blue collar. I was too art-snobbish and too ambitious. We just didn't have enough in common. And that gave me power—having the knowledge that even though I wanted him like crazy at that particular moment,

I would never want him for eternity. It wasn't Brandon's fault. He was like a starter house. You're not meant to live there forever.

Paul's different. He's the man I want who can't be replaced by any other man. I've never dared to want someone this much before. There is a brilliant sex therapist named David Schnarch who calls this phenomenon "not wanting to want." He says you might refuse to want your partner as a way of defending yourself against the knowledge that they can *walk out on you* any time they want. (Unless you chain them to something.) In the world of a sex therapist, not wanting to want leads to low sexual desire in a couple. Come to think of it, that's what it leads to in my world, too. Like with Scott, and Michael, and Kenny.

But not with Paul. Paul, I want.

It's nice to know that I must be growing psychologically if I'm willing to want someone with the intensity of my want for Paul. But it's not much of a consolation. Because the downside of wanting only one particular man is steep and rather treacherous. And that is:

If you're not careful, you might find yourself doing anything to keep him.

NEW YORK IS AWFUL. Brandon and I got here the day before yesterday, after two weeks in Dallas with one of my college friends, preceded by ten days with Yvonne in Boston (the most I'd seen her since leaving Minneapolis), preceded by three weeks on an island off the coast of Honduras, four weeks in Guatemala, four weeks in Mexico, a week in Southern California, and two weeks in Salt Lake.

The journey that brought us here began when we took HIV tests and—for the week it took to get the test results—fantasized about what we'd do if they came back positive.

"Well, I would quit my job and travel," I say.

"So would I," Brandon says back.

"Why wait until we're dying to live?"

"Yeah, why wait?"

The tests came back negative, but the idea was a pretty good one, so, on New Year's Eve turning into 1992, we locked ourselves in the bathroom at the stroke of midnight and made a pinky promise to hit the road come April.

And after four months living out of a suitcase, we are now in New York, with plans to go to Minneapolis at the end of the week to see my dad.

It's not quite as free-spirited as it sounds, though. At least not for me. Because a few days before Brandon and I made our pact to run away together I'd been called into the assistant news director's office at work.

"Tracy, I've called you in here to talk about a story you wrote for the six," Gil Hartsook says, wearing a serious expression. Not that he has any other kind.

I sit listening to him drone on, the fear needle buried so deep in my brain it's past the red even, into the sliver of white.

"It was about the Christmas Lights Festival at the convention center," Gil says, jogging my memory.

"Mm-hmm. What about it?" I'm wincing. Television news is like surgery—having to go back and revisit something you've already done is usually a bad sign.

"Well, you wrote that the Lights Festival was taking place at the Civic Center. It wasn't. It was held at the convention center."

Shit. Convention center, Civic Center. How the fuck am I supposed to know the difference? I haven't lived in Portland all *that* long.

"That's the third mistake you've made in the past two months," Gil says, tilting his head just a bit to emphasize the point. You can tell it hurts him to say this. He's a nice man, in his midthirties—the personification of a nice house in a new subdivision in a new suburb where nice people with good jobs move to raise their good children so that their nice wives can stay home instead of having to go to some stupid job just to overpay for an old house with outrageous heating bills in a hip neighborhood. In other words, Gil's life is my worst nightmare.

"I know this is your first job," he continues. "Mistakes are part of it. But not this many in this short of a time."

He's right. My love affair with Brandon has definitely had a negative impact on my job performance. I was much better when I had a gay boyfriend I didn't really want to fuck. I had a lot more energy left over for work.

"I'm sorry." I don't know what else to say. I really hope this little talk is over.

But it's not.

"You know, not everyone is cut out for this job," Gil says. "Sometimes you just have to say, 'Maybe I'm not cut out for this job.' That's what I had to do when I was a reporter." Gil looks at me earnestly and I can tell that the reporter moment was a really big deal for him. No one gets into TV news because they dream of being an assistant news director. Just like no one gets into a band to be the bassist. They all want to be Mick Jagger.

At the moment, however, it looks like I'm going to be more like the fifth Beatle.

"I'm sorry to say it, but if you make one more mistake"—he's saying this as gently as he possibly can—"we're going to have to let you go." He frowns in a kindly way.

This is the moment I decide to leave for real. I don't try to improve my performance or wait to see if I am going to make another mistake. I just start making plans.

And now we are in New York.

We are staying with (and by "staying with," I mean sleeping on the floor of) Brandon's best friend Richie, a dissolute "artist" in his thirties who left Portland a couple of months before we did.

Actually, I *was* staying at Richie's. I've just been asked to leave.

Richie and I have always had an uneasy truce in our ongoing power struggle over which of us is more important to Brandon. And being that I have a vagina and Richie does not, I win. But still, Richie maintains a certain power over Brandon, the exact nature of which I can't quite understand.

The night we got here, Brandon, Richie, and Richie's friend Allison (a girl about my age whom Brandon has always crushed out on) went out for drinks. I stayed home, not at all eager to spend the evening watching Brandon moon over Allison. I've tried to point out to him how pathetic his crush is, in the hopes of getting him to stop, but he's like a goldfish in a bowl swimming around going, "What water?" To him, trying to get a woman to approve of him is like breathing. He doesn't even know he's doing it. Ninety-five percent of the time, there's no woman he wants to approve of him more than me. But that other 5 percent of the time . . . is torture for me. I figured it would be better to just let them go out, have a drink, come home, and save myself the anxiety attack.

They stayed out until four thirty in the morning. Talk about anxiety attack! I spent the hours between twelve thirty and four thirty obsessing about Brandon's whereabouts, imagining him leaving me and never coming back, and doing what I do when faced with a situation (like my third mistake on my job) I can't handle: planning my escape.

I have an overriding survival mechanism that kicks in when I need it, and it is formidable. It's like Ripley in *Alien*. Or Sarah Connor in *The Terminator*. A powerful warrior-bitch-goddess who is going to kick in doors and mow down the monsters in order to make sure Little Me is safe and sound with a roof over her head, food to eat, and something adorable to wear from Bloomingdale's.

Nothing gets in my way. Not even Richie, Allison, and Brandon.

I wake up the next day emotionally hungover and in a fury. I have one—*one*—contact for work in New York, and I call her at eight thirty in the morning to see if she can help me get a job. She agrees to make a call to the CBS station on my behalf.

"Oh, thank you!" I say in that superbright way I have sometimes when I'm all fired up. I'm proud of myself. Usually, I have a hard time asking for help.

"Can you shut the fuck up?" Richie says from his "bedroom," a loft bed over the stove.

I don't answer. *Did you give a fuck about me last night? When you were keeping my boyfriend out until all hours without even thinking about how that would make me feel? I didn't think so.*

Instead, I go outside and smoke a cigarette. While I puff, I fantasize about living in New York. It's been a dream of mine since I was thirteen. I've always imagined myself hanging out with the beautiful people, having an amazing career, and getting my picture taken for the cool-people pages in *Interview* magazine. Now it's all going to happen.

A few minutes later the phone rings. It's my contact, calling me back to say she spoke to the executive producer in charge of hiring writers at WCBS and he is expecting my call.

"Thank you! Oh, my god, thank you so much!" I am very, very excited. Which means my voice is very, very loud. And since the telephone is mounted to the wall right under Richie's bed . . .

"Shut the fuck up, Tracy," he booms.

God, Richie's an asshole.

I have to call the executive producer right now, even if it pisses Richie off. I pick up the phone and start dialing. I couldn't give a shit if he's mad. It's nine thirty in the morning. Only losers are still asleep. Richie can kiss my sweet number-one-market newswriter ass.

The phone call goes great. I thought Richie was going to interrupt, but he didn't, which I thank him for after I hang up. The executive producer guy offered to meet me on Friday afternoon. That's the day Brandon and I are supposed to go to Minneapolis to visit my dad. But my dad's just going to have to wait.

That night I'm getting ready to go for dinner with my one "friend" in New York, a woman in her late forties who is really just a phone pal I made while at my old station in Portland. We've never actually met, but we always said if I ever came to New York we would. When

I got here, I called her and she invited me to her place for dinner. She also said I could stay with her if I needed to, but we both knew she was just being polite.

I'm sitting on the stoop, smoking a cigarette before heading over to her place in the West Village, when Brandon comes out and sits next to me.

"Um, you know that, um, friend of, um, yours?" Brandon says "um" a lot when he's nervous. "The one you're, um, going to have dinner with?"

"Yeah . . . ?" I take a long pull off my menthol. "What about her?" I exhale a thick stream of smoke.

"Richie was wondering if you could go stay with her."

I blink at Brandon slowly. I'm not sure what he's saying. "You want me to go stay with this woman I've never even met in person?"

"I don't." Brandon does this thing with his lips when he's freaking out. He rolls them over and over. He's doing that now. "It was Richie's idea. He wanted to know if . . . um . . . maybe you could ask her if you could stay with her."

"Me? Alone?" I really don't know what he means. He can't possibly mean what he's saying. "By myself?"

"Yeah . . ."

My stomach is quaking. I think maybe Brandon is asking me to leave. But he's going to stay . . . with Richie.

"But I've never even met her face to face!"

"Richie just feels like . . . there's too many people here." I hate Brandon right now for not knowing how to conjugate the verb "to be." "You mentioned that lady said you could stay at her place if you needed to, and Richie thought it would be a good idea."

He's right. I did mention that she'd said that. But she didn't fuck-ing *mean* it!

If I hadn't spent half my life up to age ten in foster care, I prob-ably would have told Brandon to just go fuck himself right then and there. But way down deep I'm so used to being the one to leave, this just feels weirdly normal, in a time-travelly kind of way. Like I just woke up and now it's 1972. Except I'm in New York. I feel sad and sick, but mostly, I'm wondering exactly how I'm going to ask this woman if I can stay with her when I haven't even met her yet.

I stub out my cigarette and go into the house. Methodically I dial the phone. When she answers, I confirm our dinner plans for the night, and then I take a deep breath and just . . . ask. If I can stay with her. I feel like I'm calling my Aunt Do, only this time, Yvonne never steps in to say the whole thing was a big mistake.

My "friend" thinks it's strange, I can tell, but she says yes.

In a couple of days, Richie and Allison are going to Portland for a week, so I will be able to go back and stay with Brandon. I'm furious with him and I don't know if I'll ever trust him again, but I don't say anything, because Tracy Ripley-Connor is already making plans.

I've been looking in the *Village Voice* for an apartment, and I find one on West Seventeenth Street that sounds great. It's $850 a month, and I have no idea how I will afford it, but I do know that where there is a will, there is a way. There is something deep inside of me that came into this world not just to survive but to conquer, and I am finally here and I'm not going to let some stupid people from Portland get in my way.

No way.

Oh, and P.S., on Friday I'm going to get the job. New York may be awful, but it also sure is great.

DEEP DOWN, PAUL AND I both want a family. Not in the sense that we want kids—we both have one child each already and that's enough for us—but in the sense that we need to belong somewhere, to someone, and to know that our life matters to another human being.

Paul's childhood was as sad as mine, in a totally different way. When, early on, I joke that I was raised by wolves, he replies, "So was I. Rich, white wolves."

Paul's dad, Richard, was an executive who moved the family all over the country, going so far as to dye his hair gray at the age of thirty-eight to interview for a CEO job. He thought he'd have a better chance if they thought he was older. He got the job.

Paul's parents had a troubled marriage. Richard was a charming and handsome liar (my words, not Paul's) of huge intelligence and even huger ambition. Paul's mother, Anne, was a young Jackie Kennedy type, a great beauty who chain-smoked, didn't eat all that much (from the looks of her), and somehow conditioned herself to stay with Paul's dad no matter what. She died, of heartbreak I think, barely out of her fifties. Paul also has an older brother who suffers from some type of mental illness involving delusions of grandeur. He was mostly functional until a couple of years ago, when he got arrested on federal charges involving fraud or conspiracy or something like that. They were dropped after it became obvious that he isn't really criminal, just crazy.

Paul has already been married, too. Not to his child's mother. To another woman whom he married as a "joke" in his early twenties after knowing her less than a month. Still, they stayed together many years before the marriage finally fizzled out. In the years since then, Paul's career took off while his personal life began a downward spiral, which is why I think he had that reckoning that led him to me. The good news about the marriage is that it is some kind of assurance that he's capable of long-term attachment. Which is more than you can say about a lot of single guys in their late thirties.

What's more, my son is smitten with Paul, and the feeling is mutual. They first met about a month after we started dating, and from the very beginning, it was clear that they had a connection. At seven, Sam is still young enough to openheartedly accept a new man into his life. It helps that Paul has a repertoire of silly voices and at heart he is a boy himself. But the fact that he also likes to play the same video games as Sam is the real deal maker.

Now that Paul and I are getting married, the three of us are spending much more time together. Sometimes we do nothing in particular, like walk the dog around downtown L.A. or go across the street for coffee and bagels. Other times we make a day of it, like when we took a trip to Six Flags. Paul took Sam on the water ride, just the two of them, while I watched. The meant-to-be quality that I experience in my relationship with Paul extends to my son, too.

We all feel it.

Recently, Paul and I were sitting on the ice-blue sofa, the one that matches the color of Paul's eyes, and Sam came up and threw his arms around me. As I snuggled him close, I said, "I love you, muffin." (That's what I call him, muffin.) In a rare display of emotion, he answered, "I love you, Mom." Then innocently, beautifully, he added, "I love you, Paul." Paul and I looked at each other, surprised. "I love you too, Sam," Paul said.

It was only a few weeks later that Paul asked me to marry him.

I suspect this feeling of family is the thing that sets me apart from the five million other women Paul dated but *didn't* ask to marry him. Paul loves me, yes. But having Sam's love and respect seems to make Paul feel really good about himself in a way that goes beyond what a woman could give him. It helps him heal the hurt little boy inside him and I think it helps soothe the pain he feels over the fact that his own son is being raised several states away. It's not all Paul's fault that the boy's mother insisted on returning to her hometown (and that Paul's work is in California), but I can tell that doesn't make him feel any less guilty or ashamed he's not there.

This family we're building—including Paul's son—is our great hope. If every relationship has a purpose—a deep underlying need that the partnership promises to fulfill—ours is to create a home.

To have and to hold.

To belong.

PAUL HAS CLEARED OUT the spare bedroom for Sam. There's not a lot of stuff in there to begin with, just a desk with a bunch of crap Paul never uses, which he's moved into the living room. That leaves just one huge thing in the room, a four-foot-by-five-foot pin screen that Paul built to use for film animation projects. It's basically a *gimongous* version of one of those little doohickeys that you press your hand or face on, causing all the little pins to give way, forming a perfect impression. The pin screen is so massive ("One of the largest in existence," Paul informs me) that it can't be moved. There is a picture "painted" into it that Paul wants to keep and Sam has been warned not to touch it. He's such a good boy, he definitely won't.

The three of us went to Ikea and picked out a bunk bed for Sam, and now Paul is in there putting it together. Every once in a while he hollers for me to come in and hold something so he can screw it together. We're all very excited about our new life. I've been doing more cooking than usual, and I'd say my roasted beets are getting pretty close to perfection.

I've given notice to my landlord that I'm moving, which is going to be a big job, since Sam and I have been living in the same place for four years. Paul's loft is full of furniture, and most of my stuff was crap to begin with, so I'm giving away almost everything. The only thing I'm really gonna miss is my washer and dryer. At Paul's place, the laundry is down the hall.

Everyone we know is so happy for us that we're getting married. The girls at the coffee place, our various buddies in the building, and of course, Tracy, my best friend, who lives in the complex—they're all stoked. Even Sam's dad is excited.

Things are going so smoothly, in fact, I could almost ignore the fact that Paul has hardly mentioned the engagement, much less anything about a wedding. I'm chalking it up to buyer's remorse, which I know he'll get over.

I just need to give him a little time.

Twelve

I Love You, Which Is
Why I'm Lying to You

I'VE HARDLY SPOKEN to my dad. It's been eight months since I got to New York and I've probably heard from him less than a half-dozen times. It's the least we've been in touch since we reconciled in 1983. That was ten years ago.

But I'm too busy to be worried. My career is on fire. In a short time, I've gone from occasional newswriting shifts at WCBS to full-time freelance work at WNBC. After a little while there, I got an additional job as the regular fill-in writer on *NBC Nightly News with Tom Brokaw*, and then, in addition to *that*, my own regular position on the weekends at *NBC Nightly News with Brian Williams*. If it sounds like I work thirteen days a week, it's because I do.

I find it hilarious that as a news writer, I have failed up so spectacularly. I wonder what old Gil Hartsook would think if he could see me now.

On the personal side, New York is like a bad boyfriend. I love it so much, but it's kind of like *meh* about me in return. I'm turning into a classic career girl—great job, cute outfits—and not a whole lot else.

Brandon and I are still together, but barely. We just can't seem to stop fighting. But we can't seem to break up, either. We moved out of Chelsea after only four months, thinking that too much togetherness was our problem. I got a roommate and moved to the East Village. Brandon moved in with Richie and Allison. That was almost four months ago.

A lonely four months.

Tonight we're fighting because Brandon doesn't want to sleep over. He never wants to sleep over anymore. And as far as I'm concerned, the whole point of having a boyfriend is to lie on my side with my head on a pillow that is perched on his shoulder and drift blissfully, safely, off to sleep. But Brandon has changed since we got to New York. I know he loves me, and he says it often. But something very basic is missing. Usually him.

Tonight we are having one of those rare nights when he's not working and I'm not working. We are smoking our after-sex cigarettes when my phone rings. It's kind of a surprise since it's nine o'clock at night, and the only person who calls me that late is right next to me, still breathing heavily from his orgasm. I pick up the phone.

"Hello?"

"Oh, Tracy. Thank god you're home."

"Aunt Winnie?" It's my dad's second-oldest sister. She used to live in another state but now has moved to Minneapolis and is living in my dad's house. She's one of my two sane aunts—she spent twenty-five years working in an insurance office and has never been shot or done crime or been to jail.

"Yeah, girl. Bad news." She takes a breath. "Your dad's been convicted."

Whoooooooooooooooooo . . . That's the whistling sound of Wile E. Coyote falling into the Grand Canyon after running right off the edge of the cliff and failing to scramble back onto solid land—which is what my guts are doing right now.

Convicted?!

I'd say *convicted* was impossible, except I know it so totally isn't. What seems impossible is that my dad has been arrested, posted bail, hired a lawyer, postponed the trial at least once or twice on technicalities, sat through opening arguments, watched a parade of witnesses, listened to closing arguments, gone to jury deliberation, and waited for a verdict *all without telling me.*

I'm a journalist. I know how slowly the criminal justice system works. This had to have been going on for at least a year. I do all the math in a split second.

"Convicted," I say. My ears are telling me I sound dead.

"Yeah, baby. They convicted him." Aunt Winnie has a raspy voice that would be superannoying if she wasn't such a nice person with such a warm personality. She's got that McMillan sunshine. "Can you believe it?" I can hear her shaking her head over the phone—*mm-mm-mm*—like Florida Evans on *Good Times.*

"Convicted. Aunt Winnie, I didn't even know! I didn't even—"

Aunt Winnie takes a breath and I can tell that she *just this moment figured out* what I'm about to say. She knows her brother. I know my dad.

"He never even told you he was arrested, did he?" She says it at the same moment I'm thinking it.

I look at Brandon. I'm kind of panicky now. I'm actually almost feeling the emotion as it's happening, which is unusual for me. Usually I feel things way after the fact, like how international phone calls used to be. They talk, and then way later, you hear it. Except with feelings. "He never told me, Aunt Winnie!" I have that shrill sound that people have on news video when they've been shocked by whatever it is that's getting them on the news in the first place.

Brandon looks at me, and I can tell from his face he knows something awful is happening. Maybe someone has been in a terrible accident. Maybe someone has died. I don't think it would ever occur to him that someone has gone to jail.

"If he had told me, I would have come to Minneapolis!" I say. "We could have seen each other!" I sound unreasonable, hysterical. Like a little girl. Brandon looks frightened. He picks up his jeans and puts one leg in, then the other. It's easier to watch him do this than to try to process what is happening on the phone.

"I'm sorry, baby. To have to be the one to call you."

"He didn't tell me!" I'm not blubbering. There are no tears coming out of my eyes, but they're coming out of my voice. "What did they convict him for?!"

"Cocaine conspiracy," she says. Of course they did. I told him they would. "And he's facing a lot of time, too. He was the ringleader."

I didn't think of this. If he's been convicted, that means he's going to be sentenced. There are sentencing guidelines. I know because of all the sentences you write as a TV news writer, probably none is written more often than this one:

ANCHOR
If convicted, so-and-so could face up to ~~five ten twenty~~ twenty-five years in prison.

It's called a "tag," and it is always the final idea of the story. The wrap-up. The culmination. The one declaration that is so final, it allows you to move your attention to the next story, the next crime, the next sentence, the next life in chaos.

"How much time is he facing?"

"Twenty-five years."

I haven't fainted in years, but this could do it. I take Brandon's hand. He's fully dressed now, shoes and everything. I'm too shocked to find this odd.

"What?! Are you sure?" My dad is fifty-seven years old. Twenty-five years would make him eighty-two on release. Most American black men celebrate their eighty-second birthday in a coffin. My dad just got life in prison. Or death.

"That's what his lawyer said. We'll find out for sure at the sentencing."

"When's that?"

"April." April is two months away.

I'm stunned. I don't know what to say. But Aunt Winnie, who has been through this numerous times—for her sister, her brother, her other brother, her nephew, and her son, not to mention the murder of her other sister and her niece—knows what to do.

Get off the phone.

"Okay, baby. I'll call you when I find out more. You take care a yourself."

"Okay. Bye."

"Bye-bye."

We hang up.

To be honest, I'm relieved to get off the phone. I want to smoke a cigarette, smoke a joint, and curl up in Brandon's arms. In that order.

I look at Brandon. "That was my aunt. My dad's been convicted. Cocaine, I guess. He's facing twenty-five years." I try to cry, but it's stunted. Like when a sneeze gets aborted right in the middle. If there's a vein that carries my tears, it's either too small for me to find it or too mangled with scar tissue to get the needle in.

Brandon doesn't say anything, but he lets me lay my head on his shoulder for a solemn ten minutes while I don't really cry. I don't know what's more disturbing: that my dad's going to spend the rest of his life in prison or that I can hardly shed a tear over it. After a little while, I get a new problem. Brandon is standing up.

"I have to go," he says.

I get up. I look at him. *Are you for real?* I'd say I'm shocked, but shock is so lame. I should just say I'm lame. "What are you talking about?" I mumble, even though I know what he's talking about. He's talking about *leaving*.

Nothing surprises me anymore.

"I have to go, Tracy. I'm sorry." He grabs his messenger bag and slings it over his shoulder.

"Where the fuck are you going?" Now I've hit a vein with something in it. Anger.

"I just have to go."

I know where he's going. To Richie's. "You're going to Richie's, aren't you? *Aren't you?!*" My roommate Jake is in the bedroom right next to mine, but I don't care if he hears me.

"Don't yell at me," Brandon says, sounding almost hurt. "I have to go." He actually has his hand on the doorknob. He's actually going to leave.

"If you walk out that door, don't ever bother to come back," I threaten. It sounds really stupid coming out of my mouth, but I mean it. "I'm serious!"

"Don't do this, Tracy. I just have to go. I'm sorry. I just can't stay."

None of this computes and I can no longer hold it together. I revert to some lower, mammalian part of the brain and go all pathetic on him. *"Why?"* I wail. "Why do you have to go right now? Please just stay with me tonight. Just tonight." I'm three now. My stuffed animals are sitting by the door. The social worker is on her way.

"I'm sorry." He is sorry. Even I can see that, and I'm practically delirious. "I'll call you tomorrow."

He leaves.

The door shuts. Behind him.

I can't believe it. And I can't cry. I curl up on my lame futon and go to sleep. Even though it's still in the couch position.

I'M HELPING PAUL get organized for his taxes. It's been some years since he's filed a return and I convinced him to go see an accountant, partly for selfish reasons—I don't want to be married to someone who owes back taxes—and partly for him, since it can't feel good to have the IRS hanging over your head. Besides, Paul *wants* to do his taxes, he just doesn't know how to go about it.

I know this because Paul saves every single receipt he gets. As soon as he is handed a receipt, it goes immediately into his right front jeans pocket, and then later, at the end of the day, he puts them into a very large drawer that is set aside expressly for this purpose. Right now there is a sideboard in the dining room with three drawers, all of them filled with receipts—from 2004, 2003, and 2002. I'm sorting through them, one year at a time, starting with this year, 2004.

I am something of a private detective and I can't help but notice that these receipts are a virtual record of his dating activities. I've been with Paul all of 2004 so there's not too much here I wasn't a part of, but 2003 and 2002 . . . now, those might be interesting.

"Does it freak you out that I'm looking through these receipts?"

"No," he says. "Should it?" I guess Paul is a lot more trusting than I am. "I have nothing to hide."

"Really? Everyone has something to hide." I'm not sure if I believe that or if I'm just being provocative. Probably I believe that everyone has stuff they'd rather not have anyone see, even if they wouldn't go so far as to hide it.

"No, really," he says. "I'm an open book."

I leave it at that, concentrating instead on picking up the tiny pieces of paper, uncrinkling them, and putting them in piles of entertainment, office supplies, and restaurant dinners. So far, the only story here is how much Paul spends on coffee. A pretty penny.

But then I pick up a restaurant receipt from January. Twenty-ninth. *That's the night after he never called me again.* I take a breath and look at Paul. He doesn't seem to notice that I've broken my smoothing-then-filing rhythm and am still holding this receipt. I sneak a longer glance at it. It's from El Carmen, the kind of Mexican restaurant that might be featured in *In Style* magazine, which is to say, packed to the gills with lonely, pretty girls who have expensive handbags and near-terminal cases of baby lust. *Ketel One vodka, $10.00. Margarita, $10.00. Two appetizers.* I remember the last time I saw him was a Thursday, which means the day after was a Friday.

I check the time on the receipt: 8:47 P.M. Definitely a date time. In fact, it must be a date, if for no other reason than Paul rarely drinks alcohol, and he certainly wouldn't drink Ketel One.

I carefully consider opening my mouth but decide against it. *Just keep your mouth shut, Tracy. He didn't do anything wrong,* I reason. He just wasn't ready to commit. He knew if he dated me he'd have to marry me, remember? *Shhhhhh.*

However, I'm now on high alert for every receipt that comes by. It doesn't take long before I find the Big One. I didn't even know I was looking for it.

May 7, 2004.

Oh shit. That day of infamy is burned into my brain forever. The Lost Weekend. I peer more closely at the receipt. It's from a café—I don't recognize the name—in Marina Del Rey. *Marina Del Rey?* That's all the way on the other side of town, near the beach. What in god's name was he doing out there? I check the time—a little after twelve noon. The food—two sandwiches. In the eight-dollar range. This is not looking good.

I decide I'd better come clean right away. "Paul. I'm looking at a receipt from May seventh." Ooh. I feel a little sick. The adrenaline surge rushes through my veins.

"May seventh?"

"The day you saw *Van Helsing*? When you said you had to lie low because you felt so drained after seeing your kid?" I'm trying to keep the accusatory edge out of my voice but failing. There's a long pause before Paul says anything.

"What do you want, Tracy?" I like how Paul cuts right to the chase.

"I want to know where you were." I don't add *and who you were with.*

"I don't remember."

"Well, I can help you out with that." I look at the receipt. "It says here you were in Marina Del Rey."

"Then I guess I was in Marina Del Rey." He's gone flat again. And cold. This makes me heat up.

"Why were you all the way out there?"

"I don't know."

It's clear he's going to stonewall me now and that makes me want to be hysterical. I want to shout, *Just tell me the fucking truth!* But I don't because I know then I'll have absolutely no chance of getting it out of him. My only hope is to move in on him so slowly that he doesn't even realize I'm there, like when you're trying to catch a butterfly. Or a bug.

"Please try to remember," I say nonthreateningly. "It can't be that hard. You came home from Texas. It was a Saturday. You were in Marina Del Rey. You ate a sandwich. Two of them. You were with someone, obviously. Who was it?"

I know Paul would never hit me, but he's looking at me like he would if he could.

"Drop it, Tracy." It's a threat. Definitely.

"I'm not going to drop it, Paul. I want an answer." He doesn't give me one. If we were Justin and Britney, now is when we would just have a dance-off. Part of what I love about Paul is that he's strong enough to resist me, but that includes times like this when I wish he wasn't.

I can't put a gun to his head and make him say the truth, so instead I go back to studying the receipt. There's gotta be something on here that will give me the answer. I check the credit card numbers against the numbers on another receipt. No match. Interesting. Paul only has one credit card, which he uses for everything. That's when I look at the signature. It's a bit smudged because it's the yellow copy of the restaurant receipt. But, upon closer inspection, it's not Paul's usual scrawl. It's . . . someone else's. It's . . . *No way* . . . Once I realize whose name it is, I wonder why I couldn't see it all along. It's *Caitlin Kelly*.

That's the girl who sent the FedEx package with the confetti and the lollipops and the photographs. The one I found when I was snooping through Paul's apartment when he was in Chicago and I was house-sitting. There was no postmark on the box, but it was clear he'd seen her in the fairly recent past and that they'd had a "thing" of some kind. At the time, I found a way to ask about her without revealing that I'd been snooping. He said she was a sweet girl who lived out of state whom he'd met through mutual friends and that they had planned to visit eventually, but in the meantime he'd gotten involved with me, so it never happened.

Well, now it's really obvious that it did.

I close my eyes in pain and cast my head to the side, over my right shoulder. Like I've just taken an invisible right uppercut to the jaw.

"I didn't sleep with her," Paul says.

Bullshit.

"I didn't. I swear."

I want so badly for this to be true. My mind is jumping through all the various possibilities. On the one hand, I have no way of proving that he slept with her. On the other, I can't imagine Paul, with whom I have had sex every time I've seen him since we met, being around a girl and *not* sleeping with her. On another hand, it's now September and we are getting married. My son has a bunk bed in the other room. I have moved out of my apartment. This Caitlin Kelly person is clearly ancient history. I would be very wise to let it go.

So I do. Right after we argue for a couple of hours.

That night we go to bed and we have our sex and when we wake up in the morning, everything is back to normal. Except for Caitlin Kelly, which I've managed to squeeze like a trash compactor into a teeny-tiny size that I can hide in the deepest recesses of my being. (Just like Daddy taught me.) Because my life is in session here, and I don't know how to stop it and I don't think I could even if I tried. So down it goes.

It's scary how easy that is.

* * *

TURNS OUT BRANDON'S been a heroin addict all this time. A fully employed, apartment-renting, bike-riding, movie-star-looking heroin addict.

I just found out.

He told me himself, now that he's in South Carolina trying to dry out or whatever you call it when you're trying to figure out what makes you put a needle in your arm. I know what makes people put needles in their arm:

Pain.

My theory is that every drug has its own explanation, based on what the drug does. Heroin is an opiate. Opiates are for pain. Nicotine makes you numb. Nicotine is for rage. Meth makes you stay up for days. Meth is for being superhuman. Marijuana dulls and has a mild hallucinogenic quality. Marijuana is for sensitive fantasists. What else? Cocaine makes you fearless. Cocaine is for the fearful. (And the grandiose.) Alcohol is a liquid depressant. Alcohol is for submerging yourself, dissolving yourself. I have had one or more of these problems at various points, sure, but you would hardly notice it, because I've surrounded myself with people who are much more extreme than me. Like Brandon.

I have only one question for myself. How could I not know?

Here's how: I didn't want to know. But that was subconscious. Like how they say we use only 10 percent of our mind and the rest is subconscious? Brandon's addiction was lost somewhere in my 90 percent.

A lot of things start to add up when I realize Brandon has been doing heroin all along. Maybe even from that very first night we stayed with Richie and Allison. I wonder if this explains Richie's hold over Brandon? And other mysteries, like how Brandon never wanted to sleep over. How even when he was there he wasn't there. And most of all, how the night of my dad's conviction Brandon had to go *no matter what.*

He had to get fixed.

Even more incredibly, I knew Brandon had been doing heroin on occasion. Because I was doing it with him! I just didn't think it was that big of a deal, and I never imagined that it was seriously out of control. Although, looking back on even my brief exposure to the drug, I should have known.

I had always sworn I would never do heroin. *My dad was a heroin dealer,* I thought. *I know* exactly *what that drug is about. No need to go there.* I'd also watched one of my best friends in college get strung out in the months leading up to graduation, with her boyfriend, a governor's son. She left suddenly and went to rehab and I never saw her again. Her experience gave me a chance to re-swear that I would never do heroin. And I didn't.

Until one night when Brandon and I are hanging out with Corey, a chef friend of ours whom I know from Salt Lake. He and Brandon are working in the same restaurant and have struck up a friendship over food and—I am about to find out—much, much more.

We are crowded into my tiny room, which is not much more than a futon with a moat around it, drinking beers, trying to figure out our next move for the night. I go to the fridge to get another beer and when I come back, Brandon is wearing his roller skates. (When he isn't riding his bike around, he's wearing his roller skates. The man just loves wheels. All kinds of them.)

"I'll be right back," he says, giving me one of his sexy-devil-troll grins. He rolls out the door and, presumably, into the elevator.

I look at Corey. "Where's he going?"

"He'll be back in a minute." Corey smiles like the Mona Lisa, which is his version of doing the Snoopy Dance. He's not real big on emotion.

While Brandon's gone, Corey and I talk a little about our mutual friends and the Salt Lake diaspora—everyone with any ambition at all leaves, unless they're Mormon—marveling at how many of us have ended up in New York. In six minutes flat, Brandon whizzes back into the room.

"That was fast," I say. I really cannot imagine where he went. I'm thinking maybe he got a bottle of champagne or something.

Instead he pulls a handful of tiny little squares of wax paper out of his satchel. There are maybe four or five of them and they look kind of beautiful, the type of thing you would find at a high-end stationery store packed with beautiful, but extravagantly unnecessary, things.

"What's that?"

"You'll see," Brandon says, unfolding one of the envelopes. It's like a teeny-tiny gift. I figure there must be something really good inside.

He opens it. It's a white powder, no more than a teaspoon. He dumps it onto one of my glass picture frames and starts arranging it into tiny—by cocaine standards—lines, each about an inch and a half long and as wide as a piece of yarn.

Twenty-seven years of saying *I'll never do heroin* instantly evaporates.

Gone.

Brandon pulls out a straw cut to one-quarter its original length. I should have wondered where this straw suddenly came from. I don't. I am too busy watching Brandon sniff a line up his nose. Corey is next.

"I want to do it!" It's the almost-bratty pleading of a younger sister, eager to do whatever it is that the big boys are doing. Corey hands me the straw.

"Take it easy," he says. He smiles, bigger this time. Not only is the drug hitting his brain, but he's also introducing me to something he knows is going to make me feel a way I've never, ever felt before.

Pain-free. Sublime. Out of this world.

And there's a power in that. Like giving a girl her first (penis-induced) orgasm.

I take the straw in my hand and inhale. I've snorted something up my nose a thousand times before—I had that semiserious coke phase in Salt Lake—so the sensation of a narcotic powder burning through my nasal cavity is like a familiar road I haven't been on in a long time. But this time that road leads somewhere completely new, like a dream where you're at your house but it's really, say, Margaret Thatcher's. And in this case, Margaret Thatcher's house is . . . awesome.

My first thought: *I never knew how much pain I had in my body until it was gone.*

My second thought: *Why is everyone so afraid of this drug?! It's not that big a deal.*

My third thought: *When can I do this again?!*

Here's what those two little lines feel like: the complete cessation of any anxiety, worry, or fear about myself, my life, my past, or my future. All while being *completely lucid*. I thought heroin was going to be like LSD, where grape jelly would be dripping down the walls and people's faces would melt. But my mind is clear, perfectly clear. Clear as a bell.

I lay back on my crappy futon and contemplate the feeling I'm having, really meditate on it. I am floating on a cloud, but it's not airy, it's firm, like one of those Tempur-Pedic mattresses. It conforms perfectly to my body—I'm enveloped by it as it exerts the perfect amount of counterpressure to make me feel fully supported and secure yet not squeezed at all.

When I describe this to a therapist, years later, he nods knowingly. "Sounds like what it feels like to be held as an infant," he observes. And it's true. Heroin is like going back to infancy, only *this* time, my needs are being met. I'm safe, and I'm not hungry, and I'm feeling no discomfort.

On second thought, maybe I better not do this again.

But of course, I do. A few more times. It's called "chipping," where you do just the right amount, just as often as you can without getting addicted. What I find out is that this amount is shockingly small. Apparently recreational heroin is the same as casual sex. Which is to say, it doesn't stay casual for long.

For me it is three times in one week. Sunday night, then Thursday night, then I used the leftovers on Friday. On Monday I wake up with the worst "flu" I've ever had. For the next several days I am the *sickest, sickest, sickest* I've ever been. I can't even *look* at food. I ache, I am nauseous, I have the chills, I can't move, and I want to die.

Die.

By that time one of my dad's posse members, Cadillac, is living in New York to pursue his acting career, after getting a series of parts in August Wilson plays that ended up on Broadway. Cadillac regularly takes me to dinner, just to keep an eye on me. He's the one who tells me what is wrong with me, a week into my "flu."

"What's the matter with you, Tracy? You're not hungry?" he says. I'm only picking at my chicken Caesar salad.

"I don't feel good." I decide to leave it at that.

"You sick?" He's eyeing me. Have you ever tried to get anything over on a fifty-seven-year-old former hustler? You can't.

"Kind of." I make eye contact with him. I'm trying to figure out if I can level with him. I think I can. "Can I ask you a question?"

"Of course, baby," Cadillac says sweetly. Like my dad, he's a little bit of a flirt. "You ask right ahead."

"Well . . ." I hesitate. "What do you do when you've been doing something you know you shouldn't be doing?"

"Like what?" He stares lasers at me. "What you been doing?"

I don't even fool around. I just come out with it. "I did heroin a few times. And now I feel like shit."

Cadillac gets this look on his face. Like it all makes sense now. "You achey? Sick feelin'?"

I nod.

"And you can't eat?"

I nod again.

"That's a jones, baby. You jonesin'." There's no judgment in his voice, which is a relief. He's just communicating a fact.

Shit. Right. Of course*! That's what this is!* It's one of those times where I know something is right the moment I hear it, even though I would never think of it on my own.

"Fuck! Are you serious? I only did it three times! I, I mean, three times in one week," I stammer. "I mean I've been doing it a little bit here and there—"

"That's all it takes," Cadillac says knowingly. "That's all it takes. Why you think it's so addictive?"

Why indeed. Because if all it takes to get as sick as I've ever been *in my life* is to do a drug three times in one week, *then that must be an evil drug*. Especially since I spent my whole life saying I would never do that drug because of my dad being a heroin dealer.

And now my boyfriend. Or should I say, my soon-to-be-ex-boyfriend.

I guess knowing something about heroin doesn't really matter, does it? It is just one sneaky drug. When you're doing it. When your man is doing it. It just creeps up on a person, and it is staggering when you find out what it is doing to you (or to your man) *right under your nose*. Suddenly, I have a lot more compassion for heroin addicts. And the people who love them.

I understand how someone can not know.

Of course, maybe I was prequalified for this type of "surprise," since I grew up in a world where forces that have been percolating for some time can "unexpectedly" culminate in a new foster home, or an arrest, or some other life-altering development. Eastern philosophy has a phrase to express this idea: "The river runs a long way underground before it comes to the surface." It means even though a thing can stay hidden a long time, it is nevertheless there and will eventually be seen.

Brandon comes back to New York for a few weeks after his South Carolina experiment and we try to reconcile, but it just won't work. After three years together, our relationship has simply run its course and there is nowhere else for it to go. One day I just say out loud what we both must be thinking: "It's over."

But not because I don't love him. I do. Because it's just not meant to be.

PAUL AND I HAVE PICKED a date—November 28, 2004. It's a Sunday, because I was doing some astrological research and I learned that Saturday is named after Saturn, which is the planet of tests and limitation. I figured why not just avoid all that and get married on a Sunday? Paul and I already have three divorces between us, so we need all the help we can get.

We've also been seeing my therapist Saundra in advance of the wedding. I suggested it after the whole Caitlin Kelly incident, and Paul agreed with no hesitation. Not that much has really come out of our sessions together (we've only had two so far), but my individual sessions have certainly gotten more interesting.

TRACY: I hate the whole thing about Caitlin Kelly.

SAUNDRA: What "whole thing"?

TRACY: How he lied. Do you think he had sex with her?

SAUNDRA: Do *you* think he had sex with her?

TRACY: Probably. Although he really didn't seem like he was lying. I hate that he lied.

SAUNDRA: You don't have to rush into this.

TRACY: We've already got the date. [I'm afraid if I don't do it now, I never will.]

SAUNDRA: Then you just need to know you're marrying a man who is a liar.

TRACY: Ugh. Does that mean I shouldn't marry him?

SAUNDRA: He's not a bad person. He just lies. You need to
take responsibility for that.

I love how Saundra breaks it down for me but doesn't tell me what
to do. Or what not to do. She just tells me the truth. Paul is a liar.
Not all the time about everything. But when he feels threatened—
when he believes he's going to lose something valuable, like me and
Sam—he compulsively hides what he thinks will cause him to be
rejected. It's all about power. Paul wants more than it is humanly
possible to have.

He wants to control me by limiting my information, which limits
my options. If I knew he spent the weekend with Caitlin Kelly I
might choose to leave. At the same time that he wants to limit my
options, he wants to keep all his open. I get that. Not that it's right,
but at least I understand it.

So, as I sit on the ice-blue sofa later, in the loft that is my home
now, just like I thought it would be when I saw that picture online, I
decide that I can take responsibility for Paul being a liar. I can marry
him, eyes open.

I believe in love.

I see him for who he is way inside, the part of him that has never
been touched by his lying dad or his fearful, wounded mother. I see
a sweet, open, talented little boy who created layer upon layer of
defenses but who wants to be loved and is tentatively taking a step
toward letting some of those defenses go. It's not going to happen
overnight.

I believe he wants a healing, or he wouldn't be with me. He
wouldn't be willing to go to therapy with me. He wouldn't be marrying me. He wouldn't be loving me. He wouldn't be loving my son.
I decide to have faith that every single thing that has happened since
the elevator doors opened is part of the answer to my prayer and

to know that—no matter what happens—I am exactly where I'm supposed to be.

Am I crazy? Probably. But not really.

I can't quite reconcile how it is that something as fucked up as my relationship with Paul is nevertheless exactly what I need to do. I want things to be tidy and logical, like they are for the Betsys of the world and that nice couple who used to live next door to me in Glendale. But I'm starting to get that I didn't come here to have Betsy's life—where the cart and the horse are in the right order, where Dick and Jane and Spot are all doing the right thing—because if I had, I would know it by now.

I came here to live a life just like the one I'm living, where it's royally complicated and not at all comprehensible unless you look with your heart. My soul needs this experience somehow, needs *Paul* somehow, and needs to keep moving toward him instead of walking away. I'm just having faith that, eventually, I'll find out why.

Thirteen

I Love You,
but I'm Ready to Start Dating

I'M PREGNANT. And it's the best thing that has ever happened to me. Not that I was "trying"—in the suburban sense of the word—for a baby. But the moment I saw that plastic pregnancy test stick with the big plus sign on it, I knew that this baby—a boy, due in April—was indeed the Plan for my life. I've never been more sure of anything in all my thirty-one years on the planet.

Indirectly, I can thank one of the senior news writers in New York for this blessed event. One day we were sitting around in the newsroom, and I asked her if she had a boyfriend. "Me?" she joked. "Haven't you heard? We lady writers call ourselves the news nuns." I didn't think being a news nun was the least bit funny, and it's only slightly oversimplifying the story to say that I decamped for Los Angeles a month later to avoid becoming one.

That was almost exactly a year ago.

The baby's daddy is one of my coworkers in TV news. Dan is thirty-two and normal. He's got flawless Mediterranean skin and dark eyes that surprise you when they turn out to be blue. And though he's a little on the short side, he's got an especially nice way about him and he's wryly funny, and I like that. We were paired together (I write, he edits) on my very first shift at KNBC-TV and I took notice of him right away because of his superior news judgment. His editing skills are network-level, which is not something you see a lot in Los Angeles. News out here, especially local news, tends to be kinda junior varsity.

I was making an exception dating Dan. I have always refused to go out with guys in TV news. They're too regular. But after three years in New York, I was very lonely and still smarting from all that "excitement." I wanted to be with someone nice for a change—you know, return to my UNG roots. Guys in New York might be dashing, they might be sexy, they might be accomplished . . . but nice? Not really. Nice modelizers, maybe. News nuns certainly need not apply.

Dan is pretty much my total opposite in every way. I am talkative, he is quiet. I am a big personality, he is low-key. He follows the rules, I break them. I'm an optimist, he's a skeptic. I think we are dating each other for the same reason—to see how the other half lives. We want to try something completely different.

After a few months the novelty begins to wear off, and we realize getting involved with your complete opposite isn't the same as it is in the movies. My quirks have become more annoying than heartwarming, and his inability to dance no longer seems so charming. Not that there are fights or fireworks—not at all. But there's no big, compelling love story to keep us together, either.

"I don't know if this is working out," he says one Sunday.

"I don't know if this is working out, either," I say back.

We agree the whole relationship has been a fine experiment but it's over and we should go back to being nice, friendly coworkers again. We break up.

The next day I'm out Rollerblading on Venice Beach, and I pop into Dan's house to see what he's up to. We live just six blocks away from each other, both of us within view of the water. He's not busy, so naturally we end up having sex on his sofa, for old times' sake. After all, yesterday was a long time ago. The whole thing happens so spontaneously, I don't even take off my Rollerblades. It's all kinds of fun and when it's over, I leave. No need to prolong the encounter. Dan and I are still opposites, and we're still broken up.

Little do I know, I am skating away with my baby.

EIGHTEEN WEEKS LATER I'm lying flat on my back. An ultrasound technician has just smeared a pile of goo onto my midsection, and now she's getting ready to mow a small, handheld paddle across my bulging belly. This is the "big" ultrasound, the one where they'll be able to tell the sex of the baby Dan and I are having. We still haven't decided if we want to know.

On the one hand, we are both in the news business, which means we like information. A lot. So much that we made it our job. We get paid to make sure there's as much information out there as the world can possibly hold. On the other hand, there's something just a little bit crunchy about us—we've both got flower child rising—and that makes us want to go "natural" for everything. Especially everything related to pregnancy and childbirth. And it's not natural to know the baby's sex in advance.

The ultrasound technician is not, evidently, thinking about any of this. Because she's only been mowing that air hockey thingy across my belly for five seconds when she says, bored, "Well, if you want to know the sex of the baby, I can tell you."

Really, lady? Why didn't you just go ahead and shout, *"It's a boy!"* and blow some New Year's Eve noisemakers? Because obviously the only way you can tell the sex of the baby that quickly is if you've got a positive identification—i.e., the presence of something, not the absence of something, the something in question being a penis. A half a centimeter long.

I look up at Dan, who is clearly excited about the thought of a baby boy. Already, his eyes are dancing with visions of father-son bonding over Dodger games and camping trips.

My thoughts are a little less idealized. Actually, I'm only having one thought, and it is this:

What in the hell *am I going to do with a boy?*

I'm the girly-girl, remember? I like fashion magazines and nail polish and ice skating. And I talk. A lot. About girl things.

What I don't know yet—lying there flat on my back—is that there is a plan. That starting this very instant, my boy child is going to bestow upon me one of the greatest gifts I've never even imagined wanting. A gift I don't even know I need.

He's going to teach me to love men.

DAN HAS NEVER BEEN to a prison before, but he's not nervous. We're in the parking lot of the Federal Correctional Institution in Oxford, Wisconsin, a medium-security prison about five hours from Minneapolis. In a few minutes Dan will meet his new father-in-law, and Freddie will meet his new grandson, Sam, now a beautiful, bouncing six-month-old.

"Are you scared to meet my dad?" I'm prodding Dan more than asking him. I have tortured Dan the whole way here with my endless ruminations on the world, which, as far as I'm concerned, is why long car rides were invented. That's when I do some of my best ruminating! But by the time we are walking into the actual prison, infant in tow, Dan is completely sick of me "just wondering" about stuff. Like how he feels about meeting my dad.

"I'm just wondering," I say innocently. I'm a little hurt that he's sick of me.

"I'm fine, Tracy." Dan's voice is flat as a skinny starlet in a cosmetic surgeon's office. We've only been married nine months, but I've already picked up on a pattern: the more I want a reaction from Dan, the less likely he is to give it to me. This is probably a great defense mechanism for living with me, but it also makes me feel invisible. I really want Dan to express some shock, or at least some *wow!*, at the fact that he is a very nice guy who has suddenly found himself schlepping into a medium-security prison. But Dan is not known for expressing shock. He's not even known for reacting.

"Really," I say to him, without even bothering to hide my contempt. "You're not the least bit surprised to find yourself here, in the middle of nowhere, about to be frisked?"

"Nope." He's annoyed with me, I can tell.

When I found out I was pregnant, Dan and I got back together. The idea was *Hey, we don't dislike each other, and we are darn good coworkers and sort of traditionalists, so why the heck not?* One thing led to another and we ended up married, but I'm pretty sure I'm not what Dan would have picked out if there had been, say, a wife store.

I do know that he really, really wanted to marry his baby that I was carrying. He just took me as part of the package. Like one of those gift-with-purchase things at the makeup counter with the lipstick shade that, while beautiful, doesn't particularly suit your coloring.

And now we're here. At the prison. "Come on," he says, picking up the heavy baby carrier. "You get the diaper bag, I'll get Sam."

This is where it would be relevant to mention that Dan's father is a Presbyterian minister who performed our wedding ceremony in the small-town church where Dan grew up. I wore a long, sleeveless brocade dress the color of half-and-half—in a size 10 to hide my bump—with a shimmering pale white, gold, and turquoise overcoat, similar to what Michelle Obama wore to the inauguration. We had twenty-eight guests, including Betsy and her husband, who now live on the East Coast.

That Dan's dad is a minister, just like Gene Ericson, makes me think it's the Tracy Ericson part of me that married Dan. Not Tracy McMillan—she's got an entirely different agenda. But somewhere in there, Tracy Ericson heard that little girls grow up to marry someone just like Daddy, and by hook or by crook, she found Dan. She thought to herself, *Now here's a guy who's just like the daddy* I *know*, and with a pair of Rollerblades and a little of my help, Tracy Ericson got her man.

I feel completely loved and accepted by Dan's people, especially his mom. Marie was a missionary in Iran in the 1950s who didn't get married until she was thirty-two. Then she had four children in five years, starting with Dan. Marie is a woman of deep faith, compassion, and intellect who is already like a surrogate mother to me. As far as shotgun mothers-in-law go, I cannot believe my luck! In fact, sometimes we joke that baby Sam came along just so the two of us could meet. All I know is, between Marie and June Ericson, I'm starting to think god puts a really nice Christian lady in my life every other time I need a new mother.

Now it's Dan's turn to meet the in-laws. It's wacky like those Ben Stiller movies, but in my case, there's only one in-law—my dad. I haven't heard from Linda in a couple of years and I long ago decided it's best to keep a safe distance from Yvonne.

"I know Freddie's really excited about this visit," I say as we head inside. "He wants to see what kind of white boy I'm dating this time." I have a terrible habit of saying controversial things whenever I want. It's one of my least endearing qualities.

"Maybe he just wants to see his grandson, Tracy," Dan suggests. He might be right, but his tone—ever-so-slightly superior—makes me feel bad. Like there's a way that normal people think and act that I know nothing about. "I doubt I'm the person your dad is thinking about right now."

"Oh yeah," I say. "He probably *is* excited to see his grandson." Especially knowing my dad, who thinks everything revolves around him. In Freddie's mind, meeting my baby will be like sitting down for a visit with his future self, the part of him that's going to be looking stylish in the year 2050.

After all of the security rigamarole, my dad makes his entrance. I haven't seen him since 1994. That was three years—and several life changes—ago. He's looking good, though. For sixty-two.

"Dan, this is Freddie," I say, presenting my dad palms-up. My dad grabs Dan's hand and pumps it vigorously.

"Hello, Dan," Freddie says.

"And . . . um . . ." I pause awkwardly. I'm not sure *what* to call my dad these days. It's fine to introduce him to someone as Freddie. But I don't want to address him—daughter to father—by his first name and I don't want to call him Dad, either. So I "write around it," which is what we do in TV news when we don't have all the facts. "And, um, this is Dan."

"Good to meet you, Mr. McMillan," Dan says respectfully. Watching this exchange, I am reminded of what I love about Dan. He is extremely fair-minded. He treats everyone the same, because he truly believes everyone is equal to everyone else. He's not wowed by your social status or how much money you have or what your job is. Dan is just as gracious and polite as he would be if my dad was a cardiologist.

"Wonderful to meet you, too," Freddie says. "My new *son*-in-law!" He's obviously tickled pink. "Now let me see my grandson! *Sammy!*"

My dad swoops up my baby and raises him high into the air, just like he did with me when I was little. Sam looks around like, *What just happened?!* "He's so cute!" Freddie chirps. "Look at him. A chip off the old block." My dad's vanity knows no limits. "And how about you, darling daughter?" Freddie gives me a hug and a big smooch on the cheek. "It's good to see you. Been a long time." There's a hint of a guilt trip in there somewhere. Which kind of pisses me off.

Fortunately, Dan's presence smooths over any prickles coming from me. Freddie's been in here four and a half years now. There's a distance that develops—for me it's a necessary distance—and it doesn't just melt away the moment I see him in person.

"So, Daniel"—Freddie doesn't bother to ask if this is Dan's name of choice—"you say your father is a minister?" He wants to know all about Dan's family, questioning him the way you imagine an Albanian peasant father questions a prospective son-in-law.

"Yes, sir. He is."

"And where does he have a church?"

"It's a small town in south New Jersey. On the way to Atlantic City, if you're familiar with that area." Dan doesn't have a "Joizy" accent at all. He says it "New *Jurr*-zee," almost overenunciating. It's a cute affectation that is very boyish and endearing.

"Sure, I've been to Atlantic City. Had a great time, too!" Freddie claps his hands together at the memory. He seems to be finding Dan charming and sweet, and I'm glad about it but not really surprised. Very few people who meet Dan don't get along with him. He is like type O blood. Universally accepted.

"Dan's town is so small, there's only one stoplight," I say.

"That small, huh?" My dad might be feigning serious interest. But more likely, he's sincere. Freddie doesn't get a whole lot of visitors. "That's really tiny."

"And," I add, "Dan was born in Beirut."

I like this part of Dan's story. At first glance he looks like just another Adam Sandler type. But his father is Lebanese, and Dan spent the first four years of his life there. It means our kid is Arab, African, and European, all at once. I can't help but feel like this makes the baby sort of evolved. "He moved to the United States when he was four."

"Is that right?" My dad's suitably impressed. Freddie is the opposite of Dan. He reacts to *everything,* usually in exactly the way you wanted him to. The pimp/hustler part of him can read your mind, and he lives to fulfill (or prey upon) your desires. At least until he gets locked up for something. "Do you speak Arabic?"

I notice with a smidgen of pride that my dad didn't ask if Dan speaks Lebanese. For a guy who only got to, like, eighth grade, Freddie's pretty knowledgeable.

"I did." Dan blushes. "But I don't remember any of it."

My dad turns to me. "You're looking good, Tracy."

"Thanks." I am wearing a brand-new pair of jeans, which might have been a mistake, because they are getting all creasy in the crotch area, which I hate. If I had worn them before, I would have known this in advance and chosen a different pair for a prison visit, which is nothing *but* sitting.

"I was worried. Those pictures you sent me—you looked a little chunky."

He means the pictures I sent of me and the baby, taken in the hospital hours after the birth! My dad is such a douche sometimes. He has no idea *what* he is saying. I tell him that with a smile on my face. "Jesus, dude. I had just given birth! You're unbelievable."

I just called my dad "dude." He deserved it.

So that's pretty much the way it goes until the visiting hours end at three P.M. My dad getting to know his son-in-law. Dan getting to know his father-in-law. My dad lovingly finding all my flaws.

And me holding my darling new baby, thinking, *I can't believe I brought my baby to prison.*

I'M GOING TO WEAR WHITE to marry Paul. I bought my dress today in a vintage wedding-dress shop in Toronto, where Paul is working on a soft drink commercial. It's from the 1950s, full-length, ivory, with a teeny-tiny waist, high neck, lace bodice, long sleeves, and two thousand buttons up the back. It looks like something Grace Kelly would wear to marry a prince. I'm just excited that, even though it took me three weddings, I will finally fulfill my fantasy of being a traditional bride.

Paul has pulled a few strings with the producer of the commercial and gotten us a suite for the long weekend. It's the most beautiful hotel room I've ever been in—the size of an apartment, with floor-to-ceiling windows and staggeringly beautiful views of Lake Ontario. I brought Sam with me, and the two of us are having a grand time eating crepes and hanging out while Paul works. We even took a day trip to Niagara Falls. Leave it to me to go to the honeymoon capital of the world right *before* I get married.

The wedding is two weeks away and things are a whirlwind. Paul gets back from Toronto next weekend, and I have talked him into making a pilgrimage to northern California to see an Indian guru who goes around the world blessing people by giving them hugs, which I think is totally punk rock. I want us to get a hug to bless our marriage. The plan is to drive up there the day Paul gets back, stay for one night, then drive back the next morning.

Nine days after that we get married.

We've kept all the wedding plans as simple as possible. There's an abandoned hotel next door, owned by the company that converted our building into lofts, where we're going to hold the ceremony. The place is a beautiful ruin—built around the turn of the century, it hasn't been inhabited in decades—with a three-story lobby, a grand center staircase, and floors made of marble. But everything else about it is destroyed. There's no electricity, and dead wires hang from the ceiling like twisted tree branches. Alabaster light streams in through the windows, some of which are broken. It's devastated and gorgeous.

We've invited just a handful of people: our closest friends, my son, and Paul's dad and stepmom. How funny that both of us have a family member who can't attend because they're institutionalized—my dad in prison, Paul's brother in a psychiatric facility—which must mean we're a perfect match. Saundra, my therapist, is officiating.

When the ceremony is over, we're all going to one of L.A.'s landmark restaurants for steaks and wedding cake. And after a night in a hotel, we'll head for a five-day honeymoon in Cabo San Lucas.

For a wedding we just started planning four weeks ago, everything has come together beautifully. Magically. Like when I said to Paul, "You know what we need for the ceremony? A candelabra." And literally two minutes later, we pass a store with a perfect pair of five-foot candelabras made of iron in the window. Like that.

All that's left now is to put the dress on and say, "I do."

Oh, and see the guru.

*　*　*

MOTHERHOOD IS MAKING ME obsessed with the electrical towers down the street. They're not far enough away from our house for my liking. They are giant sentinels of steel and electricity that seem to watch everything I do. I think about them in the middle of the night, when I wake up to nurse Sam. Sometimes I can't get back to sleep, I am thinking so hard about them. They are transmitting all of my anxiety.

Having a baby, not surprisingly, has freaked me out a little. To mother a child, I'm discovering, is a bit like accessing a 401(k) retirement account: you pull from whatever is in there, a combination of "employer contributions"—the way you were cared for by your own mother (or in my case father)—and your own ongoing deposits, i.e., whatever therapy and personal growth you've done.

I am a natural mom, in the way someone is a natural, say, tennis player: I'm warm and nurturing and comfortable caring for all of Sam's needs, but I am terribly anxious, too. Especially about leaving. I'm afraid if I go out and Sam wakes up while I am gone, he'll conclude I'm never coming back. The obvious solution is to ask myself if I am coming back—*Yeah, of course, I'm coming back!*—then rest assured that the baby will eventually figure that out when I show up in a little while, toting bags from Trader Joe's. This is what reasonable people are encouraging me to try.

But I seem incapable of understanding this. Maybe because it's not the grown woman in me who is afraid my baby will think I'm gone forever, but the baby in me who is remembering my own fear from when my parents left and then were gone "forever." Perhaps my preverbal traumas are like fossils—not only not forgotten, but *perfectly* preserved in my memory, the way a tiny etching of a shell is engraved in sedimentary rock even after thousands of years. Motherhood is the light-rail project that brings in the jackhammers, breaking up all that rock once and for all.

This makes me think that postpartum depression is when a mother has a baby and it "wakes up" that part of her that was unmothered or undermothered and thus is deeply, preverbally, achingly sad. They should call it postpartum grief. It makes sense that doctors prescribe antidepressants to "cure" it. That said, I don't think I'm depressed. Not at all.

I'm just very very concerned about the power lines.

WHEN I'M NOT OBSESSING about the power lines, I'm thinking about Gwyneth Paltrow. Of all people. I saw her once at the Sundance Film Festival, back when she was dating Brad Pitt. She was tall, and blond, and rich looking, exactly like in *Us Weekly*. At the time, I didn't think much of her one way or another.

But motherhood has forced my own "daughterhood" to the surface, and that is making me have all kinds of feelings toward Gwyneth. Like, I kind of hate her. Not actual *hate*-hate. (I'm too Minnesotan for that.) More like middle-school hate. The special type of hate for tall, blond, rich girls who date Brad Pitt that is experienced by the rest of us less-fortunates. Which is to say the vast majority of vagina-having Americans.

I know right when it started: Oscar night 1997. I'm sitting there, watching Gwyneth sashay to the podium in her pink Ralph Lauren gown, when this intense feeling arises in me. The word "envy" comes to mind, but it's really more than that. It's more like *injustice*. Not wrongly-convicted-of-murder injustice, but close. *THIS IS SO, SO, SO UNFAIR*, my mind screams. How is it that one girl—Gwynnie—can pretty much get born, go shopping, date movie stars, sail around on Valentino's yacht, then collect an Oscar, all before the age of twenty-seven? How does that happen?

Of course, I already know how, and that's precisely what's got me so upset. There's even a special term for it. Gwyneth is a *daddy's girl*.

Apparently, when you have a father who takes excellent care of you, who is dedicated to giving you what you need *and* what you want (and not just Pixy Stix between prison sentences), you grow up feeling like you should be treated very, very well. You feel *deserving*. And other people just naturally feel like you deserve stuff, too. So they give it to you.

This is obviously not quite what happened to me. But rather than mourn that, I've just decided to middle-school-hate Gwyneth.

My whole Gwyneth-Daddy obsession culminates a few years later at work. I'm supposed to be writing something for the five o'clock newscast when Gwyneth's lovely face pops up on the twelve-inch TV that sits on my desk. She's on *Oprah*. I have to watch.

I turn up the sound just as Gwyneth is sharing a story about how her dad surprised her with a father-daughter trip to Paris when she was ten. They stayed at the Ritz or something five-star like that, just the two of them. What kills me is the part where Gwyneth tells Oprah her dad's reason for the trip.

"I wanted you to see Paris for the first time with a man who will always love you," he said.

That's a quote.

My first reaction is white-hot anger—*A man who will always love me? No man will always love me. Tolerate me, maybe. Marry me if I beg him to, or if I'm pregnant. But love me so much he'll whisk me off to Paris?*

Stop it.

Then—and this surprises me—I begin to cry. Right there at my desk in the newsroom where everyone can see me. Big, clean tears, like summery white cotton. The kind good for halter tops and elephant bells.

Because Gwyneth was loved like that. And because I wasn't, but I wanted to be.

THEN THERE'S MY PARTYING, which is starting to look an awful lot like a drinking problem. Dan and I have started a band. Actually, Dan started it; I demanded membership when I saw how much fun it was and how much time he would be away from the house without me. There are almost always one or two musicians at the house now, and the band gives me a nice little cover story for my near-constant use of marijuana, and later in the day, wine.

Here's the thing about my drinking and pot smoking—you would never know. I make sure of that. It's almost like I have two lives: in one, I'm a stay-at-home mom learning the ropes of new motherhood; in the other, I'm a chick in a band. In the first life, I'm surrounded by women; in the second, I'm surrounded by men. In one, I hide my partying; in the other, it's pretty much all I do. It's like I have two opposing parts of myself: one that nurtures, and one that destroys.

I am trying to convince myself that I am freethinking, a countercultural hippie. But it's hard. I am paranoid about the next-door neighbor, a do-gooder with a brand-new master of social work degree. I have these morbid fears that she is going to smell the marijuana smoke wafting out of our garage and turn me in to Children's Services, who will take my baby away from me.

Interestingly, my morbid fear doesn't seem to be enough to make me stop doing it.

I have a bottle of wine to myself pretty much every night and smoke all kinds of weed at all hours. I try to leave at least one inch on the joint and at least one inch in the wine bottle, so I don't feel like I finished it. If I finished it, that would mean I have a problem. Most awfully, I have been doing all this drinking and weed smoking while breastfeeding Sam. I try to limit the feedings to when I'm sober, but I'm very ashamed of myself. It might sound kind of harmless—*It's just a little red wine and marijuana*—but it's not just a little and more important, *if I could stop I would*. But clearly, I can't.

As my baby grows—he's almost two now—it's getting easier and easier to just finish the bottle every night. And harder and harder to ignore the fact that, in spirit, I'm just like my own mother—except with a husband, a house, and a college degree. It's gotten to the point that I don't want to do anything without getting high first.

Like today, when I went to a toddler Halloween party. Three minutes before walking out the door, I had to smoke myself out. In the middle of the afternoon. For me, topping off my high is like freshening up my lipstick. The one last thing I have to do before I leave the house. I don't know how I would feel if I didn't do it, but I don't want to find out.

The party is being held at a very swanky house in the hills. I'm not intimidated by the house, as I have grown used to the level of wealth all around me in Los Angeles, which can border on the ridiculous. Still, I am very aware that I'm a long, loooong way from Minneapolis. But being impressed is a dead giveaway that you don't belong. So I cultivate my unimpressedness.

The crowd is made up of the women from my playgroup (most of whom have retired from whatever career they might have had, in order to become full-time moms) and their ambitious, clubby husbands, many of whom are quite successful in the music industry and seem to talk only to one another. They are a lot like the guys on the hockey team.

We all stand around discussing preschools and Teletubbies while watching our toddlers grab stuff from each other, lurch around, and occasionally fall over.

I feel weird. I know my eyes are bloodshot—there aren't enough eyedrops in the world anymore—and I'm spacey and woozy. I can hear myself saying things that sound, uh, stupid. I spend all of my mental energy making sure no one knows I'm high. Acting "normal." It never occurs to me to ask myself why I get high when I spend my whole time high acting as if I'm not high.

After an hour or so and a bunch of crudités, my high begins to subside, and some of my self-consciousness (er, paranoia) wears off. Then my worst nightmare occurs.

Nora, the pert, short-haired mother of little Olivia (or Amelia, or Isabelle, or some such turn-of-the-century name), perkily says to me, "Tracy, were you really *stoned* when you got here?"

She doesn't mean anything by it, but my stomach sinks. Or rather, drops like an elevator in an action movie where the bad guy has just cut the cable with a dozen innocent people inside, including children and old people.

"No," I lie halfheartedly. And, I hope, convincingly.

"Ohhh," Nora trills, "because you seemed, well, really stoned." She's smiling broadly. It's almost as if she, too, is a pot smoker and was hoping I'd hook her up with something. But what she's saying is way too close to the truth for me, the truth I've been trying really hard not to have to acknowledge.

Later, that night, I'm at home with Dan. The baby is asleep. I am thinking of what Nora said with an intensity that I usually save for thinking about the power lines and Gwyneth. "She knew, Dan," I say plaintively. I feel caught. I'm angry and desperate. "She *knew*!"

"Oh, Tracy, calm down." Dan's dismissing me, as usual, not so much because he's being mean but because if he doesn't, he's going to catch what I've got. Anxiety is more contagious than chicken pox.

"I'm *serious*!" I've never wanted Dan to concur with me more. "I'm a terrible mother."

I burst into tears, or what passes for tears for me—a moistness at the corners of my eyes, accompanied by a manic, stormy energy. "I don't think I can do this anymore," I say quietly. "I don't think I can."

Dan looks at me, worried. He knows that if my life changes—any part of my life—his life will change, too. And he's very well adapted to the way things are. It's like how none of your appliances work in Europe because the shape of the plug is all wrong. He's worried that if I change, his battery charger will be useless. So he tells me not to change.

"You're fine, Tracy."

"I'm not fine, Dan."

"You're fine." That's it. Dan's final answer.

I know I'm not fine. This isn't how I wanted to be a mother. I was determined to do better than my parents, and alcoholism and drug dependency—even if I can convince *you* that I'm okay—do not fit with that picture.

Here's how I know for sure. I give myself what I call the Grocery Store Survey Challenge. I imagine myself emerging from Ralph's, where there are a couple of college kids with matching T-shirts holding clipboards. They're taking a survey.

"Excuse me, ma'am, can I ask you a couple of quick questions?"

"Sure," I say. I like to think of myself as a nice person who helps out when possible.

"Great," says the girl, smiling brightly. "Okay, first question." She adopts an officious voice, like a community-organizer version of Alex Trebek. "If you were the mother of a baby and/or toddler, would you drink a bottle of wine every day?"

Oh. This one's easy. "Of course not!"

The girl checks the "of course not" box. She smiles. I think I got that one right. "Next." Her pen is poised. "How about smoking endless joints?"

I yank my neck back a couple of inches in an exaggerated gesture of *fuck no!* "No way!" I say, chuckling. The idea is so ludicrous I can laugh at it.

At least in my fantasy I can.

But in real life, it's not so easy. It's not *how much* I drink, or *how much* marijuana I smoke, or *how often* I do whatever other drugs are put in front of me—I could easily rationalize, or minimize, or justify all that, and you would believe me because it's really not all that much and I hide it well and you're probably doing even more than me because I like to hang around with people who do more than me, since they make me feel a lot better than people who don't—it's that, in my heart of hearts (per the Grocery Store Survey Challenge), I know I'd rather not be doing what I'm doing. Which leads me back to my original question. If I'd rather not be doing what I'm doing, then why am I doing it?

I already know the answer: because I can't stop.

I really don't want that to be the answer.

TURNS OUT REHAB is not really that bad. I went outpatient. Six nights a week for thirty days. Dan would come home from work, I'd hand him the baby, and he'd hand me the keys to the 1977 wood-paneled station wagon we bought on a whim for $800. Then I'd drive—in rush-hour traffic—to Van Nuys (an act of willingness if there ever was one), and sit on a folding chair from six to ten P.M. in a circle with a dozen other losers fortunate enough to still have spouses, jobs, and health insurance. Or spouses with jobs and health insurance. It is the most time I've ever spent away from Sam.

For the first hour I can't get over how bad the fluorescent lights are, but right after that this amazing thing happens: I really want to never drink again. Really. Never. And I am willing to do anything not to have to.

Almost a year later, *I'm* still going strong, but my marriage isn't. I first allow my real feelings to come to the surface during a phone call with my dad. He wants to know, as usual, how the marriage is going.

"Fine. I guess."

"You *guess*? What do you mean by that, Tracy Renee?" My dad's not stern, he's just inquisitive.

I really want to tell him what I mean by that. I want to tell *someone*. But I'm afraid to say out loud what I've known since that first night in rehab, because things that are said out loud have a way of coming true. So I crack a joke.

"Well, the marriage is fine. But I'm ready to start dating."

I laugh. My dad laughs. He knows exactly what I'm talking about.

But it's not funny. I really can't stop wanting to leave Dan. This is just the first time I've dared utter it. I'm filled with this driving urge to be alone, to ruin something, and to have sex, all at once. It's like the Pimp's Daughter has resurfaced—she's been safely contained in a Ziploc bag (of weed) all this time, and now she wants to party. But not with drugs. Those are messy and debilitating.

With men. (Like they aren't messy and debilitating.)

That part of me—the Pimp's Daughter—whispers in my ear about how different I am now, how I've changed since I've had a baby, how it's time to explore my sexuality—finally. *You've been holding back so long,* she tells me. *It's time to find out who you* really *are.* And I can't stop believing her.

But I'm not a cheater, and I'm a crummy liar, so only one choice remains.

Leaving.

I have a million "reasons" to leave: Dan only married me for the baby, Dan never really talks to me, Dan didn't want me to stop drinking, Dan's super shut-down, Dan refuses to dig deep into himself (and digging deep has now become my raison d'être), Dan's dismissive of me, Dan hardly ever spends time with me when there isn't a gaggle of band members around us. And also, did I mention Dan's super shut-down and he refuses to dig deep within himself?

Dan's a very big problem for me, apparently.

But hindsight will show me that underneath all of these reasons is a realer, larger reason. I don't know how to just *be* with a man. Oh, I *think* I do. I think that all I need to do is find a more talkative guy who "understands me" and I will be able to form a real partnership. I think it is my choices that have been the problem—my so-called "picker" is broken—because when I was drinking I just didn't know myself well enough to choose well. And that's sorta true.

But secretly I would just like to have another spin of the wheel, another roll of the dice, another walk in the park, another go at falling in love. It feels so good, and I'm not ready yet to *never* feel that again. Never is a really long time.

I'm like a kid at a carnival who throws a dart at a balloon and wins a prize and now wants to bring it back and win another one. It's not so much that I don't like the prize. It's that I really like throwing darts. I like the high of popping the balloon and hoping that this time I'm going to get the super jumbo-size stuffed animal.

I spend hours debating what to do about my marriage with girl-friends who have zero experience in any kind of successful long-term relationship. They totally support my vision for the life I'm *really* supposed to be living. It's a vision that involves two things: "getting what I want" and "getting my needs met."

ME

I really don't know what to do. I want to leave. But I feel guilty.

MY FRIEND

Guilty? It doesn't sound like your needs are being met.

ME

You're *right*. That's the question. Are my needs being met?

MY FRIEND

It doesn't sound like it. I mean, is this what you really *want*?

ME

God. Right. Is this what I want? Not really. I mean, Dan barely even talks to me. The other day, I said something about, oh, I don't know, the weather, and he didn't even look up from his newspaper!

MY FRIEND

That's, like, abusive. To be ignored like that.

ME

But what about Sam?

MY FRIEND

He's better off with two happy parents apart than miserable parents together. He'll be okay. Look how I turned out.

ME
That's true. [Deep sigh.] I guess it's over.

MY FRIEND
Sounds like it.

. . . and *scene.*

This is much, much more difficult than leaving Kenny. My guilt is so much bigger. Dan is a good person who deserves better than this, better than me, better than my crazy life. I feel terrible for getting him all mixed up in this. At least I gave him an amazing son. Which goes some, but not all, of the way toward assuaging my guilt.

Although I worry about the long-term consequences of my choice, the truth is, nothing—not even my beautiful baby boy—can stop me from going. I console myself with the knowledge that a person can only make decisions based on the information at hand. And since I believe that everything unfolds perfectly, I trust that if I was supposed to know, right now, in 1999, that Dan is a totally fine husband, I would know it.

I just wish it didn't have to end like this.

PAUL AND I AREN'T the only ones who want to see the hugging guru—there are thousands of people here. We're at an ashram set on a back road about thirty-five miles from San Francisco. People are milling about everywhere while they wait for their hugs (called *"darshan"* in Hindi), giving the place the feeling of a Grateful Dead Show, except with meditation. There are people from every walk of life here, Silicon Valley technocrats, Marin County housewives, San Francisco urban-primitives, devotees clad head to toe in Indian garb, and children—dozens upon dozens of lovely, sparkling children.

The ashram is set on acres of rolling hills, just exactly as you'd expect. It's a wonderful place to spend the day. Or it would be if I wasn't twitching with anxiety. Ever since Paul and I got here, took a seat, and started waiting for our hug, I've had this awful sense of foreboding.

"I'm going to go look at the books for sale," Paul says.

"Okay," I say. "I'll be right here."

Paul gets up and heads for the area where the vendors have set up stalls with books, jewelry, and clothing for sale, leaving me to sit in the big hall by myself. It's a very large room, about the size of the sanctuary at Hope Lutheran Church, with many rows of chairs facing forward, where the guru receives her acolytes. If you imagine one of those Renaissance period paintings with Jesus surrounded by a whole mob of people, you'll get a pretty good idea of the scene. I watch quietly as the guru clutches to her chest *each* and *every* person who comes forward to get the hug. It's pretty amazing. Then she throws a few rose petals on their heads and they're ushered off the dais as the next person comes forward. On and on. For hours.

"Are you here for the first time?" the woman next to me says. It takes me a second to realize she's talking to me. She's a nice-looking lady in her fifties, the kind who probably drives a late-model Volvo and is still married to her original husband. She's obviously looking for a little conversation. My forte.

"Yeah." I smile. "I'm here with my fiancé. We're getting married in nine days! I talked him into coming here to get a blessing for our marriage." The lady smiles at me like that's a pretty good story, which it is.

"Oh, how wonderful," she says. "Congratulations!"

"Thanks! We're excited."

"Well, this will change your life," the lady says, nodding toward the newly hugged people staggering off the stage. She turns back to her meditation.

It's not the first time I've heard that getting one of these hugs will change your life. It seems kind of an overstatement, but then again, a lot of the people saying so are wearing, like, saris.

I sit there a while longer, suddenly aware that Paul's not back yet. *Where did he go?* The familiar sensation of fear—the rapid heartbeat, the inability to take a deep breath, the scrambled thoughts—begins to descend upon me. When this happens, there's nothing I can really do but wait until it subsides. Since I've quit drinking (and it's been five-and-something years now) I've learned to listen for the exact wording of the obsessive thought as it races over and over in my mind. It's always a clue to the underlying trauma I'm reliving as an anxiety attack.

I sit and tune in to my mind's ear, which is blaring more or less what it always blares, one way or the other:

He's gone.

SAM AND I ARE BACKING out of the driveway. It's a steep driveway and you have to be really careful as you go, taking it at just the right angle, or you'll crash into someone coming down the narrow street below, or at the very least bottom out the car. I crane my neck around to look behind me, my arm slung wide over the passenger seat, which gives me a full view of my perfect little angel tucked—or should I say crammed—into his car seat in the back. His eyes are looking even more doleful than usual. I think it's because he knows.

"We're going to Daddy's new house," I say, trying to sound chipper, but it's hard. I hate lying to myself. There's nothing chipper about this. I'm in one of those moments where my choices have become super-duper real. Too real. This happens every once in a while. The surveillance camera that I use to watch myself live shuts down, and I am just left with the living itself. And in this moment, I am having to deal with the fact that I have divorced Dan, and that means that I have to fork over my baby every other weekend. He's only two and a half.

"Mommy and Daddy live in two houses now, Mommy's house"—
I point at the cute two-bedroom Dan and I signed the paperwork on
two days after I gave birth—"and Daddy's house, where we are going
right now. You're going to like it."

My kid stares at me. Sam's got an inner stillness that is more than
a little unnerving. He's so much like Dan. It figures I would end up
giving birth to the type of guy I used to date. God has an awesome
sense of humor.

I hand Sam his pacifier. "Here, dude," I say. "Take this." Without a word, he grabs it with his tiny beefy hands and pops it in his
mouth. He loves that thing.

"It's not perfect, I know," I say over my shoulder in the direction
of Sam's car seat. "And I wish it could've been different." I'm talking
to him like he understands, because I think that on a nonverbal level,
he does. "But this is how it is, and we're going to make the best of
it. Starting . . . now." I paste a big smile on my face. Not fakey, but
encouraging. I'd like to think I'm modeling how you deal with life's
imperfections. But maybe I'm just modeling how to be flawed.

Dan's living in a cute little place, a 1920s house situated on a
semibusy street about two miles away. The street level of the house
has been converted into a dog groomer and a medical supply store,
neither of which seem to have any customers. I actually found the
place. I was driving by and saw the phone number in the window.
Later, Dan called and now it's his. (In a year, I will decide I'd rather
work part-time and hang out with my son than work full-time and be
a homeowner—leading Dan and me to *swap* houses. I will move in
over the dog groomer. And Dan will move back into the little house
on the hill. Sam's life will stay as much the same as it possibly can.)

We pull into the driveway. I'm not feeling *as* sick as I thought
I would. I open up the back door and pull Sam out of his car seat.
"Come on, pumpkin. We're here."

Dan has been pushing for fifty-fifty custody, but I've managed to talk him into a more reasonable sixty-five/thirty-five. At least for another year or so. When he gets difficult on me, I am reminded that part of the reason I married him (in spite of knowing I didn't have the skills to make a marriage work) is that I really believed he might take my baby away from me. Not that Dan's a bad guy. He's just very possessive. And in my mind, because he's from a "good" family and is a "normal" person, Dan has a bigger claim to a child than I do. White makes right. Male makes right. Money makes right.

But the longer I practice my recovery, the more I am growing up. I've worked very hard—I'm now an A-student of not drinking—doing what it takes to stay sober, including therapy twice a week. It's been a year now, and the change in me has been, by all accounts, remarkable. I am a calmer, less compulsive person. Maybe four times more wacky than the average girl, but for me, it's a vast improvement.

Dan and I have more or less reverted to our original coworker relationship, except now our "work" is a child instead of a news story. When we keep things on the colleague level—and it's not hard to do—everything is cordial, friendly even. I like Dan. I always have. He's very smart and can be funny and insightful when he feels like it.

On the personal level, things sometimes get difficult, but they never really get ugly. We are both just too sensible for that. (And maybe because we were never that passionate to begin with.) Dan feels rejected, but he shouldn't, because weirdly, this couldn't be any less personal. There is no man on earth I would have stayed with. (Except for maybe—and that's a very big maybe—Matt Damon.) He's furious that I've unilaterally "ruined" his child's life, and yet, I think there's a part of him that is glad he doesn't have to be with me anymore. He secretly wants another chance to throw a dart, too.

To my face, though, when he gets mad he can't stop saying sentences containing the words "broken" and "home." When it gets confrontational, I am learning how to take responsibility for my own choices and ask myself, *What did you* think *was gonna happen by having a baby with a guy you dated for six months? You thought it was going to be easy?*

Of course not.

Nevertheless, I am totally committed to Dan. Maybe I'm not in a conjugal relationship with him, but we are in a family. And I'm committed to our family. We both are. I'd say the fact that we're civil 85 percent of the time, along with the facts that I'm not drinking and we love this child so much we're willing to deal with each other for *life* in order to make things as good as possible for him . . .

Well, it may not be perfect, but it's pretty damn good.

THE GURU SMELLS LIKE ROSES. That's the first thing I notice. Paul and I are on our knees, and two seconds ago we were nudging ourselves forward, and then suddenly it's our turn, and the guru's helpers thrust us—both of us, together—right into her arms. Now we're smushed into the guru's breast, and she is rocking us, together, back and forth, murmuring Hindi words in our ear. It seems like she's more focused on Paul, and it occurs to me that she knows he's got more pain than I do, but I dismiss the thought, because *He's a lot worse off than I am* doesn't sound like the kind of thing you should be thinking about your husband-to-be in the presence of a guru.

Twenty seconds later, the guru is sprinkling rose petals on us and the hug is over. We stand up and walk off the dais and my legs are a little like jelly, and I'm a little stunned.

"I don't feel any different," Paul says, kind of dicklike, as we try to locate our shoes in the pile right outside the door. It's not as difficult to find the shoes as it might sound, since neither of us wears Birkenstocks. "In fact, I feel exactly the same."

Ugh, I think to myself. That's exactly the kind of thing privileged white guys say when faced with a spiritual experience they don't necessarily understand. But I don't say anything, because just thinking that makes me feel judgmental and I suspect my own spiritual growth demands that I let go of judgment, at least until we're out of this ashram.

We get in the car and drive to the nearest Starbucks. We are walking out, double Americanos in hand, when Paul looks at me.

"What?" I say.

It's a really strange look on his face. One I've never seen before.

"Tracy . . ."

Paul hardly ever says my actual name. And when he does, it's not good. He says it clipped, like he's not smiling during the *Tray-* part and he's angry about the *-cy* part.

"What?!" I'm worried now, and I'm not going to bother to hide it.

"I can't."

"Can't what?!" Of course, I already know what he can't. He can't do it. He can't marry me.

"I just can't. I don't think I can. I'm just scared as fuck."

I go into super-duper calm mode. Breaking-news mode. Where all my senses are on high alert. The adrenaline is pumping. My muscles are taut. My mind is processing at double speed. After years of working in very tense TV news situations, this poised awareness is second nature in times of exceedingly high stress.

"What exactly," I ask carefully, "are you afraid of?" I have the car keys in my hand. I place my Americano in the drink holder and start the car. I pull out of the parking lot. I am on autopilot. "It's all right. You can tell me."

"I feel like . . . *glurkglurkglurkglurk . . .*"

He's talking but I can't hear him. I've taken a right and I'm instinctively heading toward San Francisco because it's nearby. And I don't know where else to go. Where do you go when the guy you love is bailing on you? You'd think I would know, since my dad gave me so much practice.

As I drive my mind jumps around from thought to thought—*My kid, the dress, my friends, my apartment, my kid, what the fuck, I knew it, my kid, my washer and dryer, my kid*—but there is one thought above all that my mind keeps coming back to: *There's nothing I can do about this. My life is imploding, and there's nothing I can do.*

Paul, meanwhile, is over there in the passenger seat giving me some kind of explanation, saying words I know the meaning of but that nonetheless are not making any sense to me. It's all something to the effect of how he's a terrible man, a bad husband, how he failed with Sarah, his first wife, and he's scared as shit that it's going to happen again, because he's a bad person, he's just bad, I don't even know how bad. He was bad to his kid's mom, and he's never been sure about me anyway, and he liked how Jennifer Maynard wore perfume, and I don't wear perfume, and . . . *glurkglurkglurk.*

There's nothing I can do about this. My life is imploding, and there's nothing I can do.

We are starving so we stop and eat dinner in San Francisco, in silence. We're going to drive home—it's the late afternoon now—but both of us are so drained we decide to just get a hotel room outside the city and leave early in the morning. We stay in an Embassy Suites, and Paul orders his usual fruit and yogurt room service, which is what he always does when he stays in a hotel. We don't have sex, but there are a few moments of seminormalcy sprinkled into the silence.

It's hard to maintain crisis mode for twelve straight hours.

In the morning I wake up at peace. That part of me that survived my crazy childhood—the foster homes, the abuses, the fear, the abandonment, the pain, and the loneliness—she's showing up, taking the keys, and driving this car back home. I'm looking out for me now. Whatever happens with Paul is whatever happens.

We ride in silence down Interstate 5. It's glorious outside. Late fall and early winter is by far the most beautiful time of year in California—the bluest possible sky, the rolling hills the color of sweet corn. I never ever get tired of the West; it means something to me, something personal, about freedom and possibilities, and now, at forty, it's starting to mean something about losses and hopes dashed.

How many car trips with how many men?

And then I start crying. I can see so perfectly, out here on the open road, what I've really believed about myself all my life—that I'm less than other people, that there's something wrong with me, that I'll always be left, and that I'll never be loved—I can see it for what it is, that it's not the truth, that it was never true, and now that I can see it, it never will be true again. Never.

I cry and I cry. For the little girl who felt like something was just so wrong with her that she manifested her deepest belief about herself as this day, and this situation, and this man, who obviously believes the same thing about himself.

I cry for both of us.

We stop for gas in Grapevine, the last big oasis before you drive over the mountains that separate the San Joaquin Valley from the L.A. megalopolis. Paul takes the keys. He'll drive the rest of the way. We've been driving four hours and still haven't said a single unnecessary word.

And then—a handful of miles from the gas station—just as we're about to enter the mountains . . .

FLURGNNRRRFFFFFFF . . . *ssssssssssssssssssssssss.*

The car rolls to a crooked, limping stop. I turn around and look out the back right window as Paul maneuvers the car to the shoulder of the interstate. We sit there for a long second. He speaks first.

"I think we have a flat tire." There's a smile in his voice, because this is, after all, really fucking funny. A flat tire.

"You're kidding me." It's not a question. It's a statement of grave, towering irony. A *flat tire*! That's hilarious! I've made this drive a dozen times, and I've never had a flat tire. Ever. And then to have a flat tire now, right now, twenty-four hours into the fight that is going to end this relationship.

Well. That kind of flat tire only happens in the movies. And not just any kind of movie. That kind of flat tire only happens in one kind of movie. A romantic comedy. And ask any film student; they'll tell you how all romantic comedies end. Because they all end the same way.

With a wedding.

IT'S ALMOST FOUR in the afternoon. The light inside the old hotel is fading—the deepest corners of the once-grand lobby are already dark. Two hundred tea lights glimmer like little stars on the floor and line the balustrade where the dozen or so guests are gathered. They're watching me.

I am walking toward the magnificent marble staircase, where Paul waits for me on the landing, twenty steps up. My dress sweeps away the rose petals strewn in my path. A Native American man plays an indigenous flute, and it's a haunting sound, especially in this place. Paul's watching me, too.

It is ten months and one day from the day we met.

Saundra steps forward and the ceremony begins. She tells the guests how much she loves me and what a special person I am, and how honored she is to be part of this special day. She talks about what marriage means, how it's a spiritual journey, and how it's really about practicing—and perfecting—your ability to love. Then my friend Herb gets up and reads something by Rumi. The whole time Paul has his long, slim fingers on the small of my back, and I can feel the pressure of his hand and it's comforting to me. He smiles at me, and I know that he loves me. And that's what matters more than anything else.

Interstate 5 seems a long, long time ago.

Paul and I have each prepared something for the ceremony. I've written a song. It's called "Happy." I've brought an acoustic guitar. I can't play for shit, but actually, the song is kind of amazing because I really mean what I'm singing.

I love
The tiny things

Like Christmas lights
And drinking tea
Who'd have thought?
That this would be mine
I can see now
Where I was blind

You sit
Over there
I would almost swear
I am right here
I'm not going anywhere

I'm happy
I'm happy
I'm happy

Paul reads from a book he bought at the ashram. He bought that book in the midst of his paralyzing fear, and the fact that he is standing here now and there is so much love in this room—you can feel it—is a testament to something greater than what is least in a person. The book contains a poem to a saint, detailing one hundred things about her that are of god. *She has the light of a million stars in her eyes. She is everything there is to know in the Universe.* And he lists twenty other things I can't remember.

But they were all about me.

We do the part where we say "I do"—he says it, and I say it—and then we kiss and people clap and wipe away their tears.

And then we turn and walk down the magnificent staircase together. Just married.

I Love You, So Obviously
You Must Have Serious Problems

I'LL ADMIT IT: I'm not very nice sometimes. It's just that when I see the words "Unknown Caller" pop up on my phone, which means my dad is calling, it starts a conditioned response of feelings that fall like dominoes in the same order every time, and the last feeling is anger. First I feel obligated to pick up the phone, then I feel guilty that I feel obligated, then I feel bad that I feel guilty, and last but not least I feel angry that I feel bad, guilty, and obligated to talk to my dad when he's the one who went and got himself put in jail. For thirty of the last forty years.

But I always pick it up anyway.

Before I quit drinking I was never angry at my dad. When people would ask me about my childhood, I would reel off the two-minute version of my story (*Mom = crazy; Dad = jail; me = foster homes*) and they would invariably say, "Wow, you're so well adjusted! Are you angry with your dad?" And I would inevitably reply, "Not at all! Isn't it amazing!? I think he's *awesome*."

But now that the chemical bubble-wrap has come off, I am discovering that I totally don't think Freddie is awesome. I think he is a selfish, vain narcissist who committed crimes so he would have the money, jewels, and clothing that would get him the women (sex) he wanted. And I'm not afraid to tell him so.

"Hey, baby!" My dad's always so excited to talk to me. Which kind of makes me sick.

"Hey."

"What, you're not happy to talk to your dad?" Freddie sounds like he wasn't expecting this. Which is obviously a defense mechanism—I haven't been very happy to hear from him since I was twelve and a half.

"I'm mad at you," I say plainly.

"Oh, you are?" His tone is like Barbara Walters in one of those after-the-Oscars interview shows. Warm and curious. "What is it?"

"Yeah, I am," I say. "It's taking me years to undo all the bullshit you created for me."

"Now, Tracy." He's a little bored. We've been over this a thousand times. "I've told you I'm sorry; what more do you want?"

"Nothing, I guess." It's not like I want him to be waterboarded or something. "I'm just not over it yet."

"Well. You're going to have to get over it." Freddie rarely uses an ungracious tone of voice, but he is now. "The past is the past."

"Yeah, except for when it's not. Like now," I say, bruised. "I'm still suffering the consequences of your obsession with women and sex." I tend to use a lot of psychological jargon when I'm putting the screws to Freddie.

"Okay, then," Freddie says in his Barbara Walters voice. "Why don't you tell me about that?"

So I tell Freddie all the things I am learning in therapy and in my reading. How he wanted *regard*. Especially from women. Not love, but regard: *to be considered or thought of in a certain way*. He wanted to be thought of as important, handsome, desirable, sexual. And he wanted power over women: to set the rules, say what happens, and judge their bodies. And how that affected me in ways too numerous to catalog in a fifteen-minute phone call. From body image to sexuality to, of course, my problems with men. How first, I chose men not like him. And now, I choose men just like him. Which sucks.

"You're a very intelligent young woman, Tracy," Freddie says.

"Is that all you can say? I'm intelligent?" Now I'm *really* pissed off.

"What do you want me to say?" And so is he—pissed—though this is as close as he's going to come to open warfare. Freddie's a lover, not a fighter. Like Paul.

"How about, 'You're right and I'm *so* sorry, Tracy. That must have sucked for you,'" I retort. "How about that?"

"You're right, Tracy," he concedes. "And I *am* so sorry."

I hate that he's so willing to apologize. That he doesn't counter-argue. Or defend. Mostly, he just listens—and as I sort through more and more of my pain in sobriety, there seems to be an endless supply of "uncoveries"—and he admits to it all, and says he is sorry, and sympathizes with my pain. It's kind of a bummer, too, because unless he fights, I can't fight back. And I really want to fight.

So, I've found a new way to show my anger—not by what I do, but by what I don't (or won't) do.

I don't send him pictures of my son. And I won't visit.

This is much more hurtful than not picking up the phone. And when he asks me why, I say, "You reap what you sow." And most of the time, he takes it silently.

Once in a while he gets angry. He tells me I am selfish and uncaring. That he is stuck in there and I am depriving him of the one thing that would brighten his day: a picture of my son.

"You don't give a shit about me," he says. "You don't care about anyone but yourself."

"That's not true," I say calmly. "I care. I'm just busy in my life. I've got a million things to do: the groceries, the carpool, the laundry, and a job to make it all work." I put a little spin on this—I want Freddie to feel ashamed that I'm out here doing all of this on my own.

"I'm your father, Tracy," he reminds me. "I'm human."

I don't really know what he means by this. Because he's my father I shouldn't be angry? To the contrary. *You're my father, so you should have protected me!* That's what I want to say. *You should have gotten your shit together! You should have let go of your pathological need for the attention of women and gotten a job driving a bus, so I wouldn't have had to suffer!* But all that's been said already. A number of times.

Then, I have a breakthrough.

"Hold on," I say. "I think I just got it."

"Got what?" He can hear something in my voice and he's grateful there may be a reprieve soon.

"Got *it*. You know how when I was little and I was just getting shuttled around here and there, or in foster care . . . And how you were out chasing women and chasing deals, and doing whatever else it is you were doing?"

"Yeah . . ." He's not sure where this is going.

"Well, that's how I am now. I'm just living. It's not that I'm *actively* ignoring you. I'm not driving to work going, *I wonder how my dad is right now, sitting in his cell, lonely and hurt that I haven't sent him a picture of Sam.* I'm just driving to work! Not thinking of you at all," I say excitedly. "That's how you were, too!

"When I was little, you weren't *actively* ignoring me. You were just doing your life. Your version of going to work and doing the laundry. You weren't doing it *to me*. You were just *doing it*." It's hard to keep up, the thoughts are coming so fast. "You see?"

"Sure, but—"

"Now the tables are turned. I'm so busy with the stuff that's in front of me, I just never quite get around to thinking about where you are or what you're doing or how all my busy-ness might be affecting you." I finally take a full breath. "But I'm not doing it *to you* either. I'm just *doing it*! Isn't that awesome? I totally get it!"

He gets it, too. Karma's a bitch.

This might not sound like a huge revelation, but it is. It has several implications.

1) It means I can begin to let go of my anger—because I can comprehend how my dad did what he did. Yes, Freddie's choices had particularly negative effects. But, in principle at least, I can see how he's not all that different from anyone else. I can bring him back into the circle of being a human being, not a monster.

2) It means I can also let go of being a victim. Because being a victim is a double-edged sword. You get to be right (and righteous), but then you're stuck there.

3) It means that one of these days, I just might go visit him.

PAUL CAN'T SEEM TO GET a job. It's been five months since we got married and in that time he's been up for five jobs and lost them all—including a huge nine-day extravaganza that would have set us up for the year. With each rejection, Paul is getting increasingly demoralized. I do my best to try to keep his spirits up.

"I suck," he says. "That's why no one wants to hire me. I ruined my career with that McDonald's job." He's talking about some job that went horribly awry not last year but the year before. "But what was I supposed to do? My brother was under arrest! I was distracted."

"It's okay. You'll get one," I say encouragingly. "Any minute now."

"You don't understand, Tracy." He says my name all clipped like he does when he's angry. He's got that irrational, closed-minded thing going on where he just *cannot* hear anything that might be hopeful. "If this keeps happening, my company will stop putting me up for jobs and start putting up someone else." Paul's face is hard. He gets mean looking when he's afraid.

He has a point. In the entertainment business, success often comes in a "run." It doesn't matter whether you are a singer, writer, director, actor, or costume designer; most people have a "moment," and unless you die early, like Elvis or Marilyn Monroe, eventually it's over. There are a few immortals, like Madonna or Clint Eastwood,

who have thirty- or forty-year runs. But most people fall a lot closer
to the Milli Vanilli end of the spectrum.

"Well, they haven't stopped putting you up for jobs yet. So why
not be willing to be one of the people who keeps working?" I'm losing
patience. I understand Paul's fear, of course I do; I grew up poor as
shit. I just hate to see him letting it rule his mind.

"I'm telling you, they've figured it out. I completely blow every
other job." Paul looks at life like he's watching CNBC, but instead
of focusing on the program, he can't stop looking at the ticker tape
crawling across the bottom of the screen that says, *You're fucked,
you're fucked, you're fucked, you're fucked . . .*

"Never expect anything you don't want," I say against my better
judgment. I know I should be quiet. Paul's in so much fear he can't
hear me. Can't I see that? Too bad I'm not known for my ability to
stop talking.

"I don't want to hear your New Age positivity bullshit, Tracy."

He isn't the first guy to say that. And he isn't the first guy to be
wrong about it, either. It's not that I'm into positive thinking. It's that
I'm into exercising free will! I may not be able to control the world,
but at least I can choose what *I'd* like to have happen. If I were Paul,
I'd visualize two big buttons, like on a game show. One is red and
says:

NEVER WORK AGAIN!

The other is green and says:

HAVE A WONDERFUL CAREER NO MATTER HOW
UNLIKELY THAT LOOKS RIGHT THIS SECOND!

Which one am I going to hit? I'm not saying I'm going to get what
I want right at this moment, but my life experience has shown me

that if I keep hitting the positive button no matter what, all kinds of cool things will happen. Like eventually I'll write a book.

This is not how Paul thinks. Paul thinks life is a book that is already written, and he's really afraid that the last page says, *Hah! I told you you were fucked! Sucker . . .* There's absolutely nothing I can say to change his mind. And I really want to change his mind. Because if he doesn't get a job (and soon), I worry about what's going to happen to us.

PAUL'S SHOWING DEFINITE SIGNS of mental problems. First off, he doesn't leave the house. Not really. I mean, he walks across the street to get a double Americano at the little coffee place every day. And he occasionally goes with me to the movies or we go to dinner at one or two places that he favors—one of them in East L.A., miles from any Hollywood types. But unless he's getting on a plane, he can usually be found sitting behind his desk. All. Day. Long. When I leave for work (that is, *when* I work—I'm down to only two days a week), he is sitting there. And when I return, he is sitting there. Looking at his computer. I try not to say too much about it, afraid to push him over the edge.

"How was your day?" I ask, like he had a "day" in the way the word is commonly used.

"Fine," he says. At least he *tries* to make it sound like he was productive. "I got some work done on the script." He means for his animated movie.

"Oh, yeah? How's it coming?" I try to sound interested. It's painful to go through the motions like this, but what other choice do I have? I can't let loose with a bunch of my fear and say what I really think—*When is something going to happen? You're going crazy! You need therapy! We can't go on like this!* It would be counterproductive. I used to think being married to a tortured, mentally ill artist seemed romantic, like in that French movie *Betty Blue* or something. Not anymore. (It took a couple of decades, but my twenties are finally over.)

It's beginning to dawn on me that Paul's agoraphobic. "I'm a hermit," he says. But that's just a nice way of putting it. I used to wonder exactly how people executed agoraphobia. Did they literally never leave the house?

Now I know—they just don't leave the house *unless they absolutely have to.* Which, on a day-to-day basis, appears simply as a "preference" to "hang out" at home. Do they not talk to anyone? No, they just arrange their lives so that they're usually only talking to someone they already know. Well.

Sam is a little young to do the math on why Paul has been home so much but I'm aware that he's probably picking up at least some of the tension around here. It helps that he lives at Dan's half the week, but still, things need to change.

Finally, six months into the marriage, six months without a job for him, and six months without ever being at home alone for me, we get some relief. Paul is going to direct another music video for the British Pop Star. This is good for two reasons. One, it'll help him rediscover his ability to manifest work. And two, it's going to be in India.

"You *have* to take me," I say when he tells me they're paying his hotel and airfare. This doesn't sound nearly as much like a polite request as I wanted it to. "I'll pay for my ticket. And stow away in your room."

"I don't know, Tracy. I'm going to be working," Paul says.

"You know I won't get in the way. I'm supergood at amusing myself," I argue. This is true. I'm an excellent traveler, and I need very little hand-holding. It's one of the few times I'd actually rather do things alone. I have more interesting experiences as a traveler when I'm not in a couple. "I *must* go," I say. I just can't imagine being left at home while Paul experiences India. "Please!?"

"I'll ask those guys," Paul says. Normally he would be fine with me coming along. But in our six months of marriage, his lack of work has made him feel like I am more of a liability than an asset. If he were struggling and unemployed alone, he'd feel a lot less terrible about it.

Then there's the fact that we were only together for ten months when we got married. And during that time he was traveling every other month. We never actually spent more than two or three weeks together at a stretch. It's hard to get tired of someone when your relationship is seventeen days on, eight days off, twenty-three days on, twelve days off. He's starting to get sick of me.

"Please?"

"I said I'll ask." Paul's tone of voice is very Case Closed.

Fine then.

It takes a full week, but he finally agrees to take me. Preparing for the trip brings a new level of purpose and bustle to our lives. Paul seems to have come alive again, which is a big relief. He sounds and looks so good, I don't even mind it when he bores me with mundane details about things like the camera equipment he is taking, which I know nothing about except that he rents it at a place called Cameras Incorporated. And the only reason I know that is because he says "Cameras Incorporated" a lot and in a way that somehow sticks in my ear.

Shrug.

Two weeks later we are in India, which is more than it's cracked up to be. Way more.

More people drying their clothes on the median of a busy six-lane street. More four-hundred-year-old banyan trees. More need to cover your head and your shoulders. More unbelievably tasty food. More contradictions, such as the impression that India is this wildly foreign place when in fact everyone speaks English. More insane poverty—and more white-gloved luxury. More cows in the street, and more cell phones. A ton of cows and a ton of cell phones.

More of all of this.

But less stress.

As I mentioned earlier, Paul and I are never better than when we're traveling, and I think I've figured out why. Because when we're traveling, women are much less of an issue. At home in Los Angeles, women are everywhere, and not just any women, but a certain type of woman—beautiful, sexy, and hungry for validation. Now that we've been together awhile, it's starting to turn into our most regularly occurring argument topic. Like at the birthday party we went to last month.

"Do you have to keep looking at that girl?" I say.

I hate parties—or maybe just when Paul's with me—but this one is being given by one of my best friends so I have to be here.

"What girl?" he answers blankly. How come he never knows which girl?

"The one you keep looking at," I say. I can tell when a woman Paul finds sexually interesting walks into a room. Several microexpressions flit across his face, he blinks once or twice, he orients his body in her direction, and his energy shifts in a way that is invisible but, at least to me, completely tangible.

I turn to get a look at the girl, but I can predict what I'm going to see, because I know what gets Paul's attention. Top three hits: dark hair, a borderline eating disorder, and bad boundaries. (I also know what doesn't get his attention: big boobs, conventionally pretty faces, and blond hair in general. He's much more *Dwell* magazine than *Playboy*.) Paul likes low self-esteem that masquerades as high self-esteem, which is to say a cocky girl who seems independent-slash-bitchy but who has dialed every knob on her outfit, facial expression, hairstyle, and manner toward gaining sexual approval from men. These girls are impossible for Paul (or me) to ignore—the visual equivalent of those guys who ride Harleys without mufflers, ripping through the streets in full sonic glory.

"Her," I say, nodding in the direction of a super-skinny chick wearing a cute pink nipped-at-the-waist blazer. She's about ten feet away, chatting with someone. She's the Banana Republic version of what Paul likes.

"Oh, her?" Paul says. "Whatever."

As we pretend to mingle, I watch the woman, who is maybe thirty-five or thirty-six, ever so slightly angle her body toward Paul. She has his attention and she knows it, but unless you are hypervigilant (like me!), you probably wouldn't detect it. As I observe the two of them doing this dance, I begin to get more and more anxious. I know if I tried to tell Paul what he was doing, he would deny it. And not necessarily because he's a liar, but because *he doesn't even know he is doing it*. Neither does she. But since I spent the first three-plus years of my life dependent on my dad—a man who walked into a room just to see if there was a woman (or three, or four) in there he'd want to fuck—I'm exceedingly attuned to that energy.

It's an energy Paul's got like crazy. It's what I love and hate about him.

What I find especially interesting about this situation is how the three of us are locked into a pattern that only one of us—me—is actually aware of. I happen to know that the woman is recently divorced; her husband (a boy-man very similar energetically to Paul) had left her for another woman a year ago. And here she is orienting herself to another woman's husband, just as some other woman did to get her man. She's obviously attracted to men like her husband. And so am I. She and I are alike that way. The crazy thing is how, if she actually "got" Paul, she would just be getting more of the same.

I find it fascinating to watch this pattern repeat itself.

When I was younger, I might have wanted to say to her, *How can you do this to me when it just happened to you? You should know better.* But what I'm thinking now is *Wow . . . is* that *what I'm like? Do I collect glances, validation, and sexual approval from men (any men, all men) like a sort of energetic hobo picking up bottles and cans for a nickel apiece? Because I really don't think I am. But if Paul is here, and this woman is here, and her husband was here, and his new girlfriend is now there . . . then I must be in all that somewhere, too.*

Mercifully, India doesn't have a lot of women without mufflers, and we spend two drama-free weeks shooting the Pop Star's video. We're all over Mumbai—on the beach, in the slums, in film production offices, in abandoned apartment buildings, in mind-boggling traffic and five-star hotels. We visit a Jain Hindu temple. And just like I have heard so many people say about India, I have a spiritual experience.

But not the kind with angels or white lights. I have one with a camera.

With nothing to do while Paul and the crew are busy, I take pictures of people everywhere we go. There's a movie I love where the main character remarks that every girl eventually goes through a photography phase. Well, I'm still in mine. When I photograph people, I shoot their faces. Really close up. I want to see what's in someone's eyes, what's in their soul.

The camera gives me a way to interact with people. One evening we are setting up in an apartment building—it's really more of a series of concrete-block rooms with doors on them—and I ask a couple of little girls if I can take their picture. They say yes, so I snap a couple of quick shots, then flip the digital camera to playback and show them the photo on the screen. It blows their minds! They shake their heads back and forth in the figure-eight-type gesture that is universal in India to mean anything from *Wow* to *What the fuck (in a good way)?* The little girls have never seen an image of themselves.

Their slightly older brothers come over and point at themselves, as if to say, "Take my picture, too." So I do. Now I'm the pied piper, because in short order, there are a half a dozen kids crowded around. They all want to see the photographs. The older boys take me by the arm and lead me back toward an open area, where women are preparing food. "Picture!" the kids say, pointing at the women, who are obviously sisters. I snap. I show the picture. They smile and giggle. And do the figure eight.

Now we're all laughing.

A few of the boys and girls head into a back room and when they reappear, they are escorting a very old woman. The grandma. They want me to take her picture. To say I am honored doesn't go nearly far enough. I'm gonna cry.

I shoot the grandma, with her rheumy eyes and her frail arms, her gray hair and her faded sari. She's beautiful. Then I show her—and her whole family—the photograph. We all smile and laugh together. We're totally connected.

It's a spiritual experience.

Standing in this amazing moment, amid these ordinary people, I am reminded once again that there is something in life that is bigger than anything, than *everything*—bigger than poverty, bigger than a language barrier, bigger than the oceans I flew across to get here— and that *something*, that indescribable something, whatever it is, is *more real* than pain, poverty, language, or even space and time.

June Ericson called that indescribable something the Lord, and it's a good thing I'm being reminded of it. I don't know it yet, standing here in this Mumbai slum, but when I return to Los Angeles, I am going to barrel headlong into a situation a lot like the one I faced when I left the Ericsons. And in order to handle it, I'm definitely gonna need a Lord.

WE'RE BACK, AND THINGS aren't right. I don't know what's wrong, but something is. I feel anxious all the time, and I am really thin. I am a normally thinnish person, but now I am skinny. Like, intervention skinny.

The video isn't over yet. The British Pop Star has flown in for another week of shooting, which necessitated a couple hundred more trips to Cameras Incorporated and the building of a giant stage and backdrop. In our living room.

While they shoot all night long, I fall asleep in the back of the loft, to the sound of that terrible song being played over, and over, and over. For some reason, on the last night of the shoot, I start feeling "bad" and throw up several times in twenty-four hours. Even though I know I'm not sick. At least not with anything viral or bacterial.

Then today, I'm on my way to the news station—I work a one P.M.–to–nine P.M. shift every Sunday—when my phone rings. It's a number I don't recognize. I pick it up.

"Tracy." It's Paul. In that clipped tone.

"Hi!"

"I'm calling from a borrowed phone," he says urgently. "I left mine in your purse. Last night at dinner. You gotta bring it back right now." Now that he mentions it, I remember him putting his phone in my purse last night right before the waitress came to take our order. It would be easy for me not to notice, since we have matching phones. The only difference is that I superglued two big rhinestones on mine. At this point, though, the rhinestones are so dirty they are easy to miss.

"Where are you?" he says, sounding very serious.

"I'm on my way to the knitting store." I want to get some new yarn to fill the boring hours in between news stories. Sundays are notoriously slow.

"Well, turn around," he says. Like a director. "I need my phone."

Huh. I'd think he would be saying that with a smile, but he's not. He means it. Which is kind of hilarious. "Turn around? I can't. I have just enough time to get to the knitting store and make it to work on time. You can meet me there." I mean at the knitting store.

"How long before you get there?"

"I'm a mile away." I'm thinking it's crazy, attempting to coordinate a meeting at the yarn store. "It would make more sense if you just waited an hour and came to my work to get it. I'll be there at one."

Paul thinks about this for a minute. Then he says, "Where's the yarn store?"

"Beverly and Alta Vista," I say, pulling the exact street out of my amazing photographic memory of the map of Los Angeles. I'm a walking, talking navigation system.

"I'll be right there." He hangs up.

I chuckle to myself. God. That's crazy, like I would *turn around* to bring Paul his phone. That's funny.

I drive another couple of blocks. It occurs to me that Paul is going to get in his car and meet me at the knitting store. The knitting store!

Paul, the borderline agoraphobic.

Driving.

To get his phone.

The phrase "any lengths" pops into my mind. It's a phrase used in the recovery world to talk about how far someone is willing to go to satisfy the addiction. It's also how far you have to be willing to go to get recovery. Paul is definitely going to any lengths to get this phone. He must *really* want this phone. I wonder why?

I reach into my purse and pull out his phone. I look at it. There's a new text message, right there. From a number with an out-of-state area code. Still tooling down Beverly, I open the phone and read the text:

Hey there, married man!

Instantly, my foot is shaking on the accelerator. How my foot has already gotten a message that my mind is still struggling to comprehend, I don't know. But my foot is shaking because it now knows why I'm so skinny.

My husband is apparently cheating on me.

My mind is racing with what to do, but it's also blank. I can't think straight. I pick up Paul's phone again and open it—

Hey there, married man!

Now something comes to mind. Hit redial. A girlish female voice picks up.

"Hello?" She's giggling. Or at least her voice is. She thinks it's the married man she just texted to say, *Hey there!*

It's not. It's me. His wife. "Hello. This is my husband's phone and you just sent a text message?"

There is a pause. The girl is obviously thinking. "Oh, I meant to dial 7771," she says apologetically. Paul's phone number ends in the digits 7774. "I must have accidentally sent it to the wrong number."

I know this is a lie. My foot is telling me so. My shrinking arms are telling me so. But this girl is not going to admit that to me, the married man's wife. Besides, it's really Paul I need to interrogate. And his actions have already told me everything I need to know.

"Oh, okay," I say pointedly to the girl. She knows I know. I know she knows I know. "Thank you, then. Bye." I hang up. I think it over for a minute—damn, she lied well! This makes me angry. Girl-on-girl violence—like cheating with another woman's man—just isn't right. I call her back. This time, she lets it go to voice mail.

Hi, this is Jessica—

I hang up. My foot is still twitching on the gas pedal.

Seconds later, I pull up to the knitting store and walk in. I'm in a daze. The woman behind the counter greets me cheerfully.

"Hello, how are you?" she says.

She doesn't know that my life just ended, I think to myself. I go through the motions of looking for some new yarn because I have no other idea what I should do. That's when I see Jean, one of my closest friends in recovery, standing right next to me. Jean is older than me, and wiser than me, and not only that, she's a therapist who has been through all kinds of stuff in her own life. She's truly a godsend at this moment. I don't know whether to be unbelievably happy that the Universe has plopped her into my world right when I need her the most or to kill myself over what is going down right now.

I throw myself into Jean's arms and spill out the story. "Paul left his phone in my purse and he called me and wanted it back right away—so bad that he's driving down here right now, and that made me suspicious, like *Why does he want that phone so badly?* so I looked at it, and there was a text message from a girl that said"—I lean in close and whisper in an acid singsongy voice—"*Hey there married man!*"

I try to steady myself. The only thing I forgot to say is that I'm freaking out. As if that needs saying.

"Oh my god," Jean says in her L.A.-via–New York accent. She hugs me. "I'm so *sawry*. I've been there, sister. Just take a breath."

She hugs me a minute while I do just that. "Now tell me again what you said. He's coming down here?"

"He's on his way right now." I'm too stunned to even cry. Jean leads me out of the store and we stand there, on Beverly Boulevard, between the upscale knittery and the upscale furniture store, so all of West Hollywood can watch me deal with my crumbling marriage.

"How long has this been going on?" Jean asks.

"I don't know." I pull out Paul's phone and show her the text. "Here it is. See for yourself." Jean flips open the phone and reads it. She's appalled on my behalf. "This really sucks, Tracy. What is he thinking?"

"I don't know! He hasn't gotten a job and I know he's been really freaked out about it, but why would he do *this*?" We're looking at each other when I see Paul's car come barreling toward us. "Oh my god, there he is."

Paul slows the car, pulls over, and rolls down the window. He sees Jean, which makes him nervous. She's not under his spell like I am. Make that like I *was*.

"Just throw it in the car," he says, meaning the phone. He sounds casual, as if I *haven't* read this Jessica person's text message and he's just going to get the phone back and go on with his life. Our life.

"No, Paul," I say. "Get out of the car. We need to talk."

His face shatters, like he knows that whatever life we had planned on November 28, 2004, is already over. And it's only July 17, 2005. He parks the car, then skulks over. In a flash I see that Paul compulsively does behaviors that cause people to think about him the way he thinks about himself—like he's a piece of shit. He can't stop.

The closer he gets, the more hysterical I am. "What the fuck are you doing, Paul? What the *fuck*!" He looks me in the eye and it's obvious—he has no idea what the fuck he's doing.

"I don't know, Tracy." He says it not apologetically, not like he's surrendering, but like he's driving a stake through my heart. He says it angrily and like I am somehow to blame.

"Well who is she?"

"She's some dumb chick who works at Cameras Incorporated." There's that name again. I know that name.

"The camera place?!" I'm having a hard time grasping that my husband of eight months is picking up counter girls at the camera-rental place. "Are you crazy?"

"Yes. Probably." He sounds more dead than crazy. Now he can't look at me.

"*Look* at me, Paul! You can't just *do* this! What about me? What about Sam? What the *fuck* are you doing?" I'm hollering. I can hear myself hollering.

And he hollers back. *"I couldn't get a job, okay? I couldn't get a job!"* He sounds pathetic.

Paul launches into a long, dramatic monologue that manages to be both totally disgusting and totally heartbreaking at the same time. "I needed to get my mojo back. And that's how I do it. I need girls. It's always been like this. When I was married to Sarah, I never worked. Maybe two or three times a year. And when we broke up and I started fuckin' girls, I started getting work like crazy. My career took off, dude. The same thing happened when I was with Cecilia." He means the mother of his child. "I got three commercials the day she moved out. And then you and I got married and I lost that big job on our honeymoon . . ." He stops speaking, adrift for a moment. I just stare at him, dumbfounded, watching as he retraces the trail of bread crumbs that brought him to this pitiful and wretched place. "I knew if I got a girl I could get a job. If I could get a girl to like me, I could get my power back."

He had to get his power back.

His logic makes perfect sense to him. And suddenly, it makes perfect sense to me, too. How I chose this man, precisely what I recognized in him when I saw his face online and I just knew that he would one day be my husband. He wasn't my husband. He was—he *is*—my father!

Getting power by getting women—that's my dad. Borrowing from a woman's regard for him in order to regard himself—that's what my dad does. He can't generate his own love for himself; he needs to borrow it from the gaze in a woman's eye. For years, my dad made his living *literally* off women's bodies. Paul wants to do that, too, just in a highly symbolic way—because he did, after all, go to Harvard.

The whole thing is epic and literary.

Paul looks up at me, and I can truly see him, for the first time since we met, without all the regard I've been giving him. It's like the mask has been pulled off and what is left is a little boy, standing in front of a yarn store, stuck in a world he doesn't really understand. Paul's going through life with the same sense of disconnect I have when I'm trying to figure out the clasp on a necklace while looking in the mirror. Things just aren't where his mind is telling him they are.

Paul's insane. That's what he is. Just like his brother in the psychiatric facility. Or to a lesser degree, his dad, who dyed his hair to be a CEO. Or my dad, who just told me last week that when he gets out of prison (which will be *soon*, he says) he wants to start a business farming earthworms. Earthworms!

This must be what a friend of Paul's was alluding to when he came up to me early in the relationship and said, "I've never seen Paul so good! This is the best 'Paul' he's ever been."

I thought this was a good thing! I guess I didn't stop to think that if you can "fix" someone—the way I fixed Paul then, and the way

Paul now wants Jessica to fix him—it can only mean one thing. He was broken to begin with.

Maybe things aren't where my mind is telling me they are, either.

THE NEXT DAY WE GO TO SEE my therapist, Saundra. She cuts right to the chase and asks Paul if he is willing to change his mind about needing women to get jobs. He's unsure.

"Well, are you willing to try to make the marriage work?" she asks.

"What does that mean?" Paul wants to know. " 'Make the marriage work.' "

"It means stop seeing the girl." Saundra carefully shifts her expression into neutral, a struggle no doubt, due to the what-the-fuckness of Paul's question.

"I'm not *really* seeing her," Paul says, trying to minimize. "We just talk on the phone." Like that changes anything. He has truly lost his mind.

"Then stop talking to her on the phone," Saundra's mouth says. Her face says, *Dude, please.*

"All right."

"You *will*?" I pipe up, startled. I hadn't expected him to agree so readily.

"Sure. Yes." He's weirdly disengaged, but it's a yes, so I'll take it.

"And you're going to need to see someone for couple's therapy," Saundra adds. "As well as individual therapy."

Paul agrees to it all. By the end he seems contrite. Like he's just passed through the well-worn stages of a spree, and this is where he's ended up—where he always ends up—at the wrong end of a woman's glare. And even though he doesn't seem to fully comprehend the consequences of his actions, he's clearly ashamed of himself.

I have some compassion for him. If I hadn't had such a run-in myself with bottles of wine and bags of pot when I had a baby I was trying to love, I wouldn't understand at all. But I have, and so I do.

Yet there's another thing I know from my own experience, and it's got me pretty worried—that without a major shift, all the shame and guilt in the world isn't gonna be enough to stop him.

PAUL AND I HAVE this amazing ability to live in impossible circumstances. We just go back about our lives. It's not that we pretend nothing happened. It's there, like a stain on the sofa that forever reminds you of the time you were careless with that Sharpie. The temptation is to feel awful every time you see the stain, but you can't or you might as well just throw out the couch. Because there's nothing you're going to do to turn the clock back to before you left the cap off.

So you throw a slipcover on it—something decent looking, from Target maybe—and hope for the best.

The hard part is dealing with the knowledge that whatever has happened, it can happen again. That has me pretty terrified most of the time, but it's a terror below the level of consciousness, the same way I imagine people in Bosnia got through the bad years with the Serbs. You know something awful can happen at any moment, and in a way you are braced for it, but until that moment comes, you just go on along as best you can.

WHEN YOU'RE DOWNTOWN, which side of the street you're on makes all the difference. The side we live on belongs to the hipsters, with their $3,000 rents and their carefully managed grime. The other side belongs to the hobos. It's full of homeless people and dirty, clogged with "apartments" made of refrigerator boxes and low-down people and dogs. But the hobo side has an excellent burger place that we like to eat from, if not at, because it's more than a little bit rough. While Paul waits for our order, Sam and I head upstairs to set the table.

Once inside the building, I realize I don't have my mailbox key, so I bolt back to get Paul's key. As I wait for a car to pass before I can cross, I see Paul pacing the sidewalk on the other side of the street. He's on the phone.

It's her.

There's something about his body language, the way he's smiling into the phone, the way he's so entranced by the discussion that he doesn't even see me standing here, watching him cheat. I turn and go back into the building.

"What's wrong, Mom?" Sam asks.

"Nothing, pumpkin," I lie. "Let's go upstairs."

"What about the mail?"

"We'll get it later."

A few minutes later Paul brings the food, and I unpack it. My burger stays mostly untouched. I'm skinny these days, like I said.

I'm getting so used to living in crisis, I go through the motions of the evening, cleaning up after dinner, loading the dishwasher, and listening to the rhythmic churn of the water inside. All the while, I'm dying to get my hands on Paul's phone, but he's got it on him, in his pocket.

Every nerve ending in my body is leaning toward Paul, the way flowers lean toward the sun. Nothing else will exist until I see that phone. Even, sad to say, my own child. I'm just glad Sam's got a TV to watch and a video game to play. I'm good for nothing until I can open that phone and find out for sure what I already know. Paul's lies are so wide and so deep, only when I can see something with my own eyes do I believe it.

Right before it's time to read to Sam before bed, Paul goes into the bathroom. He has set his phone down on the kitchen counter, so it's there, calling my name. I know I shouldn't do this right now, but I have to . . .

My heart starts its familiar race, the blood screams through my veins, and my eyes blur with whatever physiological thing happens to them when the stress hormone gets dumped into my bloodstream. My mouth is dry.

My kid is lying in bed already, waiting for his story.

I open the phone. And there it is . . . the same phone number as July 17, the day of the knitting store; I can tell from the area code. But the caller ID says "Ccollins"—that's the name of Paul's point man at work. Then I look more closely and notice there are two "C"s in Ccollins—Paul has anticipated my snooping, and he's taken steps to cover his tracks.

I'm devastated he's talking to this *Jessica* again—it's like a baseball bat to my stomach, but it's a shock to my mind as well. How can it be that this formerly rational man is going to such silly lengths to hide his need to talk to a twenty-one-year-old girl with an Ohio area code who thinks text messages to married men should be punctuated with exclamation points?

It doesn't make sense. None of this does.

Especially when there's a little boy in the other room who wants to know what happens next in *The Curious Incident of the Dog in the Night-Time.*

I go into Sam's room. I'm tense. He's lying in bed, dressed in his jammies, waiting for Paul and me to come in for our nightly reading routine. Having a routine is good for kids. It makes them feel safe, like the adults in their world can be counted on. I never had one, but I'm trying to do things differently with my son. Trying . . . and, apparently, failing. Because I have to cancel the routine tonight. There is no way I am successfully concealing the stress, the fear, the pain, and the anguish of what is going on right now.

"I'm sorry, honey. I can't read to you tonight," I say, struggling not to cry. Sam looks at me, and I can see that he's afraid. He knows something is going on, but he has no idea what. He doesn't ask.

Paul comes into the room, set to read. "Are we ready?" He doesn't know I've looked at his phone. He still thinks we're in a family together. He doesn't seem to understand what he's doing to destroy that.

"We're not reading tonight," I announce to him. I sound sick. Because I am. I give Sam a kiss on the forehead, just like I always do. "I love you, honey. I'm having a hard time tonight. I'll feel better in the morning."

He doesn't believe me.

ON SUNDAY I GO TO WORK. I'm scared to leave the house. When I'm home, I have the illusion that nothing bad can happen to us, like refusing to go to sleep so you don't have to have a nightmare. But I have to work, so off I go.

At lunch, which is at five P.M., a wave of nausea hits me right between the eyes. I see a visual of her phone number with its brand-new-in-town area code. I relive flashes of July 17—*Hey there, married man!*—of the hobo side of the street, of "Ccollins" appearing on Paul's caller ID. My whole posttraumatic thing happens—the revving heart, the shaking, the fear. I call Paul and get no answer, which makes it worse.

The eleven o'clock producer assigns me a bunch of stories, and I do them, grateful to have something to think about other than my fear. Writing the news has always been good for me this way—there's almost nothing it can't take your mind off of. No wonder there are so many twenty-four-hour news channels.

I slog through the rest of my shift, and by nine fifteen, I'm home. Paul is lying on the sofa, the one that matches his eyes. He is asleep.

"Hey," I say, leaning over to kiss him. He wakes up. He seems startled.

"How was work?"

"Fine."

Normally, Paul hugs and kisses me the moment I walk in the

door. All the insanity around here hasn't affected our sex life at all. He wants me just as much as he ever did, maybe even more. But right now he's strangely distant.

"What'd you do tonight?" I ask.

"Worked on the video. Want to see it?" I follow him over to his desk, where he shows me the latest cut of the video. Normally, he would wrap his hand absentmindedly around my leg while we watch, but not tonight.

That's when I register the shirt. He's wearing the plaid Dolce and Gabbana. His "date" shirt.

"What did you have for dinner?" I ask innocently.

"A hamburger," Paul says as he fiddles with something on the computer. "From across the street."

I don't see signs of any food having been consumed. Paul usually leaves his takeout containers on the stainless steel counter. He's not big on tidying up.

"Where are the containers?" I ask, scrutinizing him carefully for the tiny twitches and blinks that tell me when he's lying. I think I detect something, but it's hard to be sure.

"I ate it there," he says. And that's when I know for sure he's lying. Because that place is full of lowlifes and derelicts.

No one eats in there.

THAT NIGHT I WAKE UP in the middle of the night. There is only one thought in my mind—apparently the answer to a logic problem it has been working on for hours, if not days—and that thought is: *Get the receipt*. Get. The. Receipt. I know immediately what my mind is telling me to do. Paul saves all of his receipts. So if he ate somewhere tonight, somewhere other than the derelict place across the street, it will be in his pocket.

I creep out of bed and grab his pants, the lame designer jeans that made me wonder about him in the first place, the ones he wears almost every day. I reach into the front right-hand pocket. I pull out a small piece of white paper. It's a receipt. From the New Otani Hotel, just a few blocks away.

Sushi. Four glasses of sake. Total: $80 and change, plus tip.

Something shifts in me. I'm suddenly done. Free. I know enough now.

I crumple up the receipt and walk over to where Paul is sleeping, on the couch. I drop it on his chest.

"Fuck you," I say.

He opens his eyes, wide awake. He knows I know. We argue for an hour or two, but it doesn't matter. It's over. Or almost over. First we have to have the most intense sex I've ever had in my life. Where I transmit through my body all the fury, all the ache, all the worry, the love, the fear, and the horror I've ever had for, about, at, to, from, and with Paul.

Or—and this is sick, but true—for, about, at, to, from, and with Daddy.

Now it's over.

IN THE MORNING, I call Saundra, at home. She answers the phone, miraculously. I tell her what's happened. "What should I do?" I ask. I'm hungover emotionally, but I'm pretty clear, given the circumstances.

"Well, Tracy," she says, "you could do what Yoko did."

I love Yoko Ono, so I can't wait to hear what she did. Whatever it is, I'm doing it. "What did Yoko do?"

"She sent John Lennon away." Of course she did. Saundra continues, "What you can do is, if you have the strength, you can pack Paul a bag and put it by the front door. And then you call him and tell him, 'You can't do that around me.' That's what you do. If you have the strength."

I have the strength. It has taken me twenty pounds, eighteen months, and a million tears. But finally, I have the strength to let go. No, not of Paul. I've felt like this before Paul came along—maybe not as extremely, but I've felt it—and I'm sure I could find someone else who could make me feel it again. So it's not him I need to let go of.

It's Daddy.

Fifteen

I Love You,
but I Love Myself More

MY DAD IS BEING TRANSFERRED. With two-thirds of his term served, he's now eligible for the minimum level of custody—a federal prison camp. It's the last stop for a guy like my dad—who has traveled the whole circuit from maximum to medium, to minimum to prison camp—before going home. Prison camps are nice, the places you hear them joking about on late-night talk shows, where they send people like Michael Milken or Martha Stewart when they run afoul of the law. I ask my dad where exactly he thinks he's going to end up.

"There are two places they could send me—Yankton, South Dakota, or Duluth, Minnesota," he says.

"Which one's better?"

"They're both about equal, but get this—if I go to Yankton, I get a one-day furlough. They put me on the Greyhound, since there's no official prison that goes there. I checked out the route, and the bus goes from Waseca"—where he's in a minimum-security prison now—"to Omaha. Then there's a three-hour layover in Omaha. Then I get on another bus to Yankton. Altogether it's seventeen hours of freedom!"

There is something unbridled in his voice, an excitement I haven't heard in a long time, if ever. "That sounds amazing!" I say, and I mean it. I can't imagine what seventeen hours of freedom would be like after fifteen years behind bars.

"And get this—the best part is that they give me enough money for two meals!" He claps his hands together and makes this gleeful sound—the one he used to make all the time when I was a little girl. "*Hah!* Guess where I'm going to go?!"

I have no idea. "Where?"

"Kentucky Fried Chicken!" He's so happy, it breaks my heart. The years collapse and I see the two of us in the visiting room at Leavenworth—me little, him big—eating box lunches of Kentucky Fried Chicken delivered for visiting day. I haven't the heart to tell him it's called KFC now and it's not what it used to be. "I'm gonna get me some Original Recipe."

Then I get this image . . . of my dad as a little boy in an adult's body, so unable to negotiate the world that he has to be put on a bus with enough money for two meals pinned to his jacket. And when I see him like that, it all makes sense. My dad has spent all this time in jail not because he's a bad man who doesn't deserve to be let off the hook, but because he's a lonely, sad, and wounded boy hungry for nurture (*woman*) who is acutely afraid of life. A ten-foot-by-ten-foot cell is as much of the world as he is equipped to handle. Agoraphobia.

Just like Paul.

I FINISH PACKING PAUL'S big bag and leave it outside the door to the loft. I put everything he would need in there, even his pillow. He is coming to get it between three and five, but I will be gone already. My girlfriend Gigi is "babysitting" me for the evening—first we will meet some friends at a restaurant, and then I will spend the night "sleeping" in the guest room at the home of another friend, Liza. Funny how it takes a crisis to realize how loved you really are.

At the restaurant Gigi drags me to ("You'll be *fine,* it will be *good* for you"), I have a revelation. I am sitting next to a guy I've never met before, and he is making polite conversation about the Internet and some of the various blogs he is into. I've hardly heard of blogs—it's 2005—but I'm interested in them. I watch myself nodding my head and following the conversation with surprising coherence.

While the man chatters amiably, it occurs to me that even though I packed my husband's bag today and put it by the front door, firmly asserting that *you can't do that around me,* I'm not really in that much pain at the moment. By "the moment" I mean: Right. This. Second. I can follow what my table neighbor is saying as long as I'm focused on him, on Now, on whatever he is doing or saying in this very moment. It's actually quite spacious right here. In the moment.

I begin to observe more closely. Actually, I am conducting a test. I focus on the conversation. Then I focus on the bag outside the door. Then I focus on next week or next month when I will come home after work and Paul will not be sitting behind his desk. What I see is that the moment is like a radio station. The pain only happens—no, *always* happens—whenever I leave the absolute present, like the static that occurs when I click 105.6 or 105.8 instead of 105.7. One tick into the past or into the future, and it feels like I am being suffocated.

But right now, as this guy methodically mixes his wasabi into his (light) soy sauce (the one with the green top), I am fine. There is actually no pain *right here,* as he twirls his chopsticks round and round in the tiny dish. There is an ache, yes, but it's not the burning serrated-edge-knife-wound-type ache that I feel when I think about life without Paul; or about how I knew this would happen all along, but for some godforsaken reason I had to do it anyway; or how hurt and confused Sam is going to be when he finds out Paul is gone.

Nothing hurts worse than when I think about Sam. This is how it happens, isn't it? The way the exact same pain is passed down from generation to generation. My dad abandons me, then I choose a man with my dad's qualities, who then abandons me *and* my son. Now my son carries the same kind of hurt I carry, like he carries the gene that caused the gap between my two front teeth. And it's my fault. It makes me want to die.

But if I put my inability to live with the consequences of my actions above my responsibility to atone for them, I will be replicating my mother, Linda. Passing *that* pain down. Linda had to drink over what she did—and abandoned me altogether. Sam needs me. And Saundra said Sam will get through this whole thing to the exact degree that I do. He is my son; we are connected.

So I come back to sitting here, at this table full of strangers, who are eating sushi and rattling on happily about movies, and music, and normal things. After a couple of steady breaths, I can feel that I am going to be okay. All I have to do is be willing to keep bringing myself back to the present moment—at least one more time than I leave it.

SOMEWHERE IN ALL THIS I have started writing again. I've been penning songs all along, and of course, I've been writing plenty of news, but I hadn't tried a screenplay since 1999. Six years. Then on the way home from India I got the idea to write a movie about a woman who has a spiritual awakening—not by going to India, but by meeting her man's "other woman." (Tell me my intuition isn't spot-on!)

In my story a man has just died. While his wife is cleaning out his office, she accidentally hits the space bar on his computer and discovers that he has a MySpace page. With a "top friend" who is a sexy young woman. In this story, the main character, Diana, sets out to meet the other woman. She poses as a photographer conducting an art project that entails taking pictures of young girls. I won't give away too much, but interesting things happen, and both Diana and the girl are changed people by the end of the film. I titled it *The Spacebar*.

I start writing as soon as we get back from our trip and continue until two weeks after I find the text message. The movie pours out of me. It has become a place for me to work out all the fear, confusion, pain, and anger I am experiencing as a result of what's happening with Paul. In fact, I think *The Spacebar* may have indirectly hastened his departure. Because when he finished reading it, he tossed it on the sofa and said calmly, "It's good, Tracy." It almost felt as if he was jealous that I was able to take all the madness of our lives and not only make sense of it but turn it into something positive. Something artistic.

I sent the script to the one screenwriter friend I have, a mom I've known for years, who also happens to be a big deal in the business. She gave it to her agent, but he's not calling, which isn't really a surprise. Those guys are busy—everyone in town wants an agent.

But it's a big step for me to go against the Yvonne voice in my head and deign to believe that maybe something I did could be good enough—so I congratulate myself for at least being willing to be rejected. For me, that's huge progress.

And even though everything else around me appears to be in shambles, I choose to believe that this is a fresh new start for me. *The Spacebar* is evidence of it. A new me is being born—conceived the first day I saw Paul's picture and gestating ever since. As everyone knows, birth isn't very pretty. It involves blood, and guts, and agony. It hurts and it never goes according to plan. But what you get when it's over is so magnificent, so awe inspiring—a brand-new life!—that it's all worth it. Beyond worth it.

It's just hard to know that when you're in the thick of it.

SAM IS IN THERAPY. I found someone for him to talk to after the mother of one of his friends phoned me with some very disturbing news. It was just days after Paul and I split up.

"I'm calling because I thought you should know what happened with Sam today," she begins.

I've never gotten this type of call. Sam has never been a problem. He is the cautious type who becomes alarmed if the car is moving before his seat belt is buckled. Sam follows the rules—he does his homework without being told. He brushes his teeth at slumber parties. He is scrupulously honest. He's a popular member of the boy group who makes a spirited, and sometimes silly, sidekick.

What he does not make is trouble.

"What happened?" I'm nervous, because I know this can't be good.

The mother, a sweetheart named Michelle, explains how the boys had been involved in some type of minor kerfuffle and it led Sam to an emotional meltdown (to be expected under the circumstances). Michelle apparently called the boys aside to discuss what happened and, in true "progressive parenting" style, ask each one what he felt should be done about it.

"His answer really concerned me," Michelle says. "Sam said he thought he 'should just die.' I'm sure he didn't mean it literally, but still. Is everything okay?"

There are no words for the feelings that bubble up inside when you hear that your child is in that kind of emotional jeopardy, and worse, that the danger is within. "Oh my god" is all I can say. "Oh my god."

This makes me cry.

"My husband moved out this week," I say, but I can barely get the words out. "And Sam is really close to him, and I know it's having a terrible effect on him."

"Didn't you just recently get married?" Michelle, married for fifteen years, can't understand how these facts—that I'm both divorcing *and* a newlywed—could possibly reconcile themselves.

"Yes." That's all I can say: *yes*. Yes, I got us into this. And yes, I'm getting us out.

Sometimes the moment *is* where the pain is. This is one of those times.

I hang up the phone and immediately call Saundra, even though it's a Friday night. She gives me the name of a child therapist, someone in Arcadia, a good twenty-five miles east of here, but I'll do whatever it takes.

Later, I ask Sam about the incident. Gently. "Why did you say you should die, honey?"

"I don't know," Sam says. My boy doesn't talk a lot, unless it's about Pokemon. "I just did."

"Can you tell me any more about it?" I venture to ask.

"Not really."

Later, when I think about it further, I feel intuitively that Sam is picking up on all of the torment and self-hatred in this house—Paul loathes who he has become; I am startlingly thin—and it chills me down to my bones. I have always believed that children transmit the unspoken and/or repressed thoughts and feelings in a household. They are like little broadcasting towers, picking up signals and playing them back in such a way that the parents must see exactly what they can't or won't look at.

Sam is showing me where my "love" affair has taken me, and it's as bad as any drug addiction. The way I've stayed with Paul no matter what he's done—through the lies and the insanity. If I look at Paul as if he's a drug, it all makes perfect sense. I had to have it. I just had to have it.

In fact, I can look back on *all* of my relationships—the marriages, the men; the ones I got, the ones I didn't get—and I see how I have pursued my love obsession with the same single-mindedness I once used to pursue drinking and drugs. Maybe more. And now, "suddenly," on the verge of my third divorce, it's pretty goddamn obvious that I am demoralized in the same way I would be if I were still drinking. Maybe I'm not in jail, but I've got to hire a lawyer, and my kid is in trouble, and the life I built up for myself is in shambles.

Again.

Strangely, this gives me hope. Because what I know about hitting bottom is that if you can surrender, I mean really surrender, it can be the beginning of an amazing healing.

MOST DAYS I FEEL LIKE I'm in this Quentin Tarantino movie, the one where a badass martial-arts chick played by Uma Thurman is thrown into a wooden coffin and buried alive by the bad guys. Even though it's a movie (and you know that if she doesn't get out of the coffin it's going to be a really short movie), when you're watching it you totally think, *Wow, she's a goner.* Because her only hope of escape is to apply all of the kung fu lessons she's ever learned in her life. And even then, her prospects look really dim.

This is basically what I have to do now. Going through the death of my third marriage is just like being buried alive, and the coffin is my mind.

My brain, I am discovering, is my true enemy. There's an obsessive-thought *factory* up there, churning out an endless loop of negativity twenty-four hours a day and then some. *He left you for a twenty-one-year-old. You're forty-one! You're old. You're ugly. He lied to you. He cheated on you. He left you. For a twenty-one-year-old. No one will ever love you.* You get the idea. About the only thing it doesn't say is *You're fat,* and that's only because I'm pretty much starving.

The factory also produces so-called nice thoughts, fantasies, which are beautiful pictures of the way it used to be with Paul, or the way it could be if only he would come back, or the way it would have been if he'd never met that girl or maybe just gotten a job. These thoughts are just as torturous as the negative ones, if not more so, because some part of me wishes they could be true even though I already know they definitely aren't. And never will be.

Every painful feeling I'm having in this breakup—almost every tear I've shed—starts with one of these obsessive thoughts.

Which is where the kung fu comes in.

In the movie, Uma's kung fu master is a guy with gorgeous long white hair and a Fu Manchu beard named Pai Mei. Pai Mei sets up a piece of wood and tells Uma to break it in two with her bare hands. Of course she can't. She turns her knuckles bloody trying.

That's when Pai Mei tells Uma the secret to developing devastating kung fu: if she wants to break through the wood with her bare hands, she needs to stop being afraid of the wood.

"You need to make the wood afraid of you," Pai Mei says.

This is what I'm doing now. Instead of trying to get rid of the obsessive thoughts, I am using them. I am countering every single one of those agonizing fantasies and self-hating thoughts that enter my mind with four words I say to myself, sometimes silently, sometimes out loud:

I love you, Tracy.

Every. Single. Time. Which when your newlywed husband has been caught dating a girl of twenty-one can be a helluva lot of times per day. *I love you, Tracy. I love you, Tracy. I love you, Tracy.* Sometimes the emphasis is on the "I," and sometimes it's on the "love," and other times it's on the "you." Those are three different meanings, and I need to hear all of them.

After doing this for a while (like a month), what I'm finding is that if you tell yourself you love you four hundred thousand times a day, you start to look and feel and act like a person *who is loving herself.* What does that look like? Kinda happy. Kinda peaceful. Like someone drawing good people and things into her life. What doesn't it look like? It definitely does not look bitter, angry, victim-y, or depressed.

Not that there aren't still bad days or bad moments. There are. But at least there aren't bad weeks and bad months. Hell, I know women who've had bad years, even bad decades. Some of them have given up on men altogether and now have cats instead.

I guess the point of my mantra is a lot like the point of a saying in the recovery world: "You keep what you give away." In terms of busting through solid wood with your bare knuckles, it means if you think about love, you feel love. If you think about bitterness, you feel bitter. It's not that I don't experience bitterness; I do sometimes. But I'm not practicing bitterness—saying over and over, *He sucks, I'm a victim, he sucks, fuck him, he sucks.*

Even if he does suck.

It's astounding to realize that despite everything, I actually feel better than ever. I know now that the awful pain of my past break-ups—especially those where "he" left me—had less to do with the loss of those men and more to do with the washed-out bridge between me and *me.* The fact that I would just leave myself standing there, alone and vulnerable, listening to all the garbage that was being said about me, by me, is stunning.

But things are changing. Before all this Paul business, if you didn't love me, I didn't love me. I'd do anything to keep your love—I had to!—because if you deemed me unworthy of love, I wouldn't (couldn't) love myself. Like in junior high, if you didn't like my new sweater, I didn't like it either.

In the simplest of terms possible, this breakup—the "worst" thing that has ever happened to me in all my years of relationships—has taught me how to like my sweater no matter what. All I have to do is commit to the sweater. To myself. No matter what my soon-to-be-ex-husband did. Or what my thoughts are saying to me.

The implications of this are far-reaching. It means I can make a mistake, a giant mistake, and still say, *I love you, Tracy.* And I can save myself when the bad guys threaten to bury me alive.

That is some devastating kung fu.

MOVING DAY FINALLY ARRIVES two months later. Paul has been living in a hotel all this time while Sam and I stabilized emotionally and I lined up a place of our own. This might be the hardest day of my life.

Sam is safely ensconced at Dan's house, clear of any shrapnel. Thank god for Dan. He has been so good to me in all this. I swear, ten years later, Dan is teaching me what marriage really means—he knows I am way more than my flaws, and he is standing by me, pulling with me, to minimize the damage to our son *from what I've done.* And I love him for this.

My friend Tracy—Tracy Renee—comes to sit with me while I wait for the movers, and when she has to go, another friend comes to take her place. They are witnesses, but none of them can save me from the moment when I sit alone in this huge loft, sobbing.

I cry for the mess I've made. I cry for the plans I laid. I cry for the girl who thought *this* is what felt so right. It's been twenty-one months since I first wondered if I was going to like living downtown.

Well, now I know.

THE NEXT DAY, I TAKE SAM to the loft one last time. As much as I would love to just slam the door on the whole wretched affair, I know that allowing him to say good-bye to his room and to get some closure will be what's healthiest in the long run.

There's an idea in child development that you don't need—nor do you want—a perfect mother. What you want is a "good enough" mother. Someone who will make mistakes and frustrate you so that you learn how to adapt, how to cope, how to deal with life, while still in the safety of home. Sam is totally hooked up in this respect, huh?

There's another idea that goes along with the idea of a "good enough" mother: that you're *going* to make mistakes as a parent, so it's not so much about whether you do damage, it's about how you go about repairing it. Acknowledging what has happened is the first thing. Then you have to allow for grieving.

That's why I brought him here. I want to help him make the passage from the boy who had a stepdad he loved named Paul . . . to a boy who no longer does.

We stop at the bodega on the way into the building and buy one of those candles with a picture of Our Lady of Guadalupe on it. I don't even know what Our Lady of Guadalupe represents, but whatever it is, she'll do. We walk into the loft, down the long hallway, and I can't help but remember the first time I ever made this trek. I had so much hope. I really thought my dreams were about to come true. They were—just not how I thought.

Sam is quiet, but he doesn't seem morose. There are a couple of things he wants to make sure he gets while he's here.

"Don't forget my candy kit, Mom," he reminds me. He's talking about the kit we got at one of those educational stores that uses candy making to teach kids the basics of chemistry. "It's on top of the refrigerator."

He can't reach up there, so I grab it and put it on the dining room table. The table is covered with a piece of glass, under which we have slid a lot of Polaroid pictures we took over the months we were here. I pull some of them out and tuck them into my purse. We might want to look at them someday, a long, long time from now.

Sam, meanwhile, has gone into his room. There's nothing in there but the giant pin screen, the one he never did touch in months of sleeping right next to it. "Everything's gone," he says.

"It's not gone. It's in the new place." I want to cry, but I'm reluctant to make my feelings bigger than his. I remember June Ericson and how she handled the day she told me I was leaving. This is *his* moment to say good-bye, and I don't want to get in the way of that. "Come on, pumpkin. Let's do the candle."

We go back into the dining room, and I pull out the candle. I get some matches. I lay them next to the candle. I'm trying to be just a little bit ceremonious—this is a ritual, like a funeral. We're letting go of us: me, Sam, and Paul.

Because Paul is dead.

I fold my hands in prayer. "Fold your hands, muffin." He does. I'm supposed to start the prayer now and suddenly I'm at a loss for words. What are we praying for, exactly? I've never been that good at the extemporaneous. It's exactly why I never became a reporter. All those live shots! Then I remember. We're praying to acknowledge the fact that if this is happening, somehow, it is for the highest good. Because god is good. All the time.

"Dear god, we bless the time we had in this house. We bless Paul and we forgive Paul. We let him go with love and light. And so it is. Amen."

I strike a match and hand it to Sam, who lights the candle. I wipe a tear from my eye. "No one knows exactly why things in life unfold the way they do. But I *know*"—I say it a little more fiercely than I mean to—"I know that *everything* that happens is in our highest good. It's up to us to make it so." I put a hand on his back. "Do you understand, honey?"

"Yeah." I look into Sam's soulful, downturned eyes and I can see that he really does understand. Somehow. "All right," I say softly. "I think it's time to go."

"Mom?" His face is a little brighter. He's got something he wants to say before we leave. "Can I do one last thing?"

"Yeah?"

"Can I touch the pin screen?"

This I did not expect. What an amazing request! Now that we're leaving, Sam wants to do the one thing he never got to do—touch the pin screen—because we told him not to do it. Sam, a high-integrity person, held up his side of the bargain. Which is more than I can say for Paul.

"Yes, you can," I say. "You totally can."

We go into his room, and I watch as Sam takes his plump little fingers and painstakingly pushes in a few pins in the lower left-hand corner of the screen. It doesn't disturb the design on the pin screen, but it does say, *I was here.* And perhaps it adds, *Motherfuckers.*

He looks up at me and smiles. I smile back.

Now we can go.

OF COURSE, I MEET SOMEONE. I don't mean to. But I go out to a Halloween party and we strike up a conversation, and the next thing I know, the party is over. He isn't really my type. Too tall, very blond, with big muscles. The kind of guy who likes Vegas, or used to. But he's smart and he makes me laugh. And he's got a childhood like mine. His name, improbably, is Sam.

A couple of weeks later I run into him with mutual friends and we end up going for a cup of coffee. I level with him immediately. "Listen," I say. "I've been married three times. In fact, I'm married right now. As we speak."

You'd think this would send him packing immediately. But he doesn't seem all that deterred. Instead, when we get to the end of the coffee he says to me, "Can I get your phone number?"

And what occurs to me, without my wanting it to, is: *Oh shit. He's gonna want to marry me.*

When Big Sam calls and asks me out, I say yes.

Then, an hour later, I call back and say no. I feel awful about it, but who am I kidding? I'm in no position to date this guy. For one thing, Paul only left three months ago. For another, as Paul and I approach our one-year wedding anniversary, he's been wanting to ~~reconcile~~ sleep with me. For old times' sake. And I've been wanting to let him.

So I do. And after a week or two, I don't.

I just couldn't resist the opportunity to feel what it's like to have Paul want me and to not really want him back. I know exactly how lame this is. After everything that's happened? After how much pain Paul has caused me and my son?

What was I thinking?

The truth is, I'm not thinking. I'm just being human. But my ten-day relapse has shown me something very important that I could not have seen any other way: Paul is not this all-powerful love of my life. He's just a guy whose demons lined up treacherously close to mine and my dad's. And now that I'm no longer locked in a desperate battle to win Daddy's love—by getting Paul to stop lying to me and cheating on me—even the sex is only so-so.

Free at last.

Free at last.

THE TV-WRITING AGENT finally gets in touch with me—eight months later, on Paul's birthday, no less—to say he just read *The Spacebar*, he loves it, and he would like to represent me. I'm ecstatic, not only because getting an agent is the (first) Holy Grail of a Hollywood writing career, but also because it looks like all the anguish I lived through with Paul—and poured into that script—might end up yielding something good after all.

We meet for lunch. The agent tells me the next step is to send my screenplay around town and see which production companies and TV executives like it enough to take a meeting with me. The idea is that people who take meetings with me will eventually want to hire me. For something. Anything.

While I'm waiting for Hollywood to call back, I decide it might be interesting to actually carry out the photo project my main character, Diana, undertakes in *The Spacebar*. I have a camera. I have a computer. Why the heck not? It might be interesting.

So I do what Diana does in the script. I place an ad on Craigslist looking for girls to take pictures of—nothing pervy, just simple portraits of young women. I figure whatever I learn doing this project I will use as research for the next draft of *The Spacebar*. And a gallery-owner friend of mine has offered to put together an art show featuring the photos. Fun for days!

I craft my Craigslist ad to read almost exactly like Diana's—*Fine art photographer seeking subjects for a project about girls on MySpace. Please reply with link to your profile.*

The response is immediate and abundant. One hundred and twenty or so girls write me back with links to their MySpace profiles.

They all want to have their picture taken. It seems you are no one these days until someone wants to take your picture. It's the American Apparel thing—any girl can be a model. You don't have to be especially pretty, you just have to be willing to wear one of those leotards, project your sexuality into the camera, and spread your legs far enough to embarrass your mother.

My plan is to meet with a bunch of girls at a local bookstore and to photograph them in their own spaces, preferably their bedrooms. It sounds creepy, I know. But shockingly, not one girl bats an eyelash at the plan. Maybe because I seem *so* not like a pervert. Or maybe because they're all so desperate to be even a teensy bit famous.

Both, probably.

What I'm not prepared for is the shock of a lifetime.

She answers my ad. Jessica. Paul's twenty-one-year-old whatever-you-want-to-call-her. I know it's her because I saw her on Paul's MySpace profile.

I take a deep breath and calmly decide to reply to her just like everyone else. The fact that she answered the ad is just *too* goddang random and I should treat this as the opportunity of a lifetime—life imitating art imitating life. So I write Jessica back with the time and place of my open call, just like I do for the other 119 girls.

She shows up. And for one hot second it's weird. My mind wants to get hold of what is happening and start a big meta-conversation about her, and me, and him, and her, and being twenty-one versus forty-one, and . . . *blah blah blah*. But all the growth I've experienced since Paul and I split and all the meditation I've been practicing kick in, and I just stay present in the moment, giving her—*Jessica*—the same exact explanation of my project that I've given to fifty other girls today. The movie, the gallery show, the whole enchilada.

Jessica nods her head and says how she wants to be a model, and I look at the acne on her chin, the amateurish black eyeliner, and her childish gestures, and I feel a lot more like her mom (i.e., protective) than I do her rival. She's just a barely-out-of-her-teens, somewhat naïve girl from Toledo who probably felt pretty powerful to have a married director guy eating out of her hand. She did the job for Paul, though. He *has* been working again—in Toronto. Of course, he brought her along on the trip.

I later read on Jessica's blog about how she's fucking a D-list celebrity and how she's never had an orgasm with a guy but she fakes them so well no one knows. If I were her big sister, I'd tell her this is Hollywood. It's not that they don't know, sweetie, it's that they don't care.

Same story as a million girls with pretty blue eyes in this town. Maybe she'll find the validation and stardom she seeks before she ages out of the system, or maybe not. I will say this: I have absolutely no doubt in my mind that she'll probably relate to a lot of what I've written here. But not for another fifteen years. Sometime after she marries a guy she's superhot for who turns out to be just like Daddy, I mean Paul, I mean Daddy . . .

At the moment we're both acting like each of us doesn't know who the other is. For my part, it's not that I'm trying to be a crazy stalker-ish liar. It's that I'm not really sure if she does know who I am, so what am I going to say, I'm the wife of the guy you cheated with? The one who called you after discovering the *Hey there, married man!* text message? If I say that and she doesn't know who I am, that's going to be sooooo weird.

Weirder still, she may not know if *I* know who *she* is either. So should she bust out that fact right now? At Borders Books and Music? (Notably, the same one where I first met Paul, in the Art and Architecture section.) Naw. It's definitely the better part of valor for us both to keep our mouths shut. Instead, we just have a little conversation about the Diana Project. Jessica says she's very interested and she'd love to do it. By the time it's all over, I'm pretty sure she doesn't have any idea who I am.

Twenty minutes after she leaves, I get a phone call from Paul.

"So. I hear Jessica wants you to take her picture," he says curtly.

Apparently she walked out of Borders and immediately got on the horn.

I think this is hilarious. Ashton Kutcher himself couldn't have come up with anything better on *Punk'd*. "Oh yeah? I guess I'm going to take Jessica's picture then," I say.

"Over my dead body."

"You can't stop us!" I laugh out loud. I'm taunting him. I'm not big enough not to. The karmic payback of this whole thing is just too awesome. What a nightmare for Paul! The girl he cheats with and the wife he cheated on, forming a creative alliance. You couldn't make this shit up.

"She thinks you're cool," he says.

"Of course she does." I laugh. "How funny is it that of all the people in the world to answer the ad for my project, she does? Somebody up there hates you, dude."

I never do take Jessica's picture. But she does call me, and we do have a conversation. I tell her I should probably send her a fruit basket—without her, I might never have seen the truth about Paul, about my marriage, about myself.

And I might still be looking for Daddy.

Actually I don't say that last part. She's going to have to figure that out on her own.

PAUL AND I MEET AT STARBUCKS to sign the divorce papers. I choose the one near the Costco in Glendale, because I know I won't run into anyone there, and it feels like signing your divorce papers is something you should do in anonymity.

There's a strapping breeze outside and it's ever-so-slightly chilly, in the midsixties I'd guess, with a flawlessly blue sky. Southern California weather is a study in different kinds of perfect. Who knew there were so many? Paul is already seated when I walk in, clutching a manila envelope on which he's written *Our Big Divorce*. I laugh because this is funny.

"How are you?" he asks in his clipped tone, with the emphasis on the word "are." Maybe it's just me, but he seems a little embarrassed, like he knows it's his fault we are here. He has a hint of a smile. He still likes me, I can tell.

"I'm fine," I say. And I am. At this point, most of the emotion I had for Paul has cooked down. All that's left are some warmish memories, like Chinese food on a steam table.

There are a zillion papers to sign, so we get down to it. Paul has brought two pens. He gives me one of them. As we initial here and initial there, Paul cracks jokes and talks in his Donald Duck voice. I haven't heard that in a long time.

"I wonder what these people would think if we told them we were signing our divorce papers," I say, looking around at the unsuspecting Starbucks patrons. They're not getting a divorce. They're just having coffee.

When we're done signing, we walk over to a mailbox and drop the envelopes inside. It's all done now. We hug and say good-bye.

"Well. Good-bye," I say.

"So long," Paul says in a Donald Duck voice. *Woo-hoo!*

He walks me to my car. As I unlock the door, Paul continues making small talk, the way people do when they want to prolong something just a little bit longer. But my keys are in the ignition, and that's causing the warning bell to ding incessantly, so . . . it's time to go.

On my way home I can't help but reflect. None of this is really a surprise. The child in me knew all along—at some level—exactly how things would end. God knows there were signs! But that little girl in me wanted Daddy, and she knew Paul would deliver. She knew that, for her at least, there was no way around her life—there was only through it.

From where I sit now, I can see that my relationship with Paul unlocked pieces of myself—corner pieces in my jigsaw puzzle—that in forty years of living I couldn't seem to get to any other way. And with those pieces in place—like self-love, for instance—I have been able to become more myself, move forward in my career, and (perhaps best of all) be freed of the old beliefs that locked me into unworkable relationships with men.

So I have no regrets. Because it all led me here. And here is pretty damn good.

IT'S TIME TO SELL my wedding rings. I have four beautiful wedding bands: one plain gold, one platinum with five good-size diamonds, one alternating diamonds and sapphires, and one extremely thin platinum studded with itty-bitty diamonds. When we created the set, Paul and I imagined that each ring stood for one member of the family we were creating—gold was him, platinum-diamonds was me, the sapphire was Sam, and the thin band was Paul's son.

But now that the divorce is finalized and I'm starting to get low on money, I'm going to take the rings to a nice estate jewelry store near my house and sell them all. I hand them to the guy behind the counter and he takes them all into the back room. After ten minutes, he comes out.

"I'll give you eight hundred dollars," he says.

That's a fraction of their worth. I'm fine with it, though. I need the money, and to tell the truth, it's going to be nice just to get them out of the house. It's a bit jarring to be rummaging around looking for a bobby pin and come across the four rings from your third marriage.

Months later, I am walking down the street, talking on my cell phone. I pass by that same jewelry store window, absentmindedly gazing at the pretty gems. One of them catches my eye. It's lovely.

It's also mine.

I move in closer. *Yes. That was mine.* It's the platinum one with the diamonds. The one that used to signify me. Now it's tucked into a red-velvet box with a halogen light shining on it. It's been polished and cleaned. It looks just like new.

And so do I.

Sixteen

I Love You,
So I Forgive You

PAUL CALLS ME RIGHT AFTER he gets the electroconvulsive therapy. I'm peeing, but I answer the phone anyway. I want to
hear how it went.

"Good news!" he says.

Wait, don't tell me. "Let me guess—you're fine now."

"Exactly!" He not only misses the irony, he can't wait to keep
sharing. "It's like the doctors just knocked out that busy hallway between the part of my brain that thinks and the part of my brain
that despairs," he enthuses. "I have negative thoughts, but they don't
make me want to jump off a building anymore. It's awesome!"

"Wow," I say. I'm trying not to talk too much because it's really
echo-y in here and it might be weird that I'm talking to him while
sitting on the toilet. "That sounds great."

"It *is* great! I'm just . . . happy all the time!" He laughs, extra hard,
to make sure I can tell how happy he is. "It's wonderful!"

I'm not buying it. After all the years I've spent slogging through
the old traumas and the broken paradigms—I had to marry Paul to
get a healing, for god's sake!—it's not my experience that people can
just get an operation and be "cured" of their lifelong ills. No one is

ever cured of their past. It only goes into remission. And even then, only for one day.

"So what about your tortured childhood?" I snark. "Any need to go back over any of that?"

"Not really," he says, missing my scorn. I'll say one thing: that electroconvulsive thing may have successfully disconnected his sarcasm button. "That's another great thing about it. The laser just zapped all that out of there. Not that my childhood didn't happen. I just don't feel bad about it anymore."

"Great," I say.

"So," he says. "How are you?"

Paul can't honestly think I would be willing to open a serious dialogue with him! It's obvious Paul's in no shape to even talk about creating anything even approximating a healthy relationship.

What's interesting is how I *ever* thought he might have been capable of one. I think two things have happened—I've changed for the much better, and Paul's changed for the somewhat worse.

"Are you really suggesting I should date you again?" I ask him. By now I'm in the living room, sitting on the sofa.

"I think you should consider it," he says. Paul has a way of sounding rational. If you didn't know better—like if you were me, pre-Paul—you might be fooled by it. If you were me post-Paul, you'd find it fascinating. In a mental-health-evaluation sort of way.

"But what about the womanizing and the compulsive trolling on Internet dating websites? That's just gone, too?" I have no doubt Paul's still up to his old tricks. Or soon will be.

"Absolutely," he says patly. "All gone."

Just for fun, I log in to a popular dating website, the one where I met Paul. While we're still on the phone. I search Paul's zip code for men between the ages of forty-two and forty-two, since Paul is now forty-two. His picture pops up on the first page. With a flashing *Online now!* icon. Ironically (tragically?) it's the same photo I married.

Oh, Paul. Sweet, sweet Paul. You *are* a silly goose.

It's all I can do to not bust out with hysterical laughter. As a trailer-park friend of mine used to say, *Hot dog, everything's goin' normal.* And she was right; there's something comforting about knowing no one ever really changes. At least not with electroconvulsive therapy alone.

"Paul?"

"Yeah?"

"I'll love you forever, but it's over," I say.

I hang up, knowing that even though I'm going to skip the reconciliation with Paul, there is only one way to ensure that I never ever have to go there again.

I have to go make peace with my dad.

I CAN'T FIGURE OUT what to wear. My visit with my dad—the first in eleven years—is three days away, and I'm obsessed with finding an outfit. Somehow I have it in my mind that I have to look super, super cute for the visit. Complicating matters is the fact that two days ago, while walking across the street with Sam and one of his friends, I stepped into a pothole with my eighties-style boot, twisted my ankle, and went sprawling—doggie style—right in the middle of Vermont Avenue. Damn those *Purple Rain* asymmetrical pirate heels! They might look cool, but they're a real health hazard.

"Are you okay, Mom?" Sam asks in his precious perfunctory-and-yet-sincere monotone. Right this minute I know that the $8,000-a-year hippie preschool I sent him to—where they teach the kids to ask "Are you okay?" whenever another kid gets hurt—was worth every penny. The fact that he's a bona fide tween and doesn't even *care* that his mom is splayed out in front of the cutest Sunday brunchers on Los Angeles's east side is a mark of great character. Dan and I have really done something right with this kid.

"Actually, muffin, I think I'm hurt." I look down at my legs.

Both knees are skinned and bleeding, and my left hand has a not-so-adorable case of road rash. "Look."

I hold my hands out to Sam to show him. At first he doesn't say anything, but I can tell he cares. "Sorry, Mom."

"It's okay, honey." I brush myself off and stand up, a little amazed that I'm not dead already of embarrassment.

The waitress at the outdoor café has witnessed my wipeout and goes to get me some Band-Aids and Neosporin. I'm going to need two for each knee. At least. "Don't worry," the waitress says. "I ate it crossing Sunset and Alvarado last week."

I peel the wrappers off the Band-Aids and stick them on my knees. The bandages are colored the brightest blue, a shade you'd swoon over on your Greek islands getaway but wouldn't especially want to see patching up one of your knees, let alone *both* of them.

Now I'm sporting two servings of *medallion de scab*—resting on a bed of purple bruises—right where my darlingest little cotton dresses come to their summery end. At the top of my knee.

I guess I won't be wearing *those* to see Daddy.

And it's not lost on me, either, that I have managed to acquire a little girl's injury in the days leading up to my visit with him. This is so poetic-slash-cheesy-slash-karmic, if I tried to pitch it in a TV writer's room, it would probably be rejected for being too on-the-nose.

I know it seems minor, but looking good on visiting day is as ingrained in me as wearing a hat to church pre–Vatican II. And since I don't believe in coincidences, I'm left to wonder why. All I can come up with is that the Universe doesn't want me trying to be cute enough for Daddy. That maybe a pair of skinned knees is the only way I'll figure out that he will love me no matter how I look or what I have on.

At least he better.

* * *

SAM AND I ARE STAYING with Betsy. We're spending July 4 in Minneapolis, then making the three-hour drive up to the prison camp early the next morning. Betsy lives a block away from Lake Harriet with her husband Jeff and their two girls, ages eleven and nine. Looking at Betsy's daughters, especially her older one, is like getting into a time machine. She looks so much like Betsy at the same age! For all the crazy shit that's gone on in my life, it's pretty amazing that here we are, thirty-five years later, sitting in Betsy's kitchen telling the kids to go out and play.

Maybe it's just because it's summer, but I'm in love with Minneapolis. Compared to Los Angeles, it feels like someone turned off a very high-pitched noise machine that I didn't even know was on. That noise is the sound of desire—for someone else, for something else, for fame, for money, for power. It's exhausting.

We are only here for forty-eight hours, but Sam and I are doing all the things you do when you're a kid in Minneapolis. We're going fishing at Lake Harriet—tying a hook to a piece of dental floss with frozen corn as bait and dangling it right off the dock. We laugh as the tiny little sunfishes nibble it. We even catch one.

"Look, I got one!" he says, grinning. I couldn't be happier.

After that, Betsy and I take the kids swimming at Forty-sixth Street beach.

"There are no waves, Mom," Sam says while splashing in knee-high water. He's used to the Pacific fucking Ocean, which on any day of the week has waves that will literally knock you off your feet if you're not paying attention.

"I know. That's what's great about it!" I'm hollering from a few feet away, where Betsy and I are sitting in the sand, chatting about the kids—their quirks, their strengths, their weaknesses—while we watch them play in the water.

It's the same beach where Betsy's mom used to bring us when we were Sam's age. Where Betsy's mom sat in the sand, probably chatting with Ellie, her best friend, while *we* played in the water. It's also the same beach where Scott and I used to go skinny-dipping on hot summer nights, before I went away to college and ruined everything.

I am having the time of my life sitting on this beach.

Later in the afternoon, Sam and I take a long leisurely walk from Minnehaha Falls (much more impressive than I remember!) to the Mississippi River. I figure this is as good a time as any to talk about the reason we're in Minnesota: to see my dad.

"I think you're going to like your grandpa," I say by way of a conversation opener. "He's a pretty good guy."

The thing is, with my kid, an opener is just as often a closer, too. But this time, he's going for it.

"I don't really think of him as my grandpa," Sam says matter-of-factly.

"Really? What do you think of him as?"

"*Your* dad."

Damn. Sam has this way of breaking things *down*. Just calling it like it is. And he's absolutely right. As far as he's concerned, my dad is just *my* dad. Just a voice on the phone and a well-dressed guy in a couple of old photographs wearing a pinky ring. Once or twice my dad asked to speak with Sam, but it seemed a little bit weird to ask a kindergartener to talk to someone he's never met in person. Besides, Sam's not much of a phone guy.

"Yeah, I guess you're right," I say. "I can see why you'd think that."

Sam's known for a while now that Freddie is in prison. I told him—after much consulting with Saundra and Dan's mother, Marie—when he was seven. I wanted to make sure Sam was old enough to process the information when he heard it. But it's not really the kind of information *anyone* can make much sense of.

Much less a little kid.

So I change the subject to what's right in front of us—this pretty trail leading down to the Mississippi River. We see a giant old turtle tucked into an eddy in Minnehaha Creek, and we carve our names into the sandstone outcroppings along the trail's edge, the same ones I carved my name into as a little girl. And soon we're at the river, the longest one in America. I forgot how beautiful it is.

Prison will have to wait until tomorrow.

LAST TIME WE WERE in Minnesota, Sam was only five. Visiting Freddie was never an option, because he was still in prison in Wisconsin, five hours away. Besides, five is way too young for prison.

The visit was brief, a long weekend, for the purpose (I thought) of attending my twenty-year high school reunion. But really we came for a much more important reason.

To say good-bye to June.

She and Gene had long since retired to an assisted-living facility, and I phoned hoping maybe I'd be able to stop by and say hello. June had met Sam once when he was a baby, but I hadn't been back to Minneapolis since then. Gene answered the phone.

"Oh, Tracy, hello," he says, like we'd just spoken last week. "June is in the hospital. But I'm sure she'd love to see you."

I walk into the hospital room. Carl, my Ericson brother, is standing there. It's probably been fifteen years or more since I've seen him. We hug.

"Good to see you, Tracy," he says. He's got that way of speaking that all ministers have—Gene has it, Dan's dad has it, too—designed to put you at ease. "Is this your son?"

"That's Sam," I say. Sam is reticent around new people, especially adults. But Carl is great with him.

"Your mommy was just about your age when she came to live with us," he says to Sam.

Funny. I never thought of how Carl must have viewed that little girl in the Polly Flinders dress who walked into the house one January morning in 1969. He was in his early twenties then. He must be in his fifties now—still married to Missy, of course, and a grandfather a couple of times over.

"Come on in," Carl says. Then he calls out to June. "Mom, Tracy's here."

As we step more deeply into the room I see June, lying curled almost, in the bed. She has no hair. She is obviously nearing death. But she is still plenty lucid.

"I didn't know you were coming," June says. "Or I'd have bothered to put on my wig."

June is still funny. Even on her deathbed.

"It's okay," I say. I don't know what's appropriate in a situation like this. I've never really seen anyone this close to the end of life before.

June calls Sam over. "Let me see you, Sammy," she says, opening her eyes. She looks almost like a baby lying there. "Oh my. You look just like your mom. Don't you?"

Sam doesn't know what to say, either. But he is surprisingly not freaked out. June has that effect on a person. She just manifests the presence of the higher thing, the all-that-there-is. God. "You know, I always say your mommy was the smartest kid I ever had."

I'm kind of flattered, and embarrassed, at that. I don't really know what she means. It's not like June's kids were any dummies. Everyone in the family is a college grad. Several have graduate degrees. Okay, so maybe they never dismantled the sewing machine.

"And I always say you were the best mom I ever had," I counter. It's true. June saved my life. Without her, I'd probably be fulfilling the socioeconomic destiny I was born into—on Section 8, with several children, some of them wards of the state. Maybe with a crack pipe.

I certainly wouldn't be here.

We make a little more small talk, maybe five minutes' worth, before it's time to go. June is fading.

"Good-bye," I say, squeezing her hand. I know this is the last time I will see her, even if I can't totally comprehend exactly what that means.

"Sam, it's been *so* lovely to meet you," June says, in her emphatic way.

Sam just looks at her, wide-eyed. "Bye," he says.

Carl and I hug good-bye. "Say hello to everyone for me," I tell him. Even though it's been thirty years since I left the Ericsons, they are in some ways more my family than anyone else. With them I had an experience of being part of something, of belonging somewhere, of being loved unconditionally.

Back in the rental car I put the key into the ignition, but I can't quite start the car. Instead, I cry. Crystal-clear tears.

Sam sits in the backseat, strapped into the booster chair. "Why are you crying, Mom?" he asks. I don't know that he's ever seen me cry like that.

I shake my head. I can't really answer. It has something to do with the profound effect this woman has had on my life and my deep gratitude to whatever god there is for bringing me to see her one last time. That I've been allowed to experience this closure—despite being in such loose touch with the Ericsons over the years—seems like one of the more amazing gifts I've had in this lifetime. In fact, it seems like a miracle.

"Is it because she was the best mom you ever had?" Sam says, nailing it.

Yes, honey. That's exactly why. That's precisely, exactly why. Because June Ericson was the best mom I ever had. And because if you get June Ericson for a mom—even if it's only for four and a half years—you are blessed. I dry my tears and smile into the rearview mirror.

Then I start the car, knowing I am blessed.

WITH JUNE GONE, Betsy is all I have left in Minneapolis. I've completely lost touch with Linda. Dianne is here, but she's got three kids, and they're up at their lake place for the summer. Yvonne left years ago. After I went away to college, she went back to school, too, eventually graduating and taking a job in the state of Massachusetts.

She and I have lost touch, mostly, although I did see her once in 1992, and once in 1998, right before I quit drinking. Sam was just a toddler then. It was a decent visit, although the old tension was still there. We drank wine together, and that made it a little better, but maybe it's not a coincidence that I quit drinking for good a few weeks later.

A couple of years ago, during a process of going back into my past and setting things right, I sent her a letter. I'd wondered for years about my part in the relationship—how I had contributed to the way it was, and is—and what needed to be said between us. Finally, eight years after smoking my last joint, I figured it out.

I needed to thank her.

I was just a kid during the time I knew Yvonne—I was only seventeen when I left her house—and over the years I had remained in a child's state of mind when thinking about her: focused only on how she had hurt me and never really seeing the good she had done. This was unfair and unbeneficial not just to her (or the memory of her), but also to myself. It kept me stuck, casting myself in the role of Unbeloved Daughter—the one who doesn't get what she needs, the one who is raged-at, hurt, and abused.

It's easy to see how I focused on the pain and the hurt because, after all, it did hurt and it was painful. But over the years, I have become convinced that what I *think* and what I think *about* are what manifest around me. And while I can't choose what happened, I can choose how I'm going to perceive it. It's like changing the past, in a way, to unilaterally shift my focus from what Yvonne didn't do to becoming grateful for all that she did. She made sure I went to one of the best high schools in Minneapolis. She put a big emphasis on college. She filled our house with books and music and taught me about the world of the arts and the life of the mind. Things that prepared me perfectly for the world I now live in.

Setting the record straight means thanking her for that, because I never have.

So I write her a letter saying just that. I tell her how well I am doing in life and thank her for the sacrifices she made for me and the significant part she played in making me who I am today. I include a picture of Sam and a picture of me.

She writes me an e-mail a week later apologizing for "not being what I needed her to be." She says she feels guilty over what happened during those years and that "not a day goes by" when she doesn't hope for the best for me. Then she says, "Go in peace, Tracy. Go in peace."

Go in peace.

I guess she's telling me to move on without her. I feel a twinge of sadness, not because I wish that we were going to be part of each other's lives—I don't see a life of merry Christmases and summer vacations with Yvonne—but there's a part of me that loves a happy ending, and as endings go, this one isn't happy. It's just okay.

But a little time passes, and I notice that when Yvonne comes into my mind, I feel peace. Peace is good. Peace is all I've ever really wanted.

So, on second thought, an okay ending will do just fine.

PRISON CAMP IS REALLY RELAXED. It feels less like a place of punishment than it does, say, a Department of Motor Vehicles office. Except half the people are wearing prison uniforms. Other than that, the basic protocol remains the same as in federal prison 101.

My heart trembles a bit as we approach the guard. He's a clean-shaven, crew-cutted guy in his midtwenties who probably came from some small town up north and now finds himself checking the IDs of people who love people who commit crimes.

"Long way," he says, looking at my California driver's license. They probably don't get a lot of Angelenos in this place. As I slip off the little cotton sweater I have on over my white sleeveless top, he adds, "You're going to need to leave that on, ma'am."

"Huh?" I don't know what he's talking about. And I never fail to find it jarring when people call me "ma'am." When did I become old?

"Your sweater," he says, with a slightly apologetic tone. "Those are the rules."

I have forgotten that there is a dress code in prison—no tank tops, shorts, sleeveless shirts, or other clothing that might bring about too much sexy thinking. "No problem," I say. "Thanks."

Sam looks around, slightly wide-eyed. *So this is prison,* his expression seems to say. My kid is the silent type, so you're never quite sure *what* he's thinking, and it's not like you can grab him by the shoulders and ask, *"What are you thinking about this whole prison thing?!"* (Though if I thought it would yield an answer, I might.) Being Sam's mom has taught me to quiet down and know things in a whole new, unspoken language.

After signing in, we are told to take a seat. "It'll be a few minutes before we can get him down here," the guard says. "Sit wherever you want."

The room is large and light and half-filled with the usual customers: inmates, kids, and women with low self-esteem. Everything is just like I remember it—I feel right at home.

Sam and I take a seat and wait. After about ten minutes, a gray-haired, bearded man walks toward us. He seems to know who I am. *Is that him?* That's him! He has a jolly expression that I recognize, though his teeth are different than I remember. Maybe that's because Uncle Sam bought him a new set. Freddie laughs his old familiar chortle as we move in for the hug.

"Hiiiiiii!" I say, a little flummoxed at how excited I actually am to see him.

"Aw, look at my little gyurl. All growed up!" He pushes me out a foot or two, getting a better look. "You look good!" He sounds surprised. "And who's this?!"

He pulls Sam toward him, into a large but not too overwhelming hug. "My *grand*son! Oh, my. You've gotten so big." Normally

I would be thinking sarcastic thoughts, like *That's what happens in eleven years,* but the look on Freddie's face—pleased as punch—is warming my heart. "Well, you *are* a good-lookin' son of a gun," Freddie says. "A real Mack-Millan. And look at your hair!"

It's true; Sam has an amazing head of hair. He's also looking quite dapper in a pair of plaid Bermuda shorts, a green polo shirt, and brown Converse high-tops. Sam doesn't really have to try to look cute in an outfit. He just does. I guess in that way he really is a chip off my dad's old block.

"How are you, son?" My dad draws out the word "son," putting a hint of street spin on it.

"Fine." Sam looks up at my dad with a completely open, sweet, innocent face. It takes me a second to figure out who else I've seen him regard like this—then it hits me. Dan's parents! I'm stunned. It's like Sam knows he is related to this man, Freddie, and he already loves him. I wasn't expecting that at all.

"Oh, yeah?" My dad is beaming back. "You're fine?"

Sam smiles. He knows my dad is teasing him a little. "Yeah."

My dad smoothes the collar on Sam's polo shirt. "Here, son, let me fix that for you." Sam dutifully stands still while my dad presses the collar between his thumb and index finger into the perfect position. I kind of liked the collar popped, but who cares? I'm watching my personal history unfold here.

I stand there, just trying to process it all. Except for that one time when Sam was a baby, I've never been in a room with my dad *and* my son. Two generations of my family.

New feeling alert!

I never guessed coming here would be this strange form of déjà vu, where my dad is watching my son, and I am watching my dad, and I can see that the way my dad feels about Sam is the way I feel about Sam, which is also the way my dad feels about me.

It's like together we are one of those medical books where when you lay each page over the next, you get a picture of one whole body, with all of the insides. Me, my dad, my son—we're all one. The same person, just kind of split into three bodies. This is awesome, literally, because I've spent a lifetime feeling separated from everyone else—I never really felt like part of anybody else's picture. I can suddenly see how people who have mothers they know, and sisters they know, and grandmas and grandpas they know—they don't feel like a heart without a lung.

I'd say it's too bad all this is taking place in a federal prison, but it's so amazing, I don't even care.

THIS TIME MY DAD thinks I'm too skinny. At first he just hints at it. "You're so skinny," he says.

We're standing in front of the vending machines, trying to decide between the Quarter-Pound Charbroil Burger and the Chili-Cheese Dogs. Actually, my dad is trying to decide. My mind is already made up: I'm getting the hamburger. I have a weird fetish for textured vegetable protein, the kind they sneak into vending machine hamburgers to squeeze another four cents of profit out of each patty. I think it tastes good. "I noticed you were looking thin in the pictures you sent," he continues. "But now I see you in person and . . ."

Of course, I'm delighted he thinks I'm skinny. Too thin (especially since I'm definitely not) is what's known as a "quality problem" in my world. But I pretend to protest anyway.

"You should have seen me before. I used to weigh twenty pounds less than I do now," I counter. "This isn't even skinny. Guys in California like their women hungry."

"I noticed that," Freddie says. "All those Hollywood stars on TV are just . . . there's nothing to them." He looks me over one more time. He has reached a verdict. "Well," he declares, "you need to gain ten pounds." The gavel drops. "I don't like my women skinny anymore," my dad says, casting a quick glance around the room. He's obviously looking for something he *does* like. And of course he finds it. After all, he's a guy in prison, and it makes sense that a prison visiting room would be filled with women who have what guys in prison are looking for.

My dad gives a slight tilt of his head in the direction of a bottle blonde in her late twenties who is by no means fat but who could definitely survive the next Minnesota winter at around half her current calorie intake. "That's what I'm talking about," he says to me while smiling at her. She smiles back.

"Oh yeah? Well, you used to like skinny," I protest. I find it amusing and ironic that my dad is detailing how his taste in women has changed over the past fifteen years. Fifteen years he has spent in prison. "What happened?"

"I guess I changed," he says.

I'm reminded now that this is the type of conversation one ends up having with my dad, even when one is his daughter. It feels a little like we're perusing that Hot or Not website together—the one where a picture flashes on the screen and you click either "hot" or "not," at which time that picture disappears and is replaced by a photo of another candidate for hotness. Or notness.

So, so much about my life with men is starting to make sense.

ALL TOTALED, THE VISIT lasts about four hours, and we don't waste a minute of it. We play half a game of Monopoly, take another trip to the vending machines, and go outside where there's a little play area for the kids. We get our pictures taken (for a fee, a trustee inmate takes the photos and sends them to you a few weeks later), and my dad and I talk about some grown-up things while Sam wanders off to watch a Disney movie in the kid area.

Later, there's a group of three boys running around the visiting room. They look like they're having a pretty good time. Sam is usually great at making pals with other kids, so I encourage him to tag along. "Do you want to go play with those guys, Sam? They look like they're about your age."

"No, thanks," he says in his laconic way.

"Yeah. I get it," I say after a second glance. "Those boys' *dads* are in here. You're here because of your *granddad*. It's a whole different thing." Sam's been safely tucked away in the middle class all this time; and by comparison, those kids are *street*.

By the final hour, Sam and my dad are engaged in some major granddad-grandson bonding, culminating with blackjack lessons. My dad plays the dealer.

Thwack!

"Seventeen!" Freddie tosses a card down with a stylish flip of the wrist, a technique you know he must have perfected back in the day. He makes a big show of not taking another card. "I'm gonna have to hold on that bad boy. What do you want to do, son?"

It's Sam's turn now. "Hit me," he says in his cute little white-boy voice. My dad does the showy wrist-flick again, to Sam's delight. A king materializes on top of his eight.

"Eighteen!" Sam crows. "*Woot-woot!* You lose." He could not be more excited. I think to myself that this is a long way from checkers or whatever he plays with his other grandpa. The one who is a Presbyterian minister.

My dad holds his hand out. "Gimme five," he says. There's a lot of grandfatherly pride going on here. The boy is clearly bringing some skills to the game. Sam slaps my dad's hand, palm to palm. My dad then teaches him a couple of little fancy handshake moves. "Go like this," he says, making a fist and pounding it on top of Sam's. "Then like this," he says, pounding Sam's on top of his.

It's pretty damn adorable and, if you don't pay attention to the surroundings, seriously Norman Rockwell.

Too soon, the visit's over. My dad stands up and says it's time to go. "Well, baby. You drive safe now." He wipes his nose with his ever-present Kleenex. His allergies kicked up today. I'd forgotten he even had allergies. Maybe he just got allergies instead of getting emotional.

"Okay," I say. I give him a hug. "You take care of yourself."

"I will," he says. "I'll be out of here soon. Hopefully in the first part of the new year."

I don't pay attention to these things. "That would be great," I say, knowing it will never happen.

I notice that my dad is a bit distracted—it's the only sign that maybe this good-bye is affecting him. I, too, am braced against a feeling. It's not that I'm going to cry or anything. I just don't want Freddie to feel any worse than he already does that he's going back to his cell and we are going to continue on about our lives.

Freddie pulls Sam toward him and gives him a hug. "Come here, son. You be sweet for your mom, now. You're a good boy. You keep up the good work in school."

Sam hugs him. I think he had a good time getting to know Grandpa. We wave good-bye as we walk through the doors to the parking lot. My dad waves for a moment, then turns and heads through the inmates' door.

Back to whatever is behind it.

LATER, ON THE DRIVE BACK to Minneapolis, I ask Sam what he thought of his granddad.

"He was nice, I guess."

"He is nice, isn't he?" I agree. "He's always been like that. Sometimes I forget how nice he is. What was your favorite part of the visit?"

"Playing blackjack," he says impishly. Great. My dad taught my kid how to gamble. "And I liked the candy machines."

I'm flushed with this weird feeling. A feeling of shared experience with my son—I liked the candy machines, too, when I was little—and the closeness to my dad. At fortysomething, I can see that my dad was a good dad—he was just a good dad from "in there." He never gave up on me, never let me go. A lot of prison guys would have, and sooner rather than later. Freddie's kind of stellar, when you think about it.

I know this is why I stayed away from him for so long. I didn't want to feel close. There's been a safety in being alone, in being separate. No one can hurt me there. As long as I have a wall between me and Daddy, I have a wall between me and everyone, and especially between me and men.

I'm overcome with a sense of having let go of something really heavy. Something I've been carrying an awfully long time.

SIX MONTHS LATER, I'm on my way to work. I stop off for coffee at my usual place, the Casbah Café on Sunset Boulevard, just like I do every day before heading to the writers' room of the television show I'm now writing on. It's a cop drama set in 1973, so I feel right at home, even though of the eight writers on the show, only three of us actually remember 1973. Everyone else was in diapers. Or ovaries.

The phone rings, and the familiar "Unknown Caller" pops up on the caller ID. It must be my dad.

"Hello?"

"This call is from a federal prison. You will not be charged for this call . . ."

I wait for Automated Prison Recording Barbie to finish her spiel, then I press "5," just like I'm supposed to. This time, I talk first.

"Hi!" I sound chipper because I am. I'm happier to talk to my dad these days. So much tension has evaporated since our visit. And when I don't feel like talking to him, I just don't pick up the phone. Which may not be how Freddie wants it, but it's more honest, and in the end, I think we're closer for it.

"Hey, baby! How you doin'?"

"Good. I'm on my way to work. Getting my coffee."

"Well, I'm not going to keep you long," he says. "I just wanted to let you know that I got the information on that pilot program, and I put in my application."

He's talking about a law that passed recently, called the Second Chance Act. It's a big, long, complicated law, but in it, there's a provision for senior-citizen offenders. If they've done more than two-thirds of their sentence, they can apply to serve out the rest of their time in home detention. My dad's been talking about it since it was in Congress.

"Cool," I say. Then I wait for him to say something else.

"It looks like it will take some time to process my application, but I think it should come through by September 2010." He's excited, obviously. "Seventeen years, man. That's a long time. I'm ready to come home."

And just where, exactly, is home?

"I'm going to stay with your aunt Mavis." That's my Michigan aunt. I've only met her once, in 1975. But right this second, she's my favorite person in the whole world. "I've got to get a job and stay put for at least a year. To show that I can stay employed. But after I've been working a certain length of time, I can get Social Security benefits."

My dad prattles on about getting a job at age seventy-five and meeting the requirements of the pilot program, but I'm not *really* listening. I'm thinking over the fact that he just said he's getting out of prison but he's not coming here. Good. Because I only just got used to being close to him in prison. I'm not ready yet to be close to him out of it.

"That sounds good," I say. I know I sound a little bit vacant, and thankfully, my dad's not calling me on it. He doesn't even seem to notice.

"After a year, then we can talk more about what happens next," he reassures me. He knows I have mixed feelings about him just barreling into my life. I like my life. It's orderly. Plus, I have my son to think about. My dad's going to need to prove that he can stay away from crime. I don't think old age alone is going to do it.

"Oh, and have you been in touch with Cadillac?" My godfather, the actor.

"No, I haven't."

"Well, can you get me his new number? Because I'm going to need a girlfriend, and I think he can help me out with that."

This gets a reaction out of me. "You do not need a girlfriend!" I say.

"After seventeen years? I'm going to need a girlfriend." He laughs, but he's only half joking. "Have a good day at work. And give my love to Sam."

"I will."

"You be sweet, now. I love you."

"I love you, too."

We hang up. I get out of the car and head for the café. On my way inside I marvel at the fact that I'm not even thinking about a man. I'm not trying to find one. I'm not trying to lose one.

Which makes me think it's official: I no longer have daddy issues.

I Love You,

Totally and Completely

I'M IN LOVE WITH GWYNETH NOW. Okay, maybe "in love" is a bit too strong a phrase, but since I've gotten back from the prison, I am experiencing her in a whole new way. Instead of feeling taunted by her flawless life like I once was, I've decided to turn Gwyneth into my own personal walking, talking, blogging, Pilates-practicing totem of the Beloved Daughter. In the same way Native American tribes might tap into, say, wolf energy for strength and freedom and wisdom, she is someone who helps me visualize what it looks like to know you deserve every good thing life has to offer.

In other words, Gwyneth is my spirit animal.

Seeing my dad again has set me free in other ways, too. Since our last visit, I've come to accept that I'll never be able to go back and change history, but that doesn't mean there's nothing I can do to transform my past. As the bumper sticker says, it's never too late to have a good childhood. The thing is, having a "good" childhood at this stage of the game is not about somehow managing to *get* now what I wanted then. It's about *being* now what I wanted then. I have to be the parent I wish I'd had, because you keep what you give away. And I know just where to start, too, thanks to Gwyneth.

I am taking my kid to Paris.

* * *

WE ARE TRAIPSING DOWN the Champs-Elysées. Me and Sam. It's nighttime, five days before Christmas. The boulevard is jammed with people, and all the trees are festooned with pale blue lights. Behind us is the Arc de Triomphe; ahead, the Eiffel Tower, lit the color of navy blue chiffon. Paris is, as promised, magical.

My kid is begging to go to McDonald's.

"Please, Mom? Please!"

"Sam, we are *not* going to McDonald's," I say. "We're in Paris."

"Pleeeeezzzzzz . . ."

I am pretty clear that we would be fulfilling the most basic of all clichés about American tourists if, on our very first night in Paris, we eat a Happy Meal. I like to think I don't do clichés.

I manage to hustle Sam past the first McDonald's. And the Burger King. But then, when we come to *another* McDonald's, Sam asks me again. "Mom, *please?*"

And then I remember. This trip is for him.

A QUARTER POUNDER in France is called a Burger Royale. It is very, very tasty.

TEN DAYS LATER, we are on an Italian train. I am in the window seat on one side. Sam is in the other one across from me. From time to time I look up and see him, this perfect, beautiful, soulful creature sitting across from me, and I am way more human than I was the moment before.

Both of us are listening to our iPods, earphones on, our heads bobbing up and down to our personal sound tracks. Clearly, Sam is loving his song as much as I am loving mine, which makes me wonder what he is listening to. I pick the ear bud out of my right ear and give him a little slap on the knee.

"Sam," I say, leaning in.

He pulls the earphone off his left ear and leans forward. "What?"

"Which of us do you think is rocking out harder right now?"

He half smiles. Sam loves a head-to-head competition. It's the gamer in him. "I don't know. What are you listening to?"

I show him the screen on my iPod. A ruby-lipped Mick Jagger stares out from the cover of *Black and Blue.* "Middle-period Stones," I say. "'Fool to Cry.'" Pretty rockin', if you ask me.

"I'm listening to *Metallica*," he says with a spin, knowing he's got me beat. "There's *no way* you could ever win!"

"Nice," I say humbly. He's right, of course. What band rocks harder than Metallica?

We are on our way back to Paris after a wonderful and ridiculously expensive side trip to Venice. Returning has proven to be a challenge, though, thanks to the Italian train website that led me to believe there were tickets on the direct route to Paris when there most definitely were not, at least not until the week after next. Our only option, the train clerk not-so-kindly informed me, is to go to Bologna, wait three hours in the station there, catch a train to Bern, Switzerland, wait two hours, and *then* catch another train back to Paris. The whole thing is going to take eighteen hours. The direct route would have been eight.

But how can I mind? Because the train is rumbling down the tracks, and I am riding it with someone who is rocking out to Metallica while kicking ass in his video game.

"I'm pwning, Mom," Sam says. That's "winning" in video-game speak. He pumps his victorious little fist and grins at me. "*Yesss!* Woot-woot!"

I'm riding with someone I will *always* love.

IT'S NEVER BEEN MORE EVIDENT than now: my boy has taught me every single useful thing I know about men. Until my son came along, my view of men was essentially self-centered: I looked at them with my *self* in mind. And that self wanted the men in my life to talk more, emote more, chill out, stop trying to fix everything, and never *ever* want to have sex with any other woman ever again. Not to mention be devastatingly handsome, buy me a house, and have a job lucrative enough to allow me to retire immediately.

But being the mother of a baby "guy" revealed certain things to me that have changed the way I relate to men. For the better. I could write a whole book about this, and maybe someday I will. In the meantime, here are my top three epiphanies:

1. BOYS ARE DIFFERENT THAN GIRLS

Believe it or not, this one came as a shock. Growing up in the 1970s, I held it to be self-evident that girls can do anything boys can do—*because we are the same*. We're not. Duh. This led me to want my boyfriends to be more like me, because, it went without saying, my talking, feeling, relating way of being in the world was just . . . preferable!

After watching a whole group of kids grow from babies to preteens, I have decided that boys and girls have *likenesses*—in the same way, say, peanut butter and chocolate have similarities. They're not *so* different in texture or shape, and they can substitute for each other *some* of the time. (Who doesn't like chocolate spread on bread? On the other hand, who wants to drink hot peanut butter?) But when it comes right down to it, one's a bean that grows on a tree, and one's a legume that grows in the ground. Big difference. Trying to turn one into the other (which is what I'm always trying to do) is a waste of time compared to devising artful combinations of the two, which can get you, like, peanut butter cups.

My baby group proved the differences to me forever. When we first started the group, the kids were all infants—none older than nine or ten months. What I noticed right away was that (and obviously, these are just my wildly unscientific observations) the boys seemed slightly less "cooked" than the girls. Their little nervous systems were like bad cell phones—constantly dropping calls. They had a harder time sleeping, wanted (needed?) to nurse more often, and had to move around all the time. My baby boy was the most serene when he was actually sitting or lying on my body, when he was able to index his heartbeat, skin temperature, and energetic force field to mine. I provided all his food and calmed him down when he got all *ferklempt*.

Doesn't sound all that much different from a husband.

Then, as the children grew, I noticed the boys liked trucks and playing superhero. The girls liked dolls and playing princess. Obviously there were exceptions, but it's amazing that none of my girl-mom friends discovered that they could get an hour of peace by taking little Ruby to a construction site to watch the diggers scoop up dirt over here and drop it in piles over there.

Watching—really observing—these boy babies in particular, it hit me that deep inside every man I'd ever met, loved, or lived with was one of these exact same bouncing, fleshy, cooing pumpkins—an absolute innocent—all eyes, and sweetness, and need.

Depending on me for love.

Which brings me to revelation number two.

2. WOMEN HAVE INCREDIBLE POWER OVER MEN!

We act like we don't. Of course a couple of thousand years of witch burning, foot binding, and boob jobs have helped us to forget. But that's on us. A wise woman said to me once, "He needs you more than you need him, Tracy." She didn't mean one particular man, she meant *all* of them. It's not that they're weak. It's that they have such deep neural pathways along the mommy trajectory—just like our daddy pathways, but even more. Because daddies don't nurse.

As far as my boy is concerned, I am god, at least from birth to, say, age five. *God!* I am the source of everything: food, love, warmth, good feelings, bad feelings. I can bring about fear, happiness, cookies, and the toy store. The older he gets, the less unilateral power I have to create his world, but the fact that I came first makes me indelible, in the same way that five hundred years after Balboa or whoever, they still speak Spanish in South America.

Just for fun (and because, when it comes to men, god is what I've always wanted to be) I look up "god" on dictionary.com. There are nine definitions but three in particular sum up what we television writers call a story "arc"—a beginning, middle, and end—of, in this case, a man's life with women.

God

1. *The one Supreme Being, the creator and ruler of the universe.*
   Check. Mommy. Infancy through first ejaculation.
2. *Any deified person or object.*
   Check. Girls. *Maxim* through matrimony.
3. *Noun used to express disappointment, disbelief, weariness, frustration, annoyance, or the like: "God, do we have to listen to this nonsense?"*
   Check. Wife. Marriage through death.

No wonder men are scared of me. As I have watched my son face the world—with his boy heart and his boy nervous system—a deep contrition has set in. *I have been* way *too hard on men.* I have the power to hurt them—with my words, my facial expressions, my disapproval. I have been like a novice knife juggler at a day care center.

Even worse, when a man was afraid of me, I (along with many of my girlfriends) loathed him for it. I had no compassion. I couldn't imagine that maybe the poor fellow had a mother who was scary, or emotionally unstable, or who let her anger fly out just anywhere. Or that maybe he had a dad who never thought he was enough. I just saw him as weak.

I punished men for the power I had over them.

So slowly, I have begun to treat every man as if he were my son. Not in a sick way. More like, *Would I use this tone of voice with my son? Would I make this harsh face with my son? Would I be so unforgiving with my son? Would I expect my son to listen to my fears, make me feel better, provide my need for connection?*

Um, no.

Being Sam's mom has taught me to love the boy inside the man. Instead of wanting the man to love the little girl inside of me.

And that brings me to perhaps the simplest truth.

3. WHAT MEN REALLY WANT IS TO RIDE IN PEACE
(Or "What Men Really Want Is to Have Some Macaroni and Cheese and Watch Some TV")

I used to think guys were holding out on me all the time. I thought when a guy was being quiet, he was thinking really deep thoughts. Maybe about us. Or world peace, or his childhood. I suspected men kept these thoughts like a secret stash in a back room where they hid their "real" selves, and if I tried hard enough, or was awesome enough, or clever enough, or sexy enough, or pretty enough, I could get them to share it with me. I won't lie. I wanted to *own* his secret self.

I can't tell you how many times I've had some version of the following conversation with a guy who was trying to watch the game—any game—on TV.

"What are you thinkin'?" I say it casually, because I know men tense up when you ask them this.

"Nothing."

"Come on. You can tell me." I think it's a matter of gaining their confidence. I just have to show that I'm a good listener and trustworthy.

"Nothing, really."

"*No.* Really."

"No. *Really.*"

Shoot. He said that kinda forcefully. I've annoyed him. "You're mad."

"I'm not mad."

"You *are.* I can tell. You had that mad sound in your voice."

"I'm not mad."

"Don't hide it from me. I can hear the madness in your voice. You're mad!"

"God, Tracy. Do you *have* to go after me so hard all the time?! I'm just trying to watch some TV!"

Rinse. Repeat. Times three marriages and numerous live-in relationships.

Then I had the following exchange one day with my then-nine-year-old, after picking him up at school. I look into the rearview mirror to see him gazing absentmindedly out the window.

"So how was school today?"

"Fine."

"Anything interesting happen?" I'll admit, my voice carries a tad too much enthusiasm. I'm thinking, delusionally, that maybe this is the day he will give me a few paragraphs about school. What he said, what she said, what they did, and what he thought about it all.

"Mawwwm." He's using the drawn-out version of "Mom," the one he employs when he's exasperated.

"Yeah?" I say. I'll admit I'm pretty excited to hear all about it.

"Can't we just ride in peace?"

Holy shit. It's just a few words, but I'm having a revelation as big as the one I had in fifth grade when I put on my first pair of glasses. Except instead of seeing *leaves! On the trees!* I'm suddenly understanding that what Sam wants in this moment is what *every single man I've ever loved* has wanted from me. Just to be with me, in the same space as me, breathing the same air and knowing I'm there, while we just . . .

Ride in peace. Be.

I get it. Sam's not really *thinking* anything, in the sense that I, as a woman, am thinking: i.e., constantly trawling for information on the physical, mental, and/or emotional state of everyone around me. The mind of a man resembles less a ticker tape than it does an EKG. There's activity going on there, but wild swings high and low are an indication that something's wrong. They like to be right in the middle. Sam doesn't really communicate verbally. He communicates through his presence. Through being.

I decide to take this time together, on the way home, in the car, driving down the 134 freeway, as a mother-son meditation. Sure enough, a few minutes later, Sam has something to say.

"Mom . . ."

"Yeah?"

"Can I watch *Naruto* when we get home?" That's the Japanese animation show that he loves. "When my homework is done?"

"Sure, honey."

Hearing his voice again reminds me that we've been together this whole time. We just haven't been talking. It feels kind of good. Like, *We know we're here. We don't have to hear ourselves to know we're here.*

My kid is a lot deeper than I am. And then:

"Mom?"

"Yeah, pumpkin?" I say expectantly. I think maybe now that I've succeeded so well in being quiet, as a reward Sam's going to tell me something up close and personal about what happened today at school.

"Can we have macaroni and cheese for dinner?" he asks.

I inwardly laugh at myself for being so relentlessly the way I am. "Yeah, honey. We can have macaroni and cheese."

It's so much less complicated than I make it.

NEITHER OF US CAN SLEEP. It's dark, and very late, and though there is another bed, Sam is lying in mine, because this is Paris, and we are jet-lagging. At age eleven and a half, it's still okay to sleep next to your mom, a last gasp of pure childhood.

Tomorrow we are going to Versailles, which has brought up a discussion about Marie Antoinette and her public execution, which has led to a discussion of Henry VIII and his six wives, which has led to a discussion of divorce.

"You leave everyone," Sam says quietly. His tone of voice isn't superangry, but he's definitely accusing me. Over the past couple of years he has figured out that I left his dad, I left my other boyfriends, and especially, I left Paul, whom he loved. "Why do you leave, Mom?"

When I was growing up, parents never had to answer to their children. Not until Family Day at rehab, anyway. As much as it's no fun to think about where I have failed as a wife and mother, I'm glad that my kid feels comfortable asking me this. It is that much less stuff he'll have to carry around in his family-dysfunction backpack.

"Things are complicated, honey. You'll understand more when you're older." I go into a brief explanation about people with crazy childhoods, and how they have a harder time than others forming relationships, and how I'm learning a lot and working hard to heal the things in me that have made it difficult for me to stay with someone.

"Sometimes I have picked right but couldn't stay. And sometimes I have picked wrong and couldn't stay. It's complicated."

"Why did you leave Paul, Mom?" Sam has asked me this question before, but never point-blank.

I take a deep breath. It breaks my heart that my actions, my choices, have affected my child in such a profound way. I know that Paul has been recorded on his heart as the first person to disappoint him, to abandon him, to fall horribly, painfully short. To be glaringly human.

Besides me, of course.

"I had to, honey."

I've never told Sam exactly why I left. I think he knows Paul cheated, but I've never said it, because when it happened, Sam was only eight, too young for that level of disclosure. Still, I think he knows (in the way I remember "knowing" things when I was a kid), because one time, in the grocery store, near the tabloids in the magazine rack, he asked me what cheating was. But this is a whole new ball game. He's holding me accountable for the outcome of the relationship.

"I just couldn't stay," I say. "Like I said, sometimes people can, but sometimes they can't. This was one of those situations where . . . it wouldn't have been good. For any of us."

"But why, Mom?" He wants to know why. Exactly and precisely *why* I had to—and thus he had to—leave.

There's something in his voice, a quality that tells me that he is asking so pointedly because he is ready to hear the truth. Not a blaming, ugly, gory truth. But the truth that will dispel the confusion, that will allow him, going forward, to make sense of a very painful situation in a new way, that matches his going-on-twelve understanding of the world. "What happened?"

I'm facing away from him, and he is facing away from me, and there's almost no light in the room. We are almost four years and 5,600 miles away from what happened, and it seems like now is the time. I say a prayer: *God, give me the words.*

"Paul started to date a girl, honey. And when . . . when I found out, he didn't stop." That was as plain as I could say it. No judgment. No vitriol. Just the facts. None of Mommy's unfinished business, hurt, and pain spilling all over on it. Because, thank god, Mommy's dealt with it.

"Why did he do that?"

Such a simple question. So hard to answer.

"I don't know, muffin. Sometimes it's hard to know why people do things. People don't always make sense. But I couldn't keep us in that situation. It was just too destructive. Believe me, my heart was broken. I loved Paul." I pause for a minute. "I know you did, too."

There's a long silence. Which I'm careful not to just . . . fill.

"Is he married to her now?"

The question takes me by surprise, though it shouldn't. One of his friends' fathers left his wife and is still with the woman he left her for. They're married now, with kids, living happily ever after. (Or not.) This is Sam's frame of reference for people who leave people for other people.

"No. They never even had a relationship. The girl was, like, twenty-one. They were never really going to be together."

There's a silence while Sam tries to figure it out, tries again to answer his question—*Why?* And I get to ask myself, too, from where I stand today. Back then I cried. Now, I accept. Because now I get it.

Paul was *me*.

I'm the one who leaves. I left Dan. I left Kenny. I left Michael and Brandon. I chose Paul out of myself. Out of who I was. And when he was no longer me, when we were no longer a match, we left. Like one planetary body that falls out of the orbit of another. There's really no one to blame.

"Sometimes people have a hard time accepting real love, muffin. It doesn't match the way they feel about themselves inside. So they move away from the people who love them and move toward people who don't."

Sam's not saying a word. But I can feel him listening. I keep talking.

"And I understand that, because I've been like that in the past, too. Forgiving Paul is like forgiving myself." I pause. Is this too much information? I let another few seconds pass. "I know my choices have affected you, honey. I'm so, so sorry. I can't change the past. No one can. But we can make it . . ." I struggle to find the word. What can we make of the past? "We can make it count for something."

That's it. We can make the past sacred—though "sacred" is probably a little too high-concept for an eleven-year-old boy.

"No *one* person is ever to blame," I continue. "I had a part in what happened with Paul. Your dad had a part in what happened with me. That's how life is. Making mistakes—even huge ones—is what it means to be human. Otherwise we'd be, like, daisies. Or house cats." House cats don't fuck shit up. Or get married and divorced three times.

I wait for Sam to say something or to ask another question, but he doesn't. He's fallen asleep. Finally.

I lie there, staring out the window at the rooftops, thinking I might cry because even the rooftops in Paris are so damn beautiful. I feel like something good has happened. Something that never would have happened at home.

Because we don't lie awake, in the dark, jet-lagging, at home.

As I float off to sleep, Sam's foot touching mine, a sense of peace washes over me. It's the peace I've been looking for all these years. And I know it's mine to keep.